A JOURNEY TO PROF...
AND COMPASSI...

FORWARD-FACING®
—FOR—
EDUCATORS

CHERYL FULLER M.ED., REBECCA LEIMKUEHLER M.ED.
AND J. ERIC GENTRY, PHD

TABLE OF CONTENTS

DEDICATION

Cheryl

This book is dedicated to the countless teachers, custodians, counselors, bus drivers, administrators, school secretaries, cafeteria workers, and other educators that supported me as I went through school and continued into my thirty-eight years as an educator myself. I learned something valuable from every single one of you, and all of my work today is a result of your influence.

Rebecca

I would like to dedicate this book to teachers everywhere. When we took on the profession of teaching, it was to make a positive difference in the lives of those we serve. We each have the honor of shaping the lives of hundreds of children and young adults. Remember the impact we have each day on our students, hold your head up high, straighten your cape, and carry on like the superhero you are.

From all

This book is dedicated to every person who has made the tremendous personal and professional commitment to offer their life in service to the learning and growth of others. Teaching is often one of the most underappreciated professions, many times falling short of monetary rewards, verbal recognition, and public praise. But the reality is every single person has fond memories of a beloved teacher that shared the right words of encouragement, imparted just the right piece of knowledge, or responded in the most affirming way possible at a time that literally moved our lives in the direction that brought us to where we are meant to be. The selfless acts of generosity, and countless hours of dedicated work and survival of the most stressful demands possible, make educating truly the profession that creates all other professions.

We want you to continue to experience the moments of connection and joy that brought you to this profession for as many years as you choose, without the pain of burnout and compassion fatigue that can threaten the longevity of so many educators.

We dedicate this book to all of you with a debt of gratitude that can't be put into words, and we are hopeful you will find strength and healing from the skills and strategies offered here as we honor what you've already given and will continue to give to the lives of so many others. Happy educating and *thank you* for your service!

INTRODUCTION

At the time of this book's final edits before publication, our nation's educators and schools have been contending with a pandemic and its cascade of painful, concerning, and even life-threatening effects for nearly two years. As educators we've been on the frontlines during this traumatic time in history, witnessing and directly experiencing the upheaval that our schools, students, families, and communities have had to and will continue to navigate as we keep evolving to adapt to the post-COVID-19 educational landscape. This is, without a doubt, a new world—and a difficult one. Collective anxiety, depression, and aggression have all seen an uptick in our students and amongst colleagues (and society at large) as the ramifications of social isolation, fear, and grief metastasize on a worldwide scale. Educators have in many ways become the targets of unprecedented levels of defiance and other behavioral challenges from students and parents, as rates of adolescent self-harm and suicidal ideation,[1] chronic hopelessness and PTSD,[2] and domestic violence at home[3] continue to increase.

School day disruptions like stink bombs and hallway fights, gang signs being flashed between students, and the potential for lockdowns, active shooters, and the spread of COVID-19 remain in the minds of all. Social media also continues to play a role in widespread chaos at schools, as trends for classroom and facility destruction and acts of violence to be filmed and shared abound, with little to no regulations by online platforms or on a federal scale.

For these reasons and many more, we absolutely recognize the mountain that all educators are facing head-on these days, and the tough climb that lies ahead. This is a climb that won't be assuaged by the introduction of various short-lived "wellness days," or thousand-dollar bonuses and other monetary rewards that do little for long-term wellness and perpetual resilience for those going to work in schools every day. (As one of our authors and long-time educator Rebecca says, "Those measures are like putting a bandage on a bullet wound.")

What educators need in order to weather this storm, and all those to come in their chosen career, is a set of practices that are both simple and yet require focused intention for the rest of their lives to master. There is a way to look at the reality of the educational system and the widespread burnout and compassion fatigue among educators *while maintaining hope* and positive expectancy for healing and a future marked by professional resilience and trauma-informed care. The only way to thrive in perpetuity as an educator, no matter what happens inside the school or beyond it, is through these principles—*Forward-Facing® for Educators'* five steps for professional resilience. What luck that you're holding the key to your freedom and healing in your hands right now!

It is our heartfelt, soulful, and sincere intention to help you have the best year of your educational career and life (followed by every year thereafter). To help you to discover, practice, and master a set of skills that tames the intensity of the school's chaos, and helps you find traction in your movement forward to pursuing your heartfelt mission of helping kids and their families. Transformation is what happens when educators engage the Forward-Facing® process—it is both a responsibility and a right to everlasting health, peace, and joy afforded to all educators. We hope that you will join us on this life-changing journey.

Who We Are and Why We Can Help

Many of us who enter the helping professions have experienced painful events in our early lives. For some of us, this is the primary reason for entering the field—to prevent or alleviate the pain and suffering of others that we've endured in our own lives, or offer opportunities and support to our students that we might never have received ourselves. While that's a noble mission and an excellent reason to become an educator, it's also a double-edged sword. Though unaddressed and unresolved trauma from our pasts can inspire us to begin our careers with unprecedented fervor and enthusiasm, it can also sharply increase our risk of being affected by compassion fatigue.

The three of us come to you from life experiences of being of service to others: two of us (Cheryl and Rebecca) are from the world of education, and the third (Eric) has a lengthy background providing trauma treatment in the fields of healthcare, law enforcement, recovery and addiction, and in private practice with trauma survivors. We have learned and grown together, and through it have become more committed to sharing our knowledge and experiences with teachers, administrators, staff, and all educators who are doing everything possible to enhance the lives of children daily. We speak to all of you, and especially those educators who may find themselves depleted from burnout symptoms and compassion fatigue, wondering if this will be their last year working in such a challenging and demanding profession.

We want to help! We want to reconnect you to your purpose, your vision, and your own internal peace that allows you to care for yourself *in order to continue* caring for others. Here are our respective journeys so you can get to know each of us a little better before embarking on your path to healing and professional resilience.

Cheryl's Story

I've had the honor of working in education for over thirty-eight years as a teacher, counselor, principal, and educational consultant, as well as providing professional development to over 90,000 educators in North Carolina and across the United States with a variety of relevant topics to education. In the past few years, a particular focus in my work has been related to trauma-informed practices/social-emotional learning and professional resilience skills for educators. To that end, I wanted to increase my knowledge and expertise and enrolled in additional certification courses through the Arizona Trauma Institute—and it was in this arena that my professional and personal lives were profoundly impacted after coursework presented by Dr. Eric Gentry.

I came to this professional environment with a personal history of extreme physical, sexual, and emotional abuse as a child, such that I have a score of nine on the Adverse Childhood Experiences (ACE) survey. In fact, just prior to meeting Dr. Gentry I'd finished my personal trauma narrative, *Peace by Piece*. After completing Dr. Gentry's coursework, I reached out and he graciously agreed to read my book and gifted me with an endorsement and assistance in publishing. He then gave me the honor of inviting me to work with him and his colleague, Rebecca Leimkuehler, in an effort to bring the profound Forward-Facing® work to the world of education.

As another principal and educator, Rebecca and I immediately swapped stories of the overwhelming number of examples of compassion fatigue we've been noticing in more and more educators, as they struggle to balance their own lives with the constantly increasing needs and demands of their profession. We became very excited to find a way to take the strategies that have increased our own professional and personal resilience and share them with as many educators as possible. This book is our hope for all educators to begin to counter the toll our profession demands of us, so that we can all reconnect with the passion that brought us to our work in the beginning.

Rebecca's Story

I've been in education for over twenty-five years, and got into the field to make a difference in the life of a child. Over the years, however, I started to look at this concept of "making a difference in the life of a child" and realized that many of us serving in this institution of education didn't necessarily know what that meant, or how to accomplish it.

I started my career working in middle schools, where I'd spend time with my "littles," and I witnessed many adults around me judging these children. Saying that they knew everything about them, criticizing their students' behaviors, and even making comments like, "I hope they never have their own kids" about these children. I saw how burnout and compassion fatigue had taken these educators far away from their original mission of being in service to these kids, and I knew that these students really just needed someone to *see* them. To be present with them, to show them that they mattered. The educators needed healing and resilience so that they could feel healthy and regulated in their respective environments, which would then allow for a safe and co-regulatory space in the classroom to help these kids who might really be searching for an adult's guidance and support in their lives.

Then I was introduced to the CDC's Adverse Childhood Experiences (ACE) study and Marcia Stanton, the coordinator of the Arizona ACE Consortium here in my home state, and my entire life changed. I began to look into trauma-informed programs in healthcare and other fields, and saw how applicable these practices could be to the field of education. I got connected with the Arizona Trauma Institute, founded and led by Dr. Robert Rhoton, and its vice president, Dr. Eric Gentry—the creator of the Forward-Facing® methodology and founder of the Forward-Facing® Institute.

I saw the value and underpinnings of truth in an approach that was *never* about blaming teachers or blaming students, but that recognized the reality that we all have the same nervous systems that are designed to respond to traumatic experiences in order to keep us alive. My school was the first one in Arizona to become trauma-informed, bringing resiliency practices to our educators and staff for the last five years and counting.

This is how I got involved with Dr. Gentry and *Forward-Facing* for *Educators*, and I'm excited to share these methods for professional resilience with as many educators as possible—because I've personally seen the transformative and healing effects it can have for educators, their students, and our communities as a whole.

Eric's Story

Dear Educator—hello. My name is Eric Gentry. I am the developer of the Forward-Facing® Professional Resilience (FFPR) suite of programs and interventions. I have had the good fortune to help tens of thousands of professional care providers—from physicians and nurses to faith leaders, from law enforcement officers to mental health professionals—on four different continents recover from and prevent burnout and compassion fatigue. I have collaborated with colleagues over the years to publish peer-reviewed data that proves that the simple practices contained in FFPR are effective for both significantly lessening the pain associated with work-related stress, while also enhancing professional resilience and quality of life for care professionals. Forward-Facing® has become an accelerated pathway to wellbeing, and has rekindled a passion for mission for thousands of care professionals and volunteers over the past twenty-one years. However, I have not had the opportunity to assist educators in gaining and practicing these skills…until now. I am very excited to be joined by Cheryl and Rebecca in sharing this powerful work with you over the following pages.

Here's a little more about me before we begin. For those of you who understand what this means, I have an ACE (Adverse Childhood Experiences) score of nine out of ten. I was significantly traumatized throughout my childhood. I was obese, uncoordinated, socially awkward, and constantly afraid during my early years. My parents did the absolute best they could with their combination of history and circumstances, and were able to intermittently communicate to me I was loved and precious. However, more often due to their own trauma histories and inability to regulate themselves, our home frequently erupted into physical and emotional violence. In her 1992 book *Trauma and Recovery*, Dr. Judith Herman describes the state that many children who live in these environments develop into what she calls "frozen watchfulness." That certainly describes me at eight years old. In his landmark research working with traumatized children in the South Bronx in the 1980s, Dr. James Garbarino discovered that children who were able to find their way into an enduring relationship with one safe and stable adult had a better-than-even chance of developing into resilient and functional adults, while those who were unable to find this type of relationship in their environments were much more likely to succumb to self-destructive lifestyles fraught with pain and difficulty.

As I grew from childhood to adolescence, my relationship with caring teachers at the myriad of schools I attended became the only place of safety in my life. There were a handful of teachers just like you—who, throughout my development, reached beyond just teaching to connect to an awkward, afraid, obese, and isolated kid with their kindness and compassion. They helped me to feel comfortable in the presence of another human being for the first time in my life. They discovered and nurtured in me the intelligence and insight that all children have, and helped me find my voice to begin to express myself. The teachers of my early life were responsible for helping me to take the first steps from behind my fear and discover something like competence in myself as a student—a human being, instead of an alien. Teachers—just like you—saved my life.

Now, fifty years later, I have been given the opportunity to pay back and forward a little bit of this gift that was given to me. I am excited about sharing these Forward-Facing® principles and practices with you. I am excited about helping you first to see a pathway of how to work as a professional educator without having to suffer to do it, and then putting into practice simple skills that render you resilient and comfortable as you navigate through your challenging day. But mostly I am excited about helping you to diminish the pain of teaching to a level that you can regain the passion for your mission of teaching, helping, and being heroes to the children with whom you have been given the privilege to work—just as it is a privilege for me to get to work with you.

How This Book Will Heal Your Compassion Fatigue and Help You "Face Forward"

Forward-Facing® for Educators is divided into two main sections. In part I, we'll frame and reframe the problem of compassion fatigue in educators. In part II we'll explore the solution with five resilience-building strategies that will not only inoculate you against compassion fatigue, but also transform your life in profoundly positive ways.

Part I topics include:
- An overview of the landscape for educators today: the big-picture, systemic issues within the profession as well as the personal, daily stressors in classrooms and at home.
- Why the typical assumption that stress is a function of the teaching environment is erroneous, as well as the role of traumagenesis—a.k.a. painful past learning—in generating and exacerbating compassion fatigue symptoms.
- The true meaning of stress and its origins in the evolution and functioning of the human threat-response system. We will also consider how these systems can become dysregulated due to chronic overactivation, and how this increases our risk of developing compassion fatigue and other stress-related disorders.

Part II topics include:
- An overview of the five key elements of the evidence-based Forward-Facing® professional resilience skillset and how educators can master each one to remain healthy and productive.
- The conceptual, biological, cognitive, and affective aspects of step one, self-regulation, and how developing the resiliency skills of "bodyfulness" and "neuroception" will enable you to reduce and eliminate the impact of workplace stress.
- How the resiliency skills of intentionality and self-validation can improve our professional performance and enrich our lives with new meaning and purpose. Additionally, how reinvigorating our personal mission, vision, and code of honor to form our personal covenant and adopting a principle-based lifestyle are two of the most potent aspects of resilience.
- How the resiliency skill of perceptual maturation enables us to live and work with integrity, enhancing our self-empowerment and optimization while reducing our perception of the workplace as a

threatening environment.

- How compassion fatigue engenders social and professional isolation and how building the resiliency skill of support and connection can alleviate these effects and restore our connections with others.
- The physical, psychological, emotional, spiritual, professional, and integrative levels of self-care, and how these essential resiliency skills can be acquired and practiced to revitalize educators.
- How the treatment and prevention strategies of this book can be applied to a self-directed Forward-Facing® professional resilience plan to serve you in your professional and personal life for years to come.
- Our overall vision for the way leadership in education can embrace and initiate these methods to create a more efficient, empathetic, and effective system for future generations of teachers, administrators, and our students.

Forward-Facing® *for Educators* offers a gentle, self-directed, real-time treatment method that doesn't require you to painfully relive—and then wallow in—the traumatic experiences that comprise the root of all of your toxic stress, burnout, and compassion fatigue. Instead, you will learn simple, intuitive techniques that allow you to control how your brain and body react *while* you are being triggered and shifting into the natural stress response we've all been born with but rarely need.

In the chapters ahead, we'll explore the five-step Forward-Facing® process for professional resilience and examine how and why these techniques work so effectively based on our underlying biology. As we explain each concept and treatment method in detail, we'll provide specially formulated worksheets for the exploration and application of these methods in your own life. These worksheets, along with your Forward-Facing® professional resilience plan, are also compiled in Appendix I at the back of the book for ease of reference, as well as to make copies for future iterations and revisions to your work. All you need to start participating in the Forward-Facing® approach to professional resilience is a writing utensil, which we recommend grabbing now for any personal notetaking needs or insights you discover while reading. If you prefer to write down your answers to the worksheets in a separate notepad or journal instead, that will work as well.

A Critical Question for Educators and the System as a Whole

As leaders in our organizations and institutions begin to develop programs to address workplace stress, compassion fatigue, burnout, and the many corresponding issues that result from them, we want to postulate what we think is a critical question—perhaps *the* most critical question—that needs to be asked of educators and those in the teaching field: *Where does the responsibility to reduce our suffering and assure our professional fulfillment lie?* Does it belong to our leadership/institutions, or with each of us as individuals?

We believe that the answer to this fundamental question is a resounding *both*, but we have geared this book toward that which you as the reader and educator have current and complete control over: *your own personal resilience*. In the final chapter we will return to this question and expand upon the answer, but for now, we want to assert that the first line of defense against compassion fatigue lies within you. Institutions and their leadership teams have an important role to play in the future designs of our education system so that they can become more efficient and sympathetic, but these results will only be enhanced by the relief and resilience fostered individually among us.

Compassion fatigue is a real issue faced by teachers and education professionals who are performing some of the most strenuous mental and emotional work in our society today. It is not something to be ashamed of, nor is it something to keep buried within yourself until the pain is too great to bear. You are not alone, you are not defective, and this is not a permanent struggle from which you have no escape. We are extending an invitation for healing, satisfaction, and resilience that you can carry on for the duration of your career, and apply to all other areas of your personal and professional life. Join us in this journey toward renewed strength, zeal, empathy, mission, and the compassion that drew you to the education field to begin with.

PART I:
THE PROBLEM FOR EDUCATORS

CHAPTER ONE

EDUCATING OTHERS DOESN'T HAVE TO HURT

The more you care, the stronger you can be.

Jim Rohn

IT GOES WITHOUT saying that a career centered on the education of children is one of the noblest pursuits one can devote their life's work to. Teachers, administrators, school secretaries, nurses, principals, and more give of their talents, physical and mental energy, sleep and free time, and even their own wallets to shape and nurture the children and teenagers of today as they grow into the young adults of tomorrow. Educating kids can be one of the most rewarding jobs on the planet.

It can also be one of the most stressful!

Ever-growing class rosters, reductions in governmental fiscal support that seem to worsen with every year as extracurriculars are replaced with standardized testing requirements, unhealthy work environments, belligerent parents, pandemics and asynchronous learning, dangerous and destructive social media trends and "monthly challenges," all combined with the pressure of caring for dozens of students both in the classroom and out of it—there's no denying that those who dedicate themselves to education do it because of a selfless passion for helping children and shaping their young lives in a meaningful way, rather than to pursue a profession that promises more money, power, or adoration.

We value educators tremendously for a great many reasons, and would like to take some time acknowledging just how special you are. As an educator, you have an unflinching dedication to the wellbeing of your students. We recognize your heart for children, which is an indispensable quality that benefits our society presently and our future collectively. You have a positive impact on your environment, shouldering concern and care for your students

3

and their families. You've made a commitment to the success of your students, even with minimal (and shrinking!) resources to achieve this outcome. You have a dedication and hunger for lifelong learning, recognizing the value it offers your students, our communities, and our nation. You strive for excellence in your pursuits as an educator, mentor, and helper—much of which may go underappreciated or unnoticed.

Yet no matter how much dedication, raw talent, and sheer personal willpower you put forth for your career and the kids you help, the fact remains that these are not failsafe methods of protection against the burnout that working in education so often brings—and in fact, to believe yourself immune or capable of "muscling through it all" will only accelerate the development of your burnout and compassion fatigue symptoms.

The exciting news is that there *are* ways for you to inoculate yourself against burnout, traumatic stress, and compassion fatigue—they are the five Forward-Facing® methods for professional resilience that we will teach you in the latter portion of this book. In this first half we'll spend some time examining the challenges that educators face today both personally and systemically—which, by the way, are not the real sources of burnout and compassion fatigue—and discuss the physiological processes that occur when we perceive threat in the classroom or on campus (stress's *actual* origination point, and one that isn't inherently negative).

Life has been very challenging and bleak for educators as of late, but there *is* a simple solution. Once you better understand the kinds of situations that have been contributing to the widespread burnout and compassion fatigue happening for educators, as well as the inner bodily workings of your own stress response and how perceiving threat where there is little or no danger (like with your students, other faculty, or parents) can lead to post-traumatic stress, you can *truly* begin to heal while simultaneously building unshakable resilience for the future. We pledge to show you the way out of this pain and suffering!

Before we dive into all of that, however, the remainder of this first chapter includes a story told from the perspective of a fictional sixth-grade student named Freda. This narrative follows Freda's journey through a school day and her interactions with five staff members you'll meet again in future chapters, presenting the various challenges they deal with in their workplace and the negative effects that some of those challenges can produce.

This story is meant to be a celebration of the resilience and grit that educators exhibit every single day of their professional careers. It is *not* meant to disrespect educators, or to criticize or minimize the difficulties they face. Instead, we are presenting a wide range of scenarios in one narrative that you might recognize from your own professional life or that of your colleagues', as a way to bear witness to these experiences that can make your work arduous and even painful. It's our way of providing context for the many obstacles educators navigate daily on their campuses, and to demonstrate our awareness, empathy, and validation of your own hardships from this very first chapter. Our hope is that this narrative will be the beginning of *your* story to visualizing and implementing a Forward-Facing® pathway to a much more satisfying professional quality of life.

We—the three authors of this book, two of whom are long-time educators and one who is a leader in the treatment of burnout and compassion fatigue resulting from traumatic stress—have learned that the negative effects of our work *do not get better* when we deny them. Part of healing from work-related stress is the acceptance that our work is producing detrimental outcomes in our professional and personal lives. That is one of the primary purposes of Freda's story—to gently help you recognize any similarities you may have in your own work or at your own school. As you see glimpses of yourself (or your coworkers) in the below scenarios or those in upcoming narratives, you will become empowered and skilled to change, grow, and evolve into the absolute best educator you can be. Additionally, as you put the five Forward-Facing® skills for professional resilience into practice in your own life, you will become increasingly immune to the negative effects that school environments can create. You can't always leave your school to escape the stressors that come with being an educator, but once you begin implementing these five simple tools for healing and resilience, *you won't need to*.

Our ultimate goal with this book is to walk you through a transformative process that will lessen your stress, optimize your functioning, and rekindle your mission in working with children—so let the healing begin!

A Day in the Life of Freda

Freda stepped off the school bus into the bright sunshine, taking in the chaos of the elementary schoolyard on a Monday morning before her.

"Come on, Devon!" she said over her shoulder to her younger sister, pushing her backpack further up her shoulder—it barely weighed a thing at the moment, because she'd forgotten almost all her books and binders and her mom hadn't packed them any lunches for the day. They'd barely made the bus that morning because Freda had forgotten to set her alarm, and their mom was still at the hospital when they'd left. Freda's mom was a nurse who seemed to pick up more shifts nowadays than she had even during the pandemic, leaving Freda to cook almost all of the meals; do the laundry and other chores; and try to make sure Devon *actually* did her homework every night. It gave Freda little to no time to do her own, which was why she was headed straight to the principal's office this morning.

Freda waved to Devon as her little sister headed for the fourth-grade building, narrowly avoiding a collision with a few kids who raced by toward the middle of the soccer field. Freda watched as the playground monitor and several other teachers jogged over as well—two of Freda's sixth-grade classmates were in each other's faces, fighting over something to do with the last goal made.

"Kail Jensen and John Alcaraz, stop it right now!" hollered the playground monitor at the top of his lungs as he lunged between the arguing boys. "Detention slips for both of you! That's enough!"

Freda walked on, mostly indifferent to the outcome of another near-physical altercation in the schoolyard. With online classes and asynchronous learning both things of the past, she'd become used to the charged energy of the place—that simmering of her classmates' combustible emotions just below the surface. Kids who one moment could be laughing along with her if a teacher said something embarrassing or lame, but wouldn't hesitate to make *her* the butt of the joke a second later. She could rarely let her guard down; not with the other kids, and definitely not with a few of her teachers. They loved to call on Freda, asking why she was late to class or hadn't completed her homework—especially that awful Mr. Richardson. *He* was the reason she was headed to the front office right now, about to get another punishment from Mrs. Burkhart for still not having the behavior contract signed by her mom. Freda couldn't help the fact her mom rarely came home anymore! If it wasn't work, it was the new boyfriend taking up all of her mom's time. Freda hated it—she missed her dad, but he had his new family now in another state and rarely called. Sometimes she felt so lonely, scared, and stressed out that she'd lock her bedroom door and get under the covers, crying until her stomach hurt.

The five-minute warning bell for first period rang just as Freda crossed the threshold into the front office, where she saw that the school secretary, Mrs. Stanbury, was simultaneously talking on the phone and organizing papers at her desk while at least four or five different parents and their kids stood in line waiting to speak to her. Freda scanned the busy office for the principal, finally spotting Mrs. Burkhart speaking to a male teacher Freda had seen around the school but had never interacted with.

"*Six* teachers out today? Seriously? And two crosswalk guards?" Mrs. Burkhart said to the teacher, shaking her head. "Why do they always do this to me on Mondays?! Why? They *knew* the superintendent was coming today!"

"*That's* probably why," the teacher quipped. "Mr. Briguglio is not someone any of us want to start our week with."

"Well, you know where I'll be for the next hour," Mrs. Burkhart replied, rubbing at her temples as she strode toward the back of the building. Freda followed, digging in her backpack for the blank behavior contract. Freda waited a few seconds before entering as Mrs. Burkhart sank into her chair with a heavy sigh, then turned to the large computer monitor on her desk and began to tap furiously on the keyboard.

"Mrs. Burkhart?" Freda said as she went in, presenting the behavior contract immediately—she wanted to get this over with. "My mom didn't sign it."

The principal looked up from the screen and adjusted her glasses. "Freda, honey. How many times are we gonna do this? Fine, you know the drill. Lunch in the front office until you get it signed. And if I have to go to your house *personally* to hand it to your mom, I will."

"Okay," Freda said, when what she really meant was *good luck with that*. She didn't love the idea of another lunch period away from her friends, but she also had nothing to eat and only a dollar in her wallet, and secretly hoped the secretary might bring her a free lunch from the cafeteria like in the past.

Mrs. Burkhart's phone started ringing as Freda left the room, sidestepping a frowning woman who hurried toward the office with her young son in tow. Freda didn't stick around to hear *that* conversation; she really liked Mrs. Burkhart, and by the looks of it, that mom was about to unleash on the principal in a way that Freda wasn't interested in hearing.

The one-minute warning bell rang as Freda began to jog to her first class— Social Studies with Ms. Hernandez. She made it just in time, sliding into her seat as the teacher clapped to get everyone's attention.

"Good morning, class!" Ms. Hernandez said, sounding as nervous as usual. Freda noticed her voice shook most days when class began each morning; it was when everyone was the rowdiest, and the young teacher seemed almost afraid to tell the sixth-graders—some of whom were almost as tall as her—to sit down and be quiet. "Please put your phones on silent and in your backpacks if you haven't already." Many of the kids ignored her and continued tapping away on their screens, while others had distractingly loud side conversations. "Who can go make copies for me in the fifth-grade building?" Ms. Hernandez continued, which suddenly got everyone's attention. Freda shot her arm up like a bunch of others, echoing the request to "pick me, pick me!"

Ms. Hernandez chose someone else, and handed him several papers with colored tabs on them. "I need fifty of these and seventy-five of these please," she instructed the student, "and hurry! Go there and come right back."

He nodded and left the classroom as the other students went back to their phones or chatting with friends. Ms. Hernandez didn't try to stop them, instead searching through her desk's stacks of papers for the TV remote so they could all watch that morning's announcements.

Once the announcements were done and the boy still hadn't returned with the copies, Ms. Hernandez tried again to quiet everyone in the class. "Okay everyone, Jackson will be back with our assignments for the day any minute. Rachel and Brooklyn, please stop talking—what did I say about no phones in class?" She clapped again, louder and more furiously this time. "Everyone, listen to me! I need you all on your best behavior this morning, please, because we have a special and very important visitor who might stop by."

Freda dug around in her backpack for a pen and her notebook as Ms. Hernandez continued, before firing off a quick text to Devon reminding her about an important math quiz she had that day.

"Freda Whitmore, please put your phone away now!"

Freda looked up, cheeks warming instantly. "Sorry," she mumbled, dropping her phone in her backpack as Ms. Hernandez went on.

"I'm serious. No phones today, no talking when I'm talking. If you all listen to me right now, I'll bring candy in tomorrow, okay?"

The students began cheering just as the classroom door opened. Ms. Hernandez looked at it expectantly, but it still wasn't the student with her copies—it was an older man dressed in a fancy suit who Freda didn't recognize. The man said nothing as he walked to the back of the classroom with two other women, and Ms. Hernandez smiled and began to talk in a faster, high-pitched voice as she went over what they'd all be working on that day.

A few minutes later, the student finally returned with the copies and Ms. Hernandez rushed to pass them out. Two boys who Freda knew to be troublemakers laughed to each other from their seats, as one of the boy's phones dinged loudly.

"What did I say about phones, Kail?" Ms. Hernandez warned, asking them again to put the devices away. She glanced at the back of the classroom where the man and two women stood silently, before returning to her lesson. The boys cackled again, continuing to text one another with corresponding loud ringtones during most of the class.

Eventually Ms. Hernandez strode over and physically took the phones away. "You'll get these back when class is done," she practically hissed, placing the phones on top of her desk with visible frustration.

Only a short while later the bell was ringing to dismiss them, and as Freda packed up her stuff and stood to leave, she could swear Ms. Hernandez looked like she was about to cry.

"Thanks for stopping by!" the teacher said half-heartedly as the trio of adults filed out of the classroom with the students, and Freda thought it was pretty rude that none of them even responded to Ms. Hernandez. Adults could be so cranky—Freda could count on only a few fingers the grownups she actually liked, and who seemed to like *her*.

Speaking of cranky adults, her next class was History with the horrible Mr. Richardson. Freda's stomach rumbled as she headed to her locker between periods, and there was no way she'd be able to handle the next hour without some food in her stomach. Freda wove between the busy halls, digging in her backpack for her wallet to pay for something to eat. The line at the snack bar was long, which gave Freda time to mull over what she might be able to afford with one dollar. After selecting a bag of chips and buying them—at the same time as the one-minute warning bell—Freda meandered her way to class in the next building over, munching on her chips and hoping they'd make her feel better.

By the time Freda stood in front of Mr. Richardson's classroom, the final bell had just rung and she was officially late. Freda inhaled, preparing herself for the kind of reception she might receive from the grouchy History teacher. She was in *no* mood today.

"Freda Whitmore, late again," said Mr. Richardson from where he stood at the smart board as Freda slunk inside and quietly walked toward her desk at the back of the room. "I was just telling the class how frustrating it is as a teacher when our students don't respect our time. So what made you late *today*, Freda?"

The other students sat silently, some of them wide-eyed and immobile while others snickered and nodded. This was a common occurrence with Mr. Richardson—singling out his students to embarrass them for not answering correctly when they were called on, or received poor grades on tests. He'd even made one of Freda's classmates cry once, when she started to blush after he'd asked her a question. Mr. Richardson had said loudly in front of everyone, "Why is your face getting so red? Are you blushing?" until the girl had run out of the room in tears.

Freda ignored Mr. Richardson as she tossed her backpack on the ground with an audible sound and sat in her chair. She crossed her arms and glared at him. "Go on," she said finally, waving her hand at him. "Stop staring at me and teach!"

"I asked you a question," he continued, voice rising in decibel as he put the cap back on the marker in his hand. "I asked why you were late to my class *again*. I'm here on time every day, ready to do *my* job, but none of you do *your* jobs!"

"I'd come in on time if you weren't the most boring teacher alive!" Freda retorted, feeling the eyes of every person in the class glued to her. "You clearly *suck* at your job—you should probably quit!"

That got the laughter from the other kids that Freda was hoping for, but she wasn't going to stick around for her second behavior contract that month. Freda swiped her backpack off the floor and stood, dashing out of the room as Mr. Richardson yelled something back—she didn't hear what—before telling the other students to be quiet and pay attention to the lesson.

Once outside, Freda stood in the empty hallway for a few seconds as she debated where to go. She *could* hide in the girls' bathroom off the north building where most of the nearby classrooms were empty and she'd have some privacy, but the last few times Freda had gone over there, she'd run into several of the popular girls ditching class and they'd been far from welcoming.

Freda decided instead that she'd visit her favorite person at the school—the counselor, Ms. Waite. When her parents first got divorced and things were really hard at home, Freda and Devon had met with Ms. Waite separately once a week for several months to "work through their feelings." Freda had tried to keep up with semi-regular visits even after they weren't requested by the principal any longer, because she felt like Ms. Waite was the only adult who would truly *listen* to her when she talked.

When Freda arrived at Ms. Waite's office the door was closed, so she sat in one of the chairs lined up outside it. Freda could see the school counselor seated and speaking with another student through the narrow glass window on one side of the door, and hoped they'd hurry up and finish soon. She took out her phone and scrolled through her social media accounts for a while, glancing at the time every so often. After thirty-five minutes or so, the door opened and the student left. Freda got up and immediately went into the counselor's office, where Ms. Waite was busily stacking and organizing piles of papers strewn across her desk.

"Ms. Waite?"

"Freda, hi," Ms. Waite said breathlessly, barely glancing up from her stacks of paper. "How are you? I wasn't expecting you today—I don't think we had an appointment?"

"No we didn't, but I wanted to come say hi," Freda said, getting the sense Ms. Waite wasn't really available to chat. It made her feel sad and rejected, similar to how she felt whenever her mom was too busy or tired to talk on the rare days she was off from work and not at her boyfriend's house.

"Oh, that's sweet, but I've actually got to drop off these tests to all the third- and fourth-grade teachers before the lunch hour is over," Ms. Waite answered as she moved one large stack of papers on top of another one, before standing and balancing the giant amount of tests in both arms. "I have time after lunch if you want to come back then?"

Ms. Waite was already walking around her desk and headed toward the door as Freda responded. "Okay, maybe…"

"Great. Could you get the door behind me? Thank you so much," Ms. Waite said as another bell rang over the intercom to signal that lunchtime had begun. "Are you headed to the front office?"

"Yeah. My mom still couldn't sign the contract," Freda said with a frown, following after Ms. Waite as they walked through the hallways that were now jam-packed with students headed excitedly to the cafeteria.

"I'm sorry to hear that," Ms. Waite said as she broke off from Freda and angled toward the younger grades' buildings, calling out the rest over her shoulder. "You can tell me about it this afternoon!"

Freda went the other way, in the direction of the front office. The chips hadn't done much to quell her hunger earlier, and her stomach rumbled as she walked inside and made eye contact with the secretary, Mrs. Stanbury.

"Hi Freda. You know where to go," the school secretary said, and Freda nodded. She went over to the table with one chair in the corner of the large room, next to a fake, dust-covered potted plant. On the table already was a sandwich, a fruit cup, and a bottle of water, and Freda looked over gratefully to Mrs. Stanbury, but the secretary was already on the phone again.

As she sat down and ate, she surveyed the bustling office—Mrs. Burkhart on the phone in her office with the door half closed, the school nurse across the way attending to different students who showed up with fevers or injuries or requesting a COVID-19 screening, and of course the never-ending stream of parents and kids who came through the big front doors of the building.

Freda had just starting eating her fruit cup when the doors swung open and a really tall, scary-looking man strode in and walked right up to Mrs. Stanbury's desk.

"Excuse me!" he cried, either oblivious to or uncaring of the fact she was currently on the phone. "We have a problem! Hey lady, what's this—my son was suspended from the swim team?!"

Mrs. Stanbury held up a hand until she'd finished her call, and then looked up at the man. "Can I get your name please? I can try to get you in to see Mrs. Burkhart tomorrow—"

"I'm not waiting until tomorrow!" the man practically screamed, and Freda thought he might lose an eyeball based on the way they were bulging out of his head.

Mrs. Stanbury immediately pushed away from her desk and stood, walking around a corner and out of sight as the man continued to holler to whoever was nearest him in the office. Freda had never seen Mrs. Stanbury just up and leave her desk in the middle of a conversation, but then again, she'd also never been around a man so angry he screamed like that (except during a few fights between her parents when they were still together).

Freda kept eating as the commotion of the front office surrounded her, feeling a variety of emotions. Frustration, sadness, but most of all—*loneliness*. So many of the adults around her were distracted or anxious or busy, and it was like they rarely saw her.

Like she was invisible.

✖ ✚ ✖✖

After reading through Freda's story, did any of the situations her educators went through or behaviors they exhibited resonate for you? Perhaps you've gone through similar confrontations with angry parents like our school secretary and principal did, or felt intimidated by your students or upper-management faculty like our young teacher Ms. Hernandez was. Maybe you even see some comparisons between the frustration our teacher Mr. Richardson had with Freda's frequent tardiness and your own experiences with students who lacked appreciation for your diligent commitment to their success.

We recognize these and the plethora of other stressors educators come up against on a regular basis, which is why we're going to examine the scope of the problem in detail in the next chapter. We feel that in order for you to apply the Forward-Facing® principles of professional resilience at work and home most effectively, we should spend some time examining and validating the myriad of challenges educators currently face in their daily work responsibilities and nationwide due to legislative and bureaucratic decisions, community shifts, unforeseen emergencies like active shooter drills and pandemics, asynchronous learning, and more. This way you'll not only be armed with your five-step Forward-Facing® toolkit for healing your stress, burnout, and compassion fatigue indefinitely, but you'll know *exactly* when to use it.

Forward-Facing® Reflection 1:
Noticing When and Where It Hurts

After reviewing Freda's story, were there any similarities in the narrative that reminded you of situations or experiences from your own professional life? Note them down if so, as well as any emotions or physical sensations that might come up for you while recalling these memories. (This practice of getting acquainted with your thoughts and bodily sensations at any given moment is a foundational Forward-Facing® skill for resolving trauma and stress and fostering professional resilience, and is one you can begin learning to do now.)

1. Situation:

_____

_____

_____

Resulting emotions (anxiety, anger, sadness, et cetera):

_____

_____

_____

Physical sensations (muscles tensing up, jaw tightening, heart rate increasing, et cetera):

_____

_____

_____

2. Situation:

_____

_____

_____

Resulting emotions (anxiety, anger, sadness, et cetera):

_____

_____

_____

Physical sensations (muscles tensing up, jaw tightening, heart rate increasing, et cetera):

_____

_____

_____

3. Situation:

_____

_____

_____

Resulting emotions (anxiety, anger, sadness, et cetera):

_____

_____

_____

Physical sensations (muscles tensing up, jaw tightening, heart rate increasing, et cetera):

_____

_____

_____

Now we'd like you to think about any other personal work scenarios that may be entirely different from Freda's narrative above, but that still caused a stress reaction for you. If there are any you can think of, list them below as well as the resulting emotions and/or physical sensations they brought up.

4. Situation:

_____

_____

_____

Resulting emotions (anxiety, anger, sadness, et cetera):

_____

_____

_____

Physical sensations (muscles tensing up, jaw tightening, heart rate increasing, et cetera):

_____

_____

_____

5. Situation:

_____

_____

_____

Resulting emotions (anxiety, anger, sadness, et cetera):

_____

_____

_____

Physical sensations (muscles tensing up, jaw tightening, heart rate increasing, et cetera):

_____

_____

_____

CHAPTER TWO

CHALLENGES IN EDUCATION TODAY

The roots of education are bitter, but the fruit is sweet.

Aristotle

RIGHT NOW WE'RE facing a crisis in the world of education, and it's rolling toward us like a tsunami. The profession has been losing members at alarming rates, with fewer people than ever choosing to pursue a career in education.[4] Increased emphasis on standardized testing and accountability requirements, added demands to the workload, persistent underfunding that has led to school safety issues such as toxic amounts of lead in drinking water[5] and just-above-freezing classrooms in winter,[6] world health pandemics, and a decrease in respect and support for the profession are just a few of the factors convincing current and potential teachers to choose an alternate career path.

Educators are responsible for the academic learning of all other professions. You hold in your hands the intellectual paths of our nation's future doctors, lawyers, electricians, plumbers, computer analysts, inventors, other teachers, and every other profession available. If it feels as though you're carrying the weight of the world on your shoulders, maybe it's because...*you are*!

Many of the factors that make this profession difficult have challenged us since the first one-room schoolhouses came into being. The financial compensation teachers receive doesn't even *come close* to matching the level of responsibility and degree of work expected of them. And while educators and some community members continue to advocate and fight for that to change, those who choose to teach are aware of this shortcoming when they accept the job, often reminding others and themselves that "I didn't go into this profession for the income; I do it for the *outcome*!"

This extremely honorable career and life choice doesn't guarantee food in the fridge and a paid mortgage, however—and the rates at which teacher pay have stagnated while the cost of living continues to increase is another component dissuading people from entering the profession. Even compared with other service industry fields (healthcare, law enforcement, social work, et cetera), education is quickly sliding down the scale to be among the lowest-paid professions requiring a college degree in the country[7]—in some states, new teachers have starting salaries that are just above the poverty line.

With the inclusion of numerous (very important) issues such as anti-bullying, gender and racial equity frameworks, school shooting drills, suicide prevention, child abuse awareness and reporting, drug and alcohol education, and more, the amount of responsibilities at all levels—for upper-level faculty, administrative staff, and teachers—has reached unbelievable proportions. Yet as educators are asked to do so much more for their students, the typical school day, school calendar, and wages have remained the same (or lessened).

The growing sense among educators that it "just isn't worth it for the money" comes as no surprise, as the tasks expected of those in the teaching profession pile up even further. Here's Rebecca with more on this.

Rebecca: I recently provided a professional development experience where I shared a one-page document with my audience listing what was expected of teachers fifty years ago. Thankfully some of the items such as "starting and keeping the woodstove burning" had been removed since then, but the majority of the responsibilities were still present. I then held up the list of educators' job requirements today, and it was six pages long—*six times* the amount of work compared to fifty years ago!

When teachers are asked in exit interviews about the factors that led to their decision to leave the profession, the low pay is sometimes mentioned—but more frequently it's these added duties, coupled with the fact the entire system has been degrading over the last few decades.

The U.S.'s teacher shortage is only expected to worsen, with concerns growing more magnified for many of the hard-to-fill teaching jobs of special education and bilingual education. Because specialized educators can often earn so much more money in other fields, many school districts are severely lacking in the subjects of science, technology, engineering, and math (STEM) that our country's students need to compete in the evolving economy[8] and for better socioeconomic outcomes and innovative solutions for global concerns facing us now and in the near future.[9]

Simply put, the system-wide issues impacting teachers, students, and the field of education have in many ways gone unchecked in recent years, with the statistics to prove it.

Macro Challenges for Educators: The Systemic, "Big Picture" Problems

The institution of education has altered dramatically in the twenty-first century in the U.S., with many recent changes diminishing support for teachers and introducing new obstacles for success. An unprecedented number of teachers have reported feeling anxious and depressed in recent years, with much of their stress stemming from mandated curriculums, large class sizes, and standardized testing where "insufficient results" can have significant consequences for teachers and schools.[10]

The range of academic abilities within one class is wider and continues to grow, and yet the expectation for appropriate differentiation of each child's needs is greater than ever. Turnover rates have continued to climb, as environmental factors like reduced district funding and income tax breaks shift a school's financial needs and responsibilities off the federal and state departments' shoulders onto the faculty members themselves. It's *hard* to be an educator today, but don't just take our word for it—the research says so too.

School Funding and Teacher Salary Rates

- A paper published in 2017 found that although some school systems had restored funding after the recession cuts of 2008, at least twelve states had continued to **cut their "general/formula" funding by 7 percent or more per child** over the last decade.[11] The supreme court of one of these states recently ruled that the reduced funding levels were "unconstitutionally inadequate."[12]
- A 2015 report from the American Association of School Administrators stated that 83 percent of their survey's respondents **described their districts' economic situations as "inadequately funded**." This was up

from 67 percent in October of 2008.[13]

- An analysis completed by the American Federation of Teachers reported that the **average teacher's salary was lower in 2018 than in 2009** in real terms in thirty-eight states,[14] with the Economic Policy Institute finding that teachers' pay had fallen by thirty dollars per week from 1996 to 2015, while other college graduates' pay had increased by 124 dollars per week.[15]

Teacher Shortages, Turnover, and Increased Demand

- The U.S. Bureau of Labor Statistics published an article in 2018 projecting that more than **270,000 primary and secondary education teachers would leave their occupation each year** from 2016 to 2026.[16]
- A 2019 paper examining teacher shortages in the U.S. stated that while retirement accounted for one-third of "leavers" in the field, approximately two-thirds of those who'd departed did so due to **"school staffing decisions, life changes, or dissatisfactions with teaching."**[17]
- Research published in 2019 examining middle school teacher turnover rates found that **they'd risen nearly 7 percent between 2012 and 2016** alone,[18] with the National Commission on Teaching and America's Future estimating that **U.S. public schools lose more than 7 billion in turnover costs** per year.[19]
- The National Center for Education Statistics predicted that total enrollment of students in public and private elementary and secondary schools is expected to **increase by at least 2 percent—up to 57.4 million enrollees—by fall 2028**.[20]

Effects on Students, Communities, and the Economy

- An analysis studying the 2008 recession's budget cut effects on students found that a 1,000-dollar reduction in per-pupil spending led to a **decline in test scores of nearly 4 percent**. In communities where 30 percent of families were qualified as low income, **this decline rose to 12 percent**.[21]

- The same research discovered that on average, a 1,000-dollar decline in district spending was associated with 3.7 percent fewer teachers, 5.3 percent fewer instructional aides, and **12 percent fewer guidance counselors** (leading to approximately 80 more students per counselor).[22]
- A 2018 study stated that a 10 percent budget cut per high school year **led to a nearly 3 percent increase in dropout rates,**[23] with further research finding that a student who didn't graduate from high school **cost the economy approximately 240,000 dollars** over their lifetime in the form of reduced tax contributions and higher reliance on welfare and federal/state-funded healthcare.[24]

The negative trickle-down effects of these structural issues within our education system are evident in many sectors of the country's society—both economically stateside and compared to other industrialized nations, we're steadily falling behind, especially in the subjects of science, math, and reading.[25]

To illustrate these macro issues (and several "micro" issues we'll be exploring further in this chapter) in a more personalized way, let's spend some time with the principal of Freda's school, Shannon Burkhart, while she navigates her responsibilities as an upper-management educator in today's circumstances.

A Day in the Life of Mrs. Burkhart

Shannon rolled over and reached for her phone to check the time—5:40 a.m. Her alarm was set to go off at six, but as usual she found herself awake before her day was officially meant to start. She'd been feeling extra fatigued lately, and wondered if she should try to rest a few more minutes—it was Monday, after all, and she needed all the energy she could get. Instead, she tapped on her phone's screen, swiping past the three new emails in her inbox to check that day's weather forecast. She'd checked her inbox last at midnight, and figured (or rather, *hoped*) that nothing too pressing had happened in the last few hours.

I should take a shower before I read these, Shannon thought, as her index finger seemed to move of its own accord to open the most recent message.

21

She'd been trying to implement more boundaries between her work and personal time, to very little success. Sometimes it felt like a lose-lose situation—her anxiety would spike when she *didn't* read the messages as soon as she received them, yet nine times out of ten, the contents of the emails stressed her out too.

Shannon rubbed at her burning throat with her free hand as she read; her acid reflux had gotten worse this school year, and the medicine prescribed from her gastrointestinal doctor didn't even give her relief anymore. She cringed as she imagined the scolding she'd get from her doctor for not reducing her stress levels and implementing healthier eating and sleeping habits—*you're on your way to another stomach ulcer,* he'd said at their last appointment, *and that increases your chances for bad infections or even cancer. You need to take better care of yourself!* She'd promised him she'd eat more whole foods instead of the packaged stuff she snagged from the snack bar most afternoons and would no longer put in sixty-hour work weeks, but considering the fact she was already reading emails at 5:50 on a Monday morning, she had yet to implement these practices.

The first message Shannon reviewed was from the central office confirming the superintendent's visit to her campus that morning, the second from a parent demanding an immediate change in their child's teacher, and the third from veteran sixth-grade teacher Mike Richardson, who was requesting a meeting with her "as soon as possible in the day." Shannon frowned, wondering what he wanted to speak about—she knew he'd been struggling with some personal stuff at home recently, and she instantly began to worry he might be putting in his resignation. She still had two vacancies she'd been unable to fill that year, leaving those classrooms' children in the less-than-ideal situation of rotating substitute teachers for the last several months. Would she soon be adding another group to that fate?

Shannon put her phone down and headed for the shower. As the hot water hit the back of her neck, she became aware of how tense her muscles already were. She'd been a principal for almost ten years, and had always derived great joy and satisfaction from her work. Although that had been severely challenged during the pandemic that changed the landscape of teaching and threw them all for a loop for a while, Shannon had still managed to derive meaning from her work as she did her best to maintain successful learning between her students and faculty members.

Recently, however, it seemed that her symptoms of stress and anxiety were becoming more frequent and far outweighing the positive feelings and rewarding experiences she'd once had. She'd even experienced another full-blown panic attack (her third ever) a week earlier, after a busy day of meetings about her district's upcoming budget cuts. She'd made it back to her office and shut the door before the worst of it, spending the next twenty minutes in her desk chair shaking all over, sweating profusely, and suffering from the most profound, terrifying sense of dread she could imagine. Finally, she'd gathered herself enough to get up and drive home, but now the fear of more attacks flared up in the back of her mind every time she stepped foot in her office.

Shannon realized this had been a traumatic experience and she could probably benefit from therapy to work through it, but she was just so *busy*—she didn't have time for counseling at the moment. Maybe during the summer break, though in recent years any semblance of a "break" was a thing of the past as Shannon's workload seemed to multiply exponentially.

The reality was that she was accountable for *every* aspect of the functioning of her school. She was responsible for meeting the unique needs of hundreds of students and their parents, taking care of her entire staff, and upholding the school's role in the community—and all of it was becoming more overwhelming than she cared to admit.

Gone were the days of support from the very community and parents she and her teachers served; Shannon had to regularly navigate slashed budgets that sometimes didn't even allot enough funds for her classrooms' basic needs, as her teachers dealt with higher rates of disciplinary and behavior issues from students and their oftentimes angry, defensive parents. It was no surprise to Shannon that the morale amongst her remaining faculty was deteriorating, and she didn't blame them. Recently she'd found herself daydreaming about her own escape—just not showing up one day, and moving to a beach town somewhere. Sure, she'd forfeit her pension and leave her entire staff and school population high and dry, but sometimes the lure of getting away was so strong she almost considered it.

Unfortunately, these "make believe" scenarios did nothing to help her worsening anxiety and panic attacks, poor sleep, and gastrointestinal distress over the past few years, and Shannon was beginning to worry that if she *didn't* get a handle on her stress soon, she wouldn't have a choice in keeping her job or not—she might not physically be capable of doing it.

⊬ ⊕ ⊬

As was evident in the above narrative with Principal Burkhart, educators are confronting stressors in their work environments and society at large that can have lasting professional and personal consequences. This doesn't even begin to unpack the difficulties teachers deal with in their day-to-day work and home lives—things like chronic pain and mental health crises; interpersonal conflicts with coworkers, students, and family members; significant underfunding that often requires personal spending to adequately perform one's job; and a reduced quality of life and sense of purpose.

The term "micro" for these individualized issues isn't meant to diminish them at all, as they can feature significantly in an educator's lived experience and influence it arguably more so than the structural issues within the whole system.

Micro Challenges for Educators: The Day-to-Day Grind

If you were to ask new teachers why they were going into the profession, you'd likely get similar responses from most related to their love of children and/or learning. You'd probably hear phrases about "wanting to make a difference," and the excitement of "seeing the lightbulb moments" when watching a child learn something new. Teachers hold dearly to these sentiments in the midst of the many daily challenges that threaten to derail them from their mission a hundred times in a given day.

With every passing year, educators have to continue to adapt in an environment that doesn't provide many resources to help them meet their goals. Classroom supplies are often doled out piecemeal, and borrowing from others becomes a necessary part of everyday work. If you've ever watched a group of teachers at the end of a professional development training, you might be tempted to label them as "hoarders" as they cleared every table of the complimentary pens, notepads, and highlighters made available during the training. In truth, this behavior is less about hoarding and much more a reflection of the reality in which teachers work and live, constantly seeking adequate supplies due to repeated budget cuts and fiscal constraints. The frustration of working in a system where many policies, procedures, and financial decisions are made by people far removed from a teacher's day-to-day lived experience continues to disillusion many educators, who frequently have to purchase paper, pencils, and even facial tissues from their own limited wages for their students and classrooms.

Those who aren't familiar with the demands of teaching might think, "Shorter workdays, multiple breaks, and summers off? What are you complaining about?" But again, the truth is that educators' work weeks extend much longer than the traditional forty hours. The physical time spent with students, while the most fulfilling part for many, is frequently the shortest actual time commitment. Educators devote many evenings, weekends, and summer hours to researching, planning, and crafting their curriculums—it's not uncommon for teachers who also have their own children to be seen working on lesson plans while attending their child's soccer practice or band concert!

Teachers can be responsible for feeding students breakfast, lunch, and snacks between meals—because we know that when a brain is hungry, a student will have trouble engaging in learning. Furthermore, many schools across the country have installed washers and dryers and offer closets or uniform support so that students are clean, comfortable, and better equipped to study (with the teachers now in charge of clothing maintenance).

The medical issues students have at school are significantly on the rise as well, and most schools are limited in their available health services to assist with them. More children are coming to the classroom with significant allergies requiring heavy monitoring and emergency plans—multiple nut allergies, glucose intolerance, lactose intolerance, asthma, bee allergies, and more. The number of children requiring medications for anxiety and behavioral concerns *far* exceeds those of previous decades, and teachers are being asked to manage their students' behavioral health issues at alarmingly high rates. If a full-time nurse is not available on the school site (and they often are not), these physical and mental health responsibilities all fall upon the teacher.

With the increase of unique needs in the classroom for special education students, English language learners, medical concerns, gifted and talented children, and behavior management challenges, it's not unusual for teachers to spend multiple hours in consultation with other specialists assigned to work with these children—a collaborative effort that requires even more time and resources. Educators are also expected to spend additional time in trainings, learning the new procedures and policies to support each initiative as curriculums evolve. With no additional time being added to the existing calendar (or increased wages for more time spent working!), fitting all of these additional trainings and implementations into a forty-hour work week becomes virtually impossible.

Last, but certainly not least, is the recent trend of parents and communities lacking in their support of educators. Seasoned teachers likely look back with fondness to a time when they'd call a parent to discuss a behavior concern with a child, and the parent responded with an apology and a commitment to follow up with the child with conversation and consequences.

Now teachers report it is far more common when reaching out to a parent to be met with blame directed at the teacher themselves for the child's disruptive behavior. "What did you do to make them act that way?" or "I think they're bored and acting out. Why don't you teach in a way that's more entertaining, so they aren't bored?" are commonly received responses when teachers discuss a student's behavioral or academic concerns with parents.

It's beyond evident that educators are having to fight *hard* to be seen and respected for the well-educated, very hard-working professionals they truly are—and this fight is having long-term (and sometimes permanent) physical, mental, financial, and interpersonal effects.

Physical Effects for Educators

- Research examining the sleep quality of high school teachers stated that **more than half of the participants were diagnosed with sleep so poor** that it compromised their health, quality of life, and teaching performance.[26]
- A report of early childhood teachers in Oklahoma stated **that two-thirds of participants had work-related physical pain in at least one area**—these findings were consistent with research conducted in four other states.[27]
- A 2020 study found that **one in four teachers (nearly 1.5 million) had a pre-existing condition** that put them at higher risk for severe illness from COVID-19.[28]

Mental Effects for Educators

- A national survey from 2014 found that **46 percent of teachers reported high daily stress levels** during the school year.[29]

- Research examining educators' experiences during the 2020-2021 school year found that teachers **were three times more likely to experience depression** than the general adult population,[30] with a 2019 publication reporting that **higher levels of depressive symptoms in teachers were associated with poorer student wellbeing** and psychological distress.[31]
- A 2018 survey examining student-to-teacher bullying stated that 62 percent of respondents reported verbal bullying and nearly 35 percent reported physical bullying from their students, **resulting in negative emotions, disempowerment, low morale, and low work motivation**.[32]

Financial Effects for Educators

- It was estimated that 94 percent of teachers paid for classroom supplies from their own funds at some point during the 2014-2015 school year, **averaging 479 dollars out of pocket**.[33] The average yearly out-of-pocket amount **went up to 750 dollars in the 2020-2021 year** to accommodate for COVID-19 implementations such as distance and asynchronous learning, special technology and equipment, and additional supplies.[34]
- A survey analyzing teachers' out-of-pocket spending for their classrooms reported that since 2015, **teacher spending has increased by 25 percent**.[35]
- A policy in schools in California and several other U.S. states upholds that teachers who miss more than their allotted ten "sick days" per school year **must pay the costs for a substitute teacher themselves—** approximately 200 dollars a day, in some cases.[36]
- A 2017 paper investigating salary rates and the cost of living for educators in the U.S.'s 100 largest school districts found that in more than a quarter of districts, **first-year teachers couldn't afford rent for a one-bedroom apartment**,[37] while a 2019 report found that **economically anxious teachers tended to have worse attendance** and were 50 percent more likely to depart a district within two years.[38]

Interpersonal Effects for Educators

- A 2014 paper studying the effects of students' behaviors on teachers' occupational stress levels found that distant and detached behaviors from pupils led to higher levels of emotional exhaustion, depersonalization, and the **intensification of existing stress-related symptoms for teachers**.[39]
- Research on teachers' interpersonal relationships stated that those who experienced conflict with coworkers and/or students reported negative feelings of stress, sorrow, disappointment, insensitivity, and uneasiness, and **were more likely to dislike their profession and have reduced performance**.[40]
- A report published in 2019 on school climates for teachers asserted that just over one-third of participants felt there was "a great deal of cooperative effort among the staff members," with only 13.3 percent affirming they received support from parents—and that this **played a role in permanent departure from the profession**.[41]
- A study on interpersonal workplace mistreatment (defined as abusive supervision, undermining, ostracism, unwanted sexual attention, and incivility) found a **positive correlation between increased mistreatment and increased burnout**, above and beyond a teacher's inoculating personality factors of conscientiousness and agreeableness.[42]

With the evidence above to support just how taxing the situation has been (and continues to be) for educators at all levels, we wish to reiterate our deepest respect and admiration for every individual who considers pursuing this profession even in the face of such obstacles. To be an educator today speaks of your compassionate, altruistic, and mission-driven nature to help those in such great need: our nation's young people as they grow.

This selfless quality you and so many educators possess can lead to an overextension of your resources—mental, physical, and financial—as the students you teach and the administration you work for never stop needing *something* at all times. Without healthy and stable boundaries in place to protect yourself from these daily demands, toxic stress and burnout are inevitable—which is exactly what our young teacher at Freda's school, Alexandra Hernandez, is coping with at the moment.

A Day in the Life of Ms. Hernandez

Alexandra sighed in relief as the bell rang to release her class for lunch. She blinked rapidly as her sixth-graders left in a rush, hoping to quell the tears that had been threatening to fall all morning since the superintendent, Mr. Briguglio, had come in and wordlessly watched her fumble through a lesson for twenty of the most stressful minutes of her life.

Once her classroom was mercifully quiet and she could walk up and down the aisles cleaning and reorganizing the space—haphazardly thrown candy wrappers, desks and chairs out of place, a forgotten notebook she'd return to her student tomorrow—Alexandra seriously considered skipping her own shared mealtime in the teachers' lounge to hide out in her classroom alone. It was the only way she could guarantee avoidance of the snarky comments and general hostility from several of her coworkers, which had gotten worse ever since she'd stood up for Kail Jensen, the admittedly difficult student the others had all decided to hate and band together against.

While Alexandra agreed that he was an unpleasant aspect of their daily routines and had even been on the receiving end of Kail's profanity-filled verbal attacks more than once, she didn't think it was right for a bunch of adults to make it their personal mission to undermine a child's learning and possibly his entire future because he'd "made a finger gun and pretended to shoot them" or disrupted their class with the occasional angry outburst.

Sure, she was twenty-three, newly graduated, and a bit inexperienced (something they never failed to remind her about), but sometimes Alexandra wondered why any of these people had pursued the field of teaching. The others seemed to hate most aspects of their jobs, preferring to gossip with one another during breaks and disparaging her efforts any time she talked about a new lesson plan she'd designed. They'd chuckle to themselves about "how they *used* to do that" and "how much it had always cost," because the school would never give her additional funds when they hadn't even replaced the broken copy machines in two separate buildings since the start of the school year.

This treatment, coupled with the fact they almost never attended the "mandatory" after-school meetings and trainings she went to and only seemed interested in befriending her when they wanted to add *their* responsibilities to *her* workload, had made Alexandra feel more isolated, anxious, and stressed than ever.

Alexandra's phone vibrated in her pocket and she cringed, instantly aware of who it was without needing to check the screen—her roommate, surely inquiring about her share of the rent for the upcoming month. Alexandra was a bit low on funds, having underestimated how much she'd already spent of her biweekly paycheck on snacks and candy for the kids, dry-erase markers and copy paper (since the lounge was always out), and other classroom supplies. This would be the fourth time she'd borrowed money from her family this year to pay her bills, and she didn't want it to become a habit.

Some mornings she'd sit in her running car in the parking lot, calculating how badly her finances might be hit if she called out of work. That was *another* habit she didn't want to develop, but at least once a week lately, Alexandra found it hard to gather enough energy to even get out of bed, let alone teach six periods to over a hundred students. She didn't know much about depression, but the recent lack of motivation to even do things like wash and brush her hair, clean the house, or respond to her friends' and family's texts and calls had become acute enough that her roommate and parents had commented on it. She'd never felt like this before—she'd always been so *happy*. She'd wanted to help her students pursue their dreams, provide them with the support they might not be getting at home, and make a difference in their lives and in the world as a whole. Now she felt so emotionally, physically, and financially drained that any sense of mission or vision she'd once held were long-ago figments of her younger, far more naïve self.

Maybe becoming a teacher had just been one massive, expensive, depressing mistake, and Alexandra wondered whether she should quit and start over elsewhere—not only due to her financial situation, but to preserve her sanity.

✖ ✚ ✚

The profession of teaching and the educators who dedicate themselves to it are at a crossroads, just as Mrs. Burkhart and Ms. Hernandez were in their respective scenarios. As working conditions remain below where they should be (or continue to deteriorate), it can be a Herculean task just to exit your car and go into the school each morning, let alone to find time for restorative self-care amidst your compounding responsibilities in today's schools. If you find yourself daydreaming about escape or actually taking the steps to change career paths permanently, know that *you are not alone* in this unease, disharmony, and pain.

It can feel like the environmental stressors and requests for your time and energy never end—the evolving school safety protocols; district administrations that can so frequently be out of touch with the daily plight of frontline teachers, nurses, counselors, and other staff; and difficult parents or unruly students—and because you're a human being and not a machine, this can result in toxic levels of stress, burnout, and even full-blown compassion fatigue.

Coming up in chapter three, we will define these developments in more detail, and discuss why educators are experiencing symptoms of anxiety, depression, and post-traumatic stress at unprecedented rates. Most important of all is that we will then begin to unpack the foundational Forward-Facing® truth that promises you infinite healing and professional resilience in your educational career, no matter what. Because what you *think* is the problem— your environment or stressors within it, which will always remain out of your control—is actually not the problem at all. And learning that the source of your suffering is something you have *full control* over, anytime and anywhere, is an empowering realization indeed.

Forward-Facing® Reflection 2: Changes Within Our Work and Within Ourselves

Following our review of the difficult and ever-changing conditions for educators, we encourage you to spend some time thinking and writing down some of your feelings, thoughts, and observations about how your own work may have changed over time since you began. Do you have any concerns about your professional role or the field as a whole, and if so, what are they? Again, notice how your body or mind might shift in response to these kinds of thoughts, and take a few deep, slow breaths as you write to stay present and calm (this is another important tool for Forward-Facing® professional resilience discussed a little later—regulating ourselves with simple, *mindful* techniques for relaxation).

1. How I have seen education change over time:

_____

_____

_____

_____

_____

2. How I have changed in my work as an educator over time:

_____

_____

_____

_____

_____

CHAPTER THREE

WHERE SUFFERING BEGINS FOR EDUCATORS

*The greatest weapon against stress is our ability
to choose one thought over another.*

William James

It's not stress that kills us, it is our reaction to it.

Hans Selye

EDUCATORS WHO DEVOTE their careers (and so much of their personal time) to shepherding children's educations and futures, all the while persevering in the face of the many obstacles we've just unpacked in chapter two, deserve untold amounts of recognition, support, and resources from the communities they serve. Instead, what we're seeing is the exact opposite scenario: teachers contending with debilitating levels of anxiety and depression, toxic levels of traumatic stress that can have permanent physical and mental consequences, and high rates of educator burnout that regularly devolve into full-blown compassion fatigue.

If recent years have taught us anything, it's that our society continues to expect teachers to be emotionally stable, ever-present supports for their students during critical times in their development—and while crises continue to happen on a national and global scale. Whether it's asynchronous learning or significant technological shifts in the classroom, additional trainings for everything from active shooter drills to new curriculums about racial inequities and social justice, or memorizing dozens of students' special dietary needs; medications; or particular mental health diagnoses; educators today need to have superhuman levels of stamina, attention, and fortitude to meet these responsibilities.

Yet the fact remains that educators *are* human—and their energy reserves need replenishing. Unfortunately, teachers are not being provided with even a semblance of the support or education recommended to bolster them in their demanding workplaces, resulting in thousands of compassionate and mission-driven teachers who can no longer ward off the insidious effects of burnout and traumatic stress that lead to compassion fatigue.

In order to help you in your pursuit of Forward-Facing® healing and professional resilience regardless of the outside resources you may currently have access to or not, let's examine what these developments look like in greater detail—the symptoms, the triggers, and how changing your *perception* of what the problem is gives you complete control to truly heal from it.

Burnout and Compassion Fatigue: Connected but Different

There's undoubtedly a universal trait among all who pursue a career in children's education: profound care and dedication to our nation's youth, and a desire to help them in a tangible way to be healthy, happy, and successful. This empathy and passion for helping also imbues teachers with a unique vulnerability; because you care so much, you're highly susceptible to burnout and compassion fatigue in the workplace.

We've mentioned both of these several times, and while they are connected—i.e., burnout is a *factor* of compassion fatigue—they're different occurrences. Burnout refers to the negative effects resulting from an educator's interactions with a high-demand environment and the people in it. It's traditionally characterized by three dimensions:

-Feelings of exhaustion or depletion of energy.

-Reduced professional efficacy/low accomplishment at work.

-Increased mental distance or disconnection from one's job and co-workers, and/or feelings of cynicism or negativity about work (a.k.a. depersonalization).[43]

Below are some of the most frequently reported symptoms of burnout—see if any of these sound familiar and have occurred for you or your colleagues in some capacity.

Common Symptoms of Burnout

Fatigue	Hopelessness	Poor work performance
Depression	Automated/robotic	Increased errors
Malaise/general unhappiness	Cynicism	Inefficient/ineffective
Increased absenteeism or sick days	Self-medicating with alcohol/drugs/food	Not caring about quality of work/results
Irritability/anger	Loss of interest and joy	Critical of others
Anxious/stressed out	Shutting down	Deceit/dishonesty
Withdrawal and isolation	Relational difficulty	Avoiding work

If any of the above resonate at all, you're not alone—it's been estimated that between 5 and 30 percent of educators experience symptoms of burnout at any given time.[44] Left unaddressed and combined with instances of secondary traumatic stress ("witnessed" or vicariously experienced trauma, which we'll explore a little later in this chapter), burnout has a significant chance of worsening to become compassion fatigue.

But what exactly *is* compassion fatigue?

Professor Charles Figley, a pioneer in the field of traumatic stress treatment, was the first to define compassion fatigue in 1995 as "the combined effects of secondary traumatic stress and burnout."[45] Compassion fatigue can be described as a combination of psychological, physiological, moral, and spiritual damage caused by *prolonged exposure* to the "toxic" environment of caring for others in your career in education.

Compassion fatigue is not the *inevitable* consequence of working in a toxic environment—it occurs if we haven't yet built up the necessary "antibodies" of resilience needed to protect us from becoming infected. Below are a few factors of the professional teaching environment that make such defenses necessary; you'll likely recognize the parallels between these and the macro and micro problems within the education system that we listed in chapter two.

1. Performance demands that exceed human capabilities: Professional educators often work in environments that demand impeccable care and perfect outcomes for every student without exception. Of course, this is impossible. Humans are fallible. Regardless of our dedication, the quality and frequency of our training, and our experience in the field, we are bound to make mistakes occasionally. Even if we *were* able to deliver flawless teaching efforts, we could never guarantee students' perfect scores or outcomes. We can only extend our best efforts. But, especially if we hold a position of authority, our best efforts are rarely enough. We are expected to set a standard of care that is impossible for anyone to consistently achieve. The stress produced by our ongoing failure to meet this unrealistic standard is toxic to our minds and bodies, and one of the most potent infectious agents for the development of compassion fatigue.

2. Insufficient resources to meet students' needs: The unrealistic demands of the workplace and the stress this produces are compounded by the limited resources available in many teaching environments. Chief among these is the meaningful face-to-face teaching time we get with students rather than worrying about standardized testing curriculums, administrative tasks, or trainings, as well as the significantly limited resources available to us for assessing and meeting our kids' needs in the classroom. As the pressure increases from all fronts to reduce our nation's investment in education, we are continuously mandated to do more with less.

3. Ongoing exposure to stressed or traumatized students, parents, and coworkers: As educators with hundreds of students under our care and stewardship every year, many of us spend significant time with children, colleagues, and parents who are navigating their own fears, stress, and trauma. Principals and other administrators spend their days interacting with anxious teachers, bullied students, and belligerent parents. School counselors regularly listen to stories of abuse and pain from students, and carry the burden of doing all they can to provide safety and stability within their limited scope of resources. Nurses tend to injured and sick students, and are a front-line defense for testing and the prevention of illness from spreading throughout a school. As we shall discuss shortly, prolonged exposure to such powerful emotions and situations can induce secondary trauma in educators.

All of these factors can cause an imbalance in our threat-detection systems that is extremely hazardous to our health and wellbeing. Biologically speaking, compassion fatigue results when this primitive, subconscious threat response—often referred to as the "fight-or-flight response"—becomes chronically overactivated, causing us to perceive danger at work or home where none actually exists. (These bodily processes will be detailed at length in chapter four, including their evolutionarily useful survival purposes that are no longer needed in our modern workplaces.)

Let us take a moment to repeat this significant statement: *Compassion fatigue occurs when we have been perceiving threat for a significant duration of time (or at a high frequency) where there is little or no actual danger.* Acknowledging this fact is the first step to interrupting our chronically over-activated threat response and creating space to heal.

Typical symptoms of compassion fatigue have similarities with those of burnout, but to a much more severe degree. Those who've been in the teaching field for a substantial amount of time may certainly recognize these having occurred at some point for themselves or coworkers.

1. Physical symptoms: You may feel so tired and physically depleted that you find it increasingly difficult to drag yourself out of bed and go to work or to maintain your normal exercise regimen. You may also feel restless and have trouble sleeping, or notice that your desire for sex and your enjoyment of intimacy have diminished significantly.

2. Psychological and emotional symptoms: You may be able to fall asleep, but are later awakened by work-related nightmares that leave you feeling anxious, cynical, and pessimistic about the day to come. You may also find that your self-confidence and self-esteem are shaken when you experience difficulty making decisions that once came easily, or discover that the decisions you're making are poor ones. To compensate, you may shut down emotionally. You might turn to overeating, excessive use of alcohol, or drugs to allay your pervasive sense of anxiety and unease. As your self-image and self-control erode, you may find yourself exploding in rage at friends and family members, thus damaging loving relationships that could otherwise sustain you and help you heal. Or you may compensate by isolating yourself so that no one can see how ashamed and self-destructive you've become.

3. Professional symptoms: Your performance at work may suffer because you're distracted and unable to focus. Perhaps you find yourself becoming increasingly erratic, irritable, and short-tempered with your colleagues and students. You may be unable to put aside the demands of the school during off-hours, or obsess over imagined slights and perceived failures that make you wish you had the courage to simply march into your principal or superintendent's office and quit once and for all.

4. Spiritual symptoms: You may find yourself losing faith in the spiritual traditions and fundamental values that once anchored you to your community and provided solace, meaning, and purpose to your life. When friends and family notice your evident distress, you may strike out in anger and then isolate yourself, consumed with shame and confusion at your uncharacteristic loss of self-control.

Symptoms like these can be sneaky, infecting our lives gradually until our resources are depleted and we're thrown into crisis. By the time we realize that something has gone seriously wrong, we may feel so demoralized and discouraged that we lose hope of ever finding a way out and plan to leave the profession altogether.

Such is the case for our veteran teacher, Mr. Richardson, whose multitude of acute and chronic compassion fatigue symptoms have led to many distressing situations and unhealthy perceptions both at school and home in the narrative below.

A Day in the Life of Mr. Richardson

Mike unscrewed the cap off the orange bottle of anti-anxiety medication, checking to make sure no one else in the parking lot was close by before tossing back double his prescribed dose and chasing the pills with his soda. Mike sighed audibly as his blood pressure reduced in the following minutes, his near-blinding anger and panic from earlier ebbing to a more manageable degree. He kept replaying the scene from earlier that day over and over in his mind—Freda Whitmore's late arrival to class, and the insults she'd hurled at him. *I'd come in on time if you weren't the most boring teacher alive!* she'd shouted while the other kids laughed at his expense. *You clearly suck at your job—you should probably quit!*

What the twelve-year-old probably didn't realize was that Mike was seriously considering that very thing. He was just waiting for the principal to respond to that morning's email request for a meeting, at which point he'd most likely hand in his resignation unless Shannon could somehow talk him off the ledge. Six years of college for a master's degree followed by twenty-five years of teaching at the same school (a feat unto itself), and *this* was what he had to show for it? Struggling to convince himself to return to his classroom without anti-anxiety pills at lunchtime, and counting down the minutes until he could potentially walk away from a career (and retirement benefits) he'd spent his entire adult life building.

If he was honest with himself, things had been crumbling for a while. Bianca had moved out several months back almost immediately after their daughter left for college, leaving Mike to stew in his resentment and fear that any knock on the door could be someone serving him divorce papers. Even before Bianca left, Mike had drawn away from her and their circle of friends and stopped attending their Bible studies and church events. He just couldn't muster up the energy to meet their demands anymore—to act like he cared when others shared their personal challenges, to get vulnerable enough to ask for prayer or support himself, to be the once-jovial Mike who used to drop everything to help someone the moment they asked. Now if he wasn't simmering with right-under-the-surface rage at the many people who slighted him on a daily basis, he felt *flat*. Unmotivated. Disconnected from himself, his family, his students, and his colleagues. Why put so much effort into a marriage, a career, friendships, or parenting when everyone was only out to get him or use him? He was sick—*physically* sick!—of them all, and he didn't deserve such inhumane treatment.

Mike looked down when his phone vibrated—finally, a response from Shannon saying she had some availability the following day. He mused over what he might say in the meeting: *I can no longer tolerate this position or the disrespectful students who don't deserve my expertise!* Maybe detailing to her how much money he *could* have been making all these years with his education and experience, and for a quarter of the time he spent teaching, grading, and attending miscellaneous (uncompensated) trainings each month. He could tell her all about the personal costs he'd incurred and barely been able to pay for in recent years—at least a dozen sessions of couples' therapy at Bianca's behest (he was convinced they'd just been an excuse for his wife to disparage him under the guise of "therapy"), and many medications and visits to various medical professionals for chronic pain, digestive and intestinal issues, and his recent Type II diabetes and high blood pressure diagnoses. He was certain these issues—and the ways he'd been self-medicating with junk food, sweets, and increasing amounts of alcohol on weekends—were the result of his unfulfilling career and the students and needy coworkers who seemed intent on making his life hell.

Mike typed out an answer to the principal that they could meet the following day during his planning time before hurriedly eating the rest of his burger and fries and finishing off his thirty-two-ounce soda. He didn't want to admit that Freda's accusation had hit the deepest, most sensitive fear he carried: that he was a bad teacher. It was true that he did recycle his lessons, and he was pretty sure a student or two had cried after his admonishments for their poor behavior. Sometimes he could barely stomach the sound of his own uninspired voice, identifying for a moment with his students when their eyes glazed over or they snuck their phones from their backpacks, thinking he couldn't see.

He'd morphed so far from the man he'd once been that when he looked in the mirror, it was like meeting the gaze of a stranger. Mike was without a wife and daughter, without his friends or support groups, and without a purpose or mission that held real meaning any longer. He was lost, and truly had no idea how to find himself again—if that was even possible.

✖ ✚ ✜

Burnout and compassion fatigue should be understood as the natural and inevitable consequences of caring for others in the profession of education. They are *not* signs of weakness, character flaws, a moral failing, or a pathology—they are indicators of an overactivated nervous system that's been "on" and perceiving threat for too long.

Now we'll delve into what causes our bodies and brains to develop this response to those workplace situations, environmental factors, and interactions with others that have been deemed "dangerous" and activate our threat response. It's called painful past learning or *traumagenesis*, and is the origination point of *all* our stress, regardless of what happens in or out of the classroom.

Painful Past Learning:
The Genesis of Traumatic Stress

As we stated earlier in the chapter, vicariously experienced or "witnessed" trauma was cited by traumatic stress expert Charles Figley as the second precursor to compassion fatigue. While other professionals working high-demand jobs do experience symptoms of burnout, those of us tasked with caring for our students (and the myriad responsibilities this entails, ranging from feeding and clothing our kids to lockdown drills to monitoring for serious allergies and contagious illnesses) are exposed to a different sort of threat than the environmental stressors commonly associated with burnout.

Therefore, educators must acknowledge, understand, and find ways to prevent and heal from the specific effects of secondary or "witnessed" trauma in order to achieve professional resilience and a high quality of life, starting with the comprehension of this concept of traumagenesis.

Put simply, traumagenesis is the concept that any pain-producing learning experience in our life will teach us to perceive future situations with any similarities to that first experience as a present-day threat.

Painful (i.e., perceivably threatening) life experiences + learning = Perceived threat in similar future situations.

Traumagenesis doesn't just include those stressful events that occur to us *personally*—we can also be deeply affected by witnessed or secondary trauma (for example, when one of our students comes to class with signs of physical abuse or neglect and our reports to CPS seem to go unanswered), or even spending time in an environment near other traumatized people—like the teachers' lounge when everyone is stressed out because the superintendent is visiting campus.

These three categories of traumagenesis can occur alone or in combination, all resulting in significant post-traumatic symptoms that contribute to burnout and compassion fatigue.

1. Primary traumatic stress: This trauma is directly experienced by you during one or more situations that threaten your wellbeing, and over which you have little to no control. Primary traumatic stress can include exposure to one-time traumatic events like physical or verbal assault from a student, an active shooter warning that puts the school into lockdown, or a natural disaster that puts you and your students at risk—these types of instances are called "big-T" trauma.

It can also occur over a longer period with repetitive, smaller occurrences of trauma, known as "little-t" trauma. Encounters with argumentative or belittling parents during meetings, regular exposure to viruses or other illnesses, budget cuts that put your financial security in jeopardy, or virtual harassment from students would all be examples of this type of trauma.

2. Secondary traumatic stress: This is personally witnessed trauma that directly threatens someone else's wellbeing. It can be witnessed in vivo (i.e. at the real-time site of the trauma, such as a parent scolding their child harshly in front of you until they cry), via forms of media, or by listening to another's narrative of their traumatic experiences.

3. Environmental trauma: This type of trauma occurs when in proximity to people who are suffering from anxiety and their own chronically overactivated nervous systems. You might not witness them being actively traumatized, but their mere presence while in a dysregulated state can traumatize you.

How do you feel while you spend time with someone who is very anxious? Now contrast that with how you feel when you spend time with someone who is mellow and soft-spoken. Human beings are herd animals, and when one of the herd begins perceiving threat, they will set off the threat response of those in their periphery.

Think about the last time you were in a crowded airport during the holidays—the hustle, the frantic travelers, the woman bemoaning the loss of her bags to an official while a family races by, terrified they are going to miss their flight. Even with your ticket secured, your bag checked, and your terminal identified, being surrounded by others in a dysregulated state will inevitably influence your own state of being. Many of us find ourselves exhausted after a day of travel, and *this* is the primary reason for that exhaustion—we've been in a high-energy state all day long.

Now imagine the fact that in some schools many educators are doing this *six or more times a day* with every transition between classes as soon as the bell rings. There's a stampede of students gathering their materials and hurrying out into the hall as we try to keep order between periods, sometimes with fights ensuing or kids screaming as everyone tries to get where they need to go (or avoid where they need to go) as quickly as possible.

This is the sequence painful past learning takes: Once we encounter disturbing and/or threatening stimuli, whether it is personally experienced, witnessed, or a facet of our environment, those components will forever after influence how we see the world and the people in it. This means that a student witnessing a teacher "calling out" or criticizing another child can be just as traumatizing as if it had happened to the student themselves. The trauma doesn't just occur for the child being confronted in a harsh manner, but for every child in the room hearing and seeing the experience. The same goes for teachers who might have repeated exposure to a colleague across the hall who continuously yells at their students. The teacher isn't even in the same room as their angry and dysregulated colleague, but being in the same vicinity as them can have a "contagious" traumatizing effect.

When we work in a consistently stressful environment like education, we are encountering *thousands* of these perceived threats (where there is little to no actual danger) and remaining in our fight-or-flight "survival mode" for longer periods of time, which creates hyper-attunement to the perceived threats. It is a self-perpetuating cycle, and one that can only be halted through diligent and mindful self-regulation and relaxation (this is the first step to Forward-Facing® professional resilience, and is taught in chapter six).

The development of traumatic stress is just as insidious as burnout—on a day-to-day basis, we may not be aware of the negative effects beginning to occur from our interactions with others who are navigating their own traumagenesis. Over time these effects build up, snowballing until our own personal threshold of resilience is reached (everyone's is different). It's like water creeping higher and higher toward the top of a dam—if there is no additional outlet and the rain does not stop, it *will* overflow. In the case of toxic amounts of secondary traumatic stress and burnout, a breached threshold results in the manifestation of compassion fatigue and/or a host of other detrimental physical and mental effects.

There is considerable research pointing to toxic amounts of stress as the root cause for many diseases, psychological problems, and immune system dysfunctions, ranging from severe depression and cognitive impairment to increased risk of cardiovascular disease and autoimmune disorders.

There are two facets to examine when it comes to toxic amounts of traumatic stress: immediate/present symptoms, and long-term effects. While the graphs below aren't exhaustive, they provide a framework for some of the most common symptoms and long-term effects that can arise from experiencing post-traumatic stress too frequently or for too long.

(Note: It's worth mentioning that for most educators experiencing post-traumatic stress symptoms from their work, they are at subclinical levels that can be treated without the support of a mental health professional. There are some individuals at the far end of the spectrum, however, who may be navigating diagnosable PTSD as dictated by specific criteria including regular and frequent flashbacks, high levels of disturbance that severely impact daily living, dissociative episodes, suicidal ideation or attempts, and/or other symptoms. Please refer to chapter five for a list of resources to receive professional care for these symptoms and/or other scenarios when trained support would be most beneficial and necessary.)

Symptoms of Toxic Amounts of Traumatic Stress

Physical	Emotional/Cognitive	Behavioral
- Skin conditions such as acne/eczema	- Feeling overwhelmed and/or a loss of control	- Unhealthy eating (overeating or undereating)
- Sleep difficulties/insomnia	- Increased irritability/anger	- Drug, tobacco, and/or alcohol use
- Stomachache	- Anxiety/racing thoughts	- Social withdrawal
- Chest pains	- Depression or sadness	- Isolating oneself from others
- Fatigue	- Restlessness	- Exercising less often
- Muscle pain and tension	- Feeling bad about yourself/worthless	- Sleeping too much or too little
- Headaches and migraines	- Mood instability	- Procrastinating/neglecting responsibilities
- Indigestion/nausea	- Decreased sex drive	- Compulsions/addictive behaviors
- Increased sweating	- Loss of motivation	- Aggressive or angry outbursts
- Weakened immune system	- Forgetfulness and disorganization	- Nail biting, pacing, or other nervous habits
- Neck and back pain	- Dissociative episodes	

Long-Term Effects of Toxic Amounts of Traumatic Stress

Physical	Emotional/Cognitive	Behavioral
- Early death	- Suicidal ideation	- Anxiety disorders
- Hardening of arteries	- Suicide attempts	- Eating disorders
- Abnormal heart rate/high blood pressure	- Burnout/ compassion fatigue	- Substance dependence - and/or abuse
- Heart disease	- Schizophrenia	- Alcoholism
- Obesity	- Alzheimer's disease	- Impotence/sexual arousal disorder
- Asthma and arthritis flare-ups	- Personality disorders	- Neuroticism
- Ulcers and/or irritable bowel syndrome (IBS)	- Major depressive disorder (MDD)	- Involvement in near-fatal/fatal accidents
- Fertility issues	- Post-traumatic stress disorder (PTSD)	- Decreased hygienic practices
- Inflammation	- Psychosis/brief psychotic disorder	- Reduced work efficiency/ productivity
- Diabetes		- Gambling

Another group of educators at risk for toxic amounts of traumatic stress include the school counselors, social workers, and nurses witnessing their students' pain and suffering every day in their lines of care work. We'll spend some time now with our school counselor, Ms. Waite, to see how the traumatic stress from her job, combined with untreated childhood trauma, have led to dissociation and isolation from vital support systems in her life, as she tries to muscle her way through an unsustainable workload on her own.

A Day in the Life of Ms. Waite

Holly swallowed to relieve the lump in her throat as she strode away from one of her favorite students, Freda Whitmore, her arms aching with the weight of the standardized tests she needed to pass out to the third- and fourth-grade classes in the next forty minutes. She'd told Freda to return to her office that afternoon, but Holly honestly didn't know how she'd find the time (or the energy, to be quite honest) to see the sixth-grader for an impromptu meeting on a busy Monday afternoon.

Holly took a shaky breath and made her way toward her colleague's classroom first. Sierra was a fourth-grade teacher who was also in her late thirties like Holly was, and they had similarly quiet temperaments and had grown to be good friends since Sierra started at the school two years prior.

Holly was still reeling from a counseling appointment she'd had with another sixth-grade student that day, who'd revealed they were struggling with self-harm behaviors and disordered eating and had hinted there was abuse that had been happening at home for a while. It was a scenario Holly found herself in so often now—stories of domestic violence or messy divorces, bullying online and in person, neglectful parents who were rarely home or battling addictions, a lack of food or sufficient clothing or hygiene products, and even several students whose families were living out of motels or in campgrounds because they'd lost their housing since the pandemic.

She felt like a container, with her students and their parents and even her coworkers pouring their problems into her, day after day. She wasn't sure how much more she could hold, and this overflow had only become more evident in recent years, as nightmares and flashbacks from her own childhood trauma following her older brother's drug overdose and sudden death had started resurfacing. Sometimes she'd wake up in the middle of the night drenched in sweat and shaking all over, while other times during stressful appointments with angry parents or struggling students she'd dissociate, her entire body going numb as it felt like she'd stepped out of herself and was watching from somewhere else.

Though Holly had a supportive long-time partner and friends like Sierra she knew she was supposed to confide in about the pains of her past and present, she couldn't bring herself to add any more stress to their busy lives. Instead she buried it all beneath an impossibly busy schedule, trying to fix all of her students' problems herself rather than referring them out to other specialists or social workers. She'd given her personal cell number to several of her most at-risk students to call if they felt they were in danger during outside-of-school hours, and had spent hundreds of her own funds on snacks and toiletries to hand out as needed for that school year alone. In some ways, Holly thought that if she helped as many hurting students as possible, it might somehow heal her own pain and stress without her needing to address it directly.

When she wasn't attending to her students, Holly's administrative tasks also never seemed to end. Whether she was managing the standardized testing for dozens of classrooms, reporting to Child Protective Services or the police when a student's safety or health were suspected to be in jeopardy, keeping up on her counseling notes, or filing paperwork for various resources for her students, Holly was putting in twelve-hour workdays regularly.

Her partner, James, had recently started to complain about how little time she had for him, and that when they were together she seemed "checked out."

"You need to set some boundaries with your time," he'd scolded her a month earlier during a rare occasion when she was free for dinner. "You seem overwhelmed, and you're working too much."

"I'm fine," Holly had rebuffed, moving her hand away from his when he tried to hold it. "I'm helping my students. I can't just 'stop being there' for them—they need me. You don't know what it's like."

"Then *tell* me what it's like," James had said, reaching again for her hand. Holly let him grasp it, but shook her head and kept her mouth shut. She never wanted to burden James with what was going on, not to mention the counselor-student confidentiality and ethical boundaries she always needed to keep in mind.

Holly was isolated, that was true. A bit of it was due to her position's confidentiality requirements, but she knew most of her seclusion from others was self-imposed. Sometimes when Holly went for long periods of time without a break she'd crash, arriving home on a Friday afternoon and leaving her phone in the car for the entire weekend. She wouldn't go out to grab it until Sunday night, scrolling through the dozens of worried texts and calls from James (unless he'd already shown up to her house to check on her, which he'd done numerous times lately), plus a barrage of work and personal emails and the occasional *Hey, you doin' okay?* text from Sierra or another of Holly's friends.

Doing just fine, sorry been swamped with work! she'd reply, adding a stream of smiley-face emojis to hopefully make her lies more convincing.

Holly rearranged her face now as Sierra's classroom door came into view, trying to ensure the smile pasted on her mouth actually reached her eyes. It was a practice she'd developed during her chaotic, turbulent childhood and adolescent years when adults would ask if she was all right, or give her their condolences following the news of her brother's passing. She'd smile and nod, but quickly learned if the smile didn't reach her eyes they'd keep asking questions. She'd gotten significantly more convincing since then, but Holly could tell her façade was slipping...and she wasn't sure how much longer she could keep it in place.

⚒ ✚ ⚒

In an ideal world, the most effective treatment for burnout, secondary traumatic stress, and compassion fatigue is prevention—*keeping our daily stressful or traumatic experiences from ever encoding as such in our memories*. The wonderful news is that this prevention *is* possible, and it starts with a shift in your perception from that which you cannot control, like your environment or the people in it, to that which you *can*: your body and brain's response to it all.

Shifting Your Perception to Heal Yourself: You *Are* in Control

If you were to ask an educator whether their symptoms of stress and burnout were results of their environment, you'd likely get a resounding and unanimous *yes*! (Or a roll of the eyes at such a silly question.) Much of the research on burnout identifies workplace factors as the primary cause of these debilitating symptoms, a sentiment echoed by the many thousands of professionals at the start of their participation in Eric's Forward-Facing® Professional Resilience workshop over the years. But as we've mentioned several times already (and what all attendees to the workshop are taught in quick succession), the cause of your burnout, traumatic stress, and compassion fatigue is *not* your work environment—and the moment you believe it is, you become a victim of your workplace and all that transpires there.

Early on in Eric's formative work for treating burnout and compassion fatigue, he and several colleagues developed an alternative definition that offers the opportunity for individual resistance against the effects of a toxic environment. According to this definition, compassion fatigue is the "chronic condition of *perceived* demands outweighing *perceived* resources." (Eric and his colleagues also developed an individualized treatment protocol called the Accelerated Recovery Program for Compassion Fatigue, or ARP, that is available through the Forward-Facing® Institute for interested educators— please see Appendix II for more information on this.)

Let's break this down. We all know colleagues who are burned out. They believe their work is stressful, and that the demands placed upon them are the cause of their suffering. They might make statements like, "if only they would stop pulling me into meetings and just give me the time to actually do my job," or "they keep adding students to my classes and I don't know how I'm supposed to meet all of their needs," or "any more paperwork and I'll never leave my office!"

It is not the workplace or the demands that are debilitating these intelligent and sentient educators—*it is their perception*. How do these professionals perceive their work? As a series of overwhelming and insurmountable demands. How do they perceive the resources provided to them? Too little, too late.

Many professionals who are experiencing burnout and compassion fatigue become demoralized by their demanding environment and gradually devolve to a myopic focus on the problem. Just like our veteran teacher Mr. Richardson, they can recite to you everything that's wrong with students, co-workers, and workplace—sometimes without taking responsibility for any of their own decisions that played a part in this unhappiness.

Unfortunately, the only hope they have for a better quality of life is by: 1) leaving their work; 2) surviving until retirement; or 3) clinging to a rescue fantasy that the world will finally acknowledge these problems in education and step up to fix them. This is a sad and hopeless state, one with a low percentage of resolution for the professional. These suffering educators are using all their energy and capacity simply to survive their workday, rather than to find joy, peace, purpose, love, and meaning in their daily responsibilities.

The fact is that for the remainder of our careers, we will most often find ourselves unable to instigate much change in workplace policy, dictate our own schedule, select our interactions, or adjust the demands that our work levies upon us. When we tear our attention away from these things that are beyond our control and begin to focus upon that which we *can* control—our body and brain—we can gain some traction in diminishing the effects the work environment has upon us to lessen our symptoms.

⚓ ⚓ ⚓

For many educators like veteran teacher Mr. Richardson and school counselor Ms. Waite, the pain, suffering, interpersonal conflicts, misperceptions, and dissociative or unhealthy coping behaviors due to their burnout and toxic levels of secondary traumatic stress at work can feel inescapable at best and wholly incapacitating at worst. But as you now know, the real cause of any compassion fatigue an educator might be experiencing is due to their *perception* of the environment rather than the environment itself. This recognition charts the path for a significant shift toward healing oneself and constructing an unshakeable professional and personal resilience that lasts a lifetime.

The next piece of the puzzle is a better understanding of the *real* origins of all of your stress: the cascade of physiological processes occurring in your body and brain when you perceive a threat, so that you might interrupt them when there's little to no actual danger. No matter what might be happening around you in the environment—a surprise visit from the superintendent, a student who tries to embarrass you, a counseling session with a child who is hurting, or a barrage of urgent emails the moment you wake up on a Monday morning—you'll soon possess all the tools needed to shift out of survival mode immediately, thus regaining access to your highest cognitive functioning and behaving as your best self at all times.

The key to resolving all of your suffering and protecting yourself from accruing any more is within reach—onward with us to the next chapter!

Forward-Facing® Reflection 3: Spotting Elements of Compassion Fatigue

Now can be a time to reflect on this chapter's sections on compassion fatigue and burnout to see if you spot any elements of either in your own life. Refer to the earlier descriptions as well as the chart on toxic stress, writing down any symptoms that you might've experienced before or are currently experiencing. As you spend some time journaling about this, take deep breaths and practice a mindset of positive expectancy that healing is possible and *will* happen for you very soon.

1. Physical symptoms:

_____
_____
_____
_____

2. Psychological and emotional symptoms:

_____
_____
_____
_____

3. Professional symptoms:

_____
_____
_____
_____

4. Spiritual symptoms:

_____
_____
_____
_____

CHAPTER FOUR

"WHEN THE CLASSROOM FEELS DANGEROUS": PERCEIVED THREAT AND THE NERVOUS SYSTEM

The key to change...is to let go of fear.

Rosanne Cash

He who is not every day conquering some fear has not learned the secret of life.

Ralph Waldo Emerson

THE HUMAN BRAIN and nervous systems are marvels of engineering, with billions of cells interacting seamlessly to manage our bodies, interpret signals from our senses, and endow us with consciousness, reasoning, and a mission-driven desire to nurture our students and help them thrive. When it comes to perceiving and responding to threats, however, the most primitive parts of our brain and body instantly take over with one goal in mind: *survival*. Gone are our abilities to access deep cognitive functions like rationale and logic, to self-soothe or reflect, or to devise a detailed, well-thought-out plan to handle a disagreement with a student, teacher, or coworker with grace and empathy. Once the fight-or-flight response is activated, our body and brain's goal, one honed by millennia of evolution, is to stay alive (whether we realize it or not).

It's important to mention that *without* this unconscious threat response, we'd never experience the exhilarating anticipation of the first day of the school year, or the nervous thrill and subsequent relief following an important presentation we executed perfectly in front of our students, parents, or colleagues. We wouldn't howl with glee during rollercoasters, nor would we feel butterflies in our stomach when arriving at the airport to set off on a summer vacation to an exciting new locale. All of these situations trigger our fight-or-flight response, and if we didn't have it in limited and appropriate measure, we wouldn't enjoy the highest heights of passion, energy, and elation, or really feel much at all.

A short bout of mild stress can sometimes be highly beneficial, sharpening our concentration, helping us learn and teach, or preparing our muscles for quick and decisive action. This relationship between optimal performance and the physical and mental arousal induced by stress was first identified by American psychologists Robert Mearns Yerkes and John Dillingham Dodson back in 1908, with contemporary psychologists refining and codifying these insights as the "Yerkes-Dodson Law" or "Yerkes-Dodson Curve."

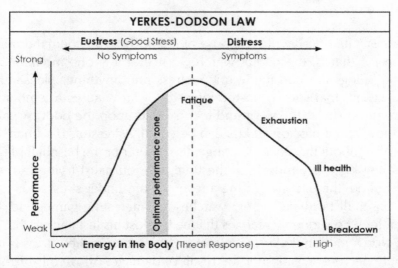

As any quick online review of the curve will reveal, low levels of arousal are *necessary* and *useful* for good performance. No one quickly diagnoses an ill-feeling student, responds to a surprise lockdown drill with efficiency, or successfully orchestrates a boardroom meeting with the district's directors while they are napping.

However, once the energy in our bodies climbs beyond optimal levels, our performance drops precipitously. This occurs sooner when we are engaged in complex and challenging tasks, especially those that are mentally and/or physically demanding. Yerkes and Dodson found that those undertakings requiring memory, concentration, and problem-solving were best completed at a lower point along the curve, while physically exerting (but simpler) tasks were excelled at with a higher arousal level. For every task there's an optimal level of arousal at which we're likely to perform our best— and *enjoy* ourselves while doing it.

Building off this idea of "good" and "bad" stress was Austrian-Canadian endocrinologist Hans Selye, who in 1936 defined the term of stress as "the nonspecific response of the body to any demand."

Selye expanded on this idea further in the seventies by classifying stress into two categories: distress (negative stress), and eustress (positive stress).

In Selye's book *Stress Without Distress*, he described how stress occurs at any moment that we are experiencing bodily arousal—even when the source is a positive one:

Stress is "the nonspecific response of the body to any demand made upon it," that is, the rate at which we live at any one moment. All living beings are constantly under stress and anything, pleasant or unpleasant, that speeds up the intensity of life, causes a temporary increase in stress, the wear and tear exerted upon the body. A painful blow and a passionate kiss can be equally stressful. The financier worrying about the stock exchange, the laborer or the baseball player straining his every muscle to the limit, the journalist trying to meet a deadline, the patient fighting a fever, all are under stress. But so is the baseball fan who merely watches an interesting game, and the gambler who suddenly realizes that he has lost his last cent or that he has won a million dollars. Contrary to widespread belief, stress is not simply nervous tension nor the result of damage. Above all, stress is not something to be necessarily avoided. It is associated with the expression of all our innate drives. Stress ensues as long as a demand is made on any part of the body. Indeed, complete freedom from stress is death!

Similarly to Yerkes and Dodson before him, Selye advocated for stress as a potentially enhancing factor of human interaction and existence, but one that was easily forced out of balance. This is an even truer sentiment in our high-demand, ever-evolving workplaces, with the problem arising when we're *chronically* activated.

Just like Mrs. Burkhart experiencing a panic attack following a jam-packed day of budget meetings or long-time teacher Mr. Richardson feeling frustrated and underappreciated when Freda arrived late to class, an overactivated, distressed brain-and-body system will lead us to view every interaction as a potential threat—oftentimes when there's no real danger at all.

Your Brain "On" Stress

Without diving too deeply into the abounding intricacies of neuroscience and biology, there are two main processes we'd like to explain further when examining our brain "on" stress: the amygdala's role in addressing trauma and cataloguing traumatic situations for future contexts, and the emergence of the "lizard brain" when a threat is perceived, as well as the behavioral effects that result because of the lizard brain's suppression of our executive cognitive functioning.

1. The amygdala: When we encounter anything frightening or painful in our lives (traumagenesis), this tiny but powerful cluster of neurons (sometimes referred to as the "fear center") in the temporal lobe of our brain takes charge, setting off impulses that dictate not only our reaction in the present moment, but the way we will interpret certain threatening situations in the future. Let's break things down a little further to understand the amygdala's role in threat perception, and why it's designed to behave this way.

- **What the amygdala does**: This structure plays a huge role in helping us form and store long-term memories associated with emotional events. As a part of our innate threat-detection system, the amygdala is given control during any type of emotion-inducing (re: stressful) situation to create and store a powerful memory that includes all of the sights, sounds, smells, feelings, and other physical and emotional sensations experienced during that emotional experience.

- **Why the amygdala does this**: The amygdala catalogues all of these situational details in order to *protect us and keep us alive* if and when any other threat that is remotely similar to the first painful experience presents itself. Here's a relatively minor example of this process: As children we might not have realized a glowing-red stovetop was hot, but after accidentally putting our hand on the scalding surface and experiencing the searing pain of our skin being burned, we'd never

55

again forget about the potential danger of that stovetop. Additionally, we'd be cautious around all other surfaces/items that even *slightly* resembled that stovetop, in order to avoid re-experiencing that kind of pain ever again. It is in the amygdala that this type of emotional learning about potential threat and pain occurs, and these are the lessons that majorly influence our perceptions of danger in present and future contexts.

-   **The long-term ramifications of the amygdala's role in the stress response**: Memories that are created in the amygdala over the hippocampus—the region where non-stress-induced memories are made and stored—means that we end up with these traumatic and stressful memories that are lodged or "stuck" in our consciousness, never being properly processed to remove their disturbing qualities so that we can move on. Instead, these "charged" memories retain their sharpness, continuously surfacing and resurfacing to keep our fight-or-flight response activated, oftentimes for much longer and more frequent occurrences as time goes on. (When individuals battling post-traumatic stress or PTSD talk about flashbacks or nightmares, *this* is the process they're referring to.)

Once we begin to comprehend how many painful learning experiences we have in our pasts, we can start to appreciate how and why we perceive so many threats in the present day that lead to toxic levels of stress and compassion fatigue. Understanding the amygdala's encoding process and how it manifests as perceived threat in the present leads to the discovery that it is our painful past learning—not our colleagues, students, their parents, or our school system—that is the cause of all our stress.

2. The lizard brain: Technically referred to as the limbic system, this deeply primitive part of the brain (referred to as the "lizard brain" or "reptilian brain" because of its similarity to the primeval brain structure a reptile possesses) manages a majority of our emotions, addictions, moods, and other mental and emotional processes, all of which are affected when our fight-or-flight response becomes activated.

-   **What the lizard brain does**: When we perceive threat and the lizard brain takes over, our access to a host of higher cognitive functions like reasoning, self-control, creativity, and self-reflection is subdued or restricted altogether, while behaviors including impulsivity, aggression, black-and-white thinking, snap judgments and criticisms, and reactivity become substantially heightened.

- **Why the lizard brain does this**: We experience a reduction in these cognitive abilities because of one reason only: to better equip us for survival. In prehistoric times when life or death depended on how quickly we fought or ran from a wild animal or attackers, all of our mental energy was directed toward *reacting fast* and without hesitation, clarification, or rumination. Sitting and wondering whether oncoming strangers wielding weapons were *actually* hostile or not would get you killed back then—so our brains and bodies evolved to assume this was always the case. When someone accidentally cuts you off in traffic and you're suddenly overcome with this intense, rageful desire to ram their car and scream obscenities at them, it's because your lizard brain is saying, "This person means you harm! This person is dangerous! This person is a threat, and you must attack them or escape this situation before they hurt you!"

- **The long-term ramifications of lizard brain activation**: It takes no stretch of the imagination to deduce that a reduction in higher cognitive functioning like rationale, self-soothing abilities, and self-control due to toxic levels of stress is going to lead to some serious and potentially life-threatening consequences. When we repeatedly perceive threat in our daily lives and operate from the lizard brain for significant amounts of time, the behavioral ramifications are far-reaching and can become ingrained in our brain's processing pathways—things like irritability and angry outbursts, hypervigilance and paranoia, concentration problems, avoidance or detachment during social situations, risky behaviors, and depression or suicidal thoughts/ideation.

Here's Cheryl with a personal story about her experience with a teacher who was operating from the lizard brain during a classroom emergency, and the ways this affected the teacher's thought processes and behaviors.

Cheryl: One day while I was working as a principal a few years back, I stepped out of my office to see my secretary answering the intercom from a teacher's classroom. This was a highly intelligent, respected, and competent teacher. However, a student in her class had passed out and was having a seizure on her floor. The teacher was so concerned for the student and traumatized by the event that this highly skilled individual just kept asking over the intercom for someone to provide her with the phone number for 9-1-1 so she could call for help. Her lizard brain was so activated that she could not cognitively access the knowledge that she needed to dial the numbers 9-1-1, and not the traditional nine-digit phone number that she was used to doing in other situations.

The physiological reactions from amygdala and lizard brain activation were undoubtedly useful and less problematic for ancient humans, whose decision-making options were mostly limited to fighting or fleeing. But in our modern world of parent-teacher conferences, distance learning, standardized testing requirements, and yes, students who might be having a health emergency in our classrooms, the situation is quite different. The kinds of threats we commonly encounter today are much more complex and abstract, and we need full access to our reasoning and communication capabilities to respond efficiently, effectively, safely, and healthfully. Unfortunately for us, however, we're going up against a millennia-old body-and-brain system that operates entirely on instinct and below the reach of our conscious control: the autonomic nervous system.

The Autonomic Nervous System and Its Role in Stress

Until recently, the mental health and medical fields viewed this human threat-response system as consisting of two interacting neural networks that played complementary and opposing roles. They are called the sympathetic nervous system (SNS) and parasympathetic nervous system (PNS), and together they form the autonomic nervous system (ANS).

1. The SNS: More commonly known as the "fight-or-flight response" we've been referencing for some time now, the SNS is a bi-directional neural pathway that stretches from the brain stem and spinal cord to virtually every major organ system, including the heart, lungs, liver, stomach, intestines, reproductive organs, and more. One of the SNS's chief responsibilities is to activate these organs into a heightened state of readiness whenever we perceive a threat to our safety and survival. This threat-detection process occurs extremely quickly, and almost entirely below our conscious awareness.

The fight-or-flight response begins with threat detection in a part of the brain known as the anterior cingulate cortex (ACC). The ACC is situated in a unique position, because it has connections to both the "emotional" limbic system—the lizard brain—and the "cognitive" prefrontal cortex.

Once alerted to a potential threat, the ACC sends a signal to the brain's temporal lobe, where the amygdala is. The amygdala then immediately starts creating a powerful memory about the experience for current and future reference.

At the same time as our brain's swift response to a perceived threat, our body is also undergoing a rapid shift designed to optimize our physical capabilities for strength and speed. Our heart rate and blood pressure spike as sugars and fats pour into our bloodstream to furnish us with a burst of energy. Blood is diverted away from our skin surface to our muscles, and our clotting function is accelerated to reduce the possibility of blood loss due to injury. Our muscle tension increases to prepare us for maximum sustained effort, and our immune system mobilizes to fight off infection in case our skin surface is punctured or damaged.

All of these changes are marvels of the human machine. Almost all functioning—speed, dexterity, senses, and strength—improves with the *activation* of the SNS…for about thirty seconds! That's right, the SNS was built to be utilized for about thirty seconds to get us out of danger by involuntarily utilizing aggression (fight) or avoidance (flight). If the SNS stays activated beyond that time, then we begin to experience diminished effectiveness of these capacities along with a toxic increase of stress symptoms.

This short-term mobilization of our SNS *does* have its costs. When it's activated, not only is the lizard brain restricting us from our abilities to reason, analyze, and make choices based on judgment and prior experience, but our visual acuity, impulse control, fine motor control, and communication skills are hindered as well. Below are some more brain-and-body changes that occur when the SNS is activated:

Physical
- Acceleration of heart and lung action.
- Pupil dilation.
- Constriction of peripheral blood vessels throughout the body.
- Auditory exclusion (loss of hearing).
- Tunnel vision (loss of peripheral vision).
- Inhibition of digestive system functioning.
- Inhibition of the lacrimal gland that produces saliva and tears.
- General effects on the sphincters of the body.

Brain mechanics
- Increased basal ganglia and thalamic functioning (responsible for coordinating voluntary movement).
- Decreased frontal lobe activity, including executive functioning, fine motor control, and emotional regulation.
- Decreased temporal lobe activity, with reduced language and speech capabilities.

Other effects
- Increased obsessive and compulsive thoughts and behaviors.
- Decreased speed, agility, and strength.
- Constricted thoughts and behaviors.
- Increased fatigue.

2. The PNS: Once the immediate danger has passed, a second system comes into play. Like the SNS, the PNS is a bi-directional neural pathway that runs between our spinal cord and our major organ systems. The PNS plays an opposing role to that of the SNS, calming our bodies and conserving our energy resources for more routine processes, such as digestion and reproduction. For this reason, the PNS is sometimes referred to as the "feed-and-breed system."

With the PNS at the controls, our heart rate slows back down, our muscles relax, and our blood pressure, blood chemistry, and immune systems return to normal. Our higher brain centers also come back online, restoring our abilities to think, assess, interact with others, and behave in accordance with our values and aspirations. The PNS is also the part of the nervous system that is responsible for healing and repair.

Ideally, this hand-off from the SNS to the PNS occurs efficiently, smoothly returning our bodies and brains to their pre-threat conditions. This process of regaining physical and mental equilibrium between the SNS and PNS is referred to as "homeostasis." Helping people to spend more and more time in the PNS and restore their homeostasis is *the* antidote to toxic amounts of stress and compassion fatigue, and is one of the primary goals and outcomes of the five Forward-Facing® steps for professional resilience you'll soon learn.

There's another facet to our physiological threat response that's gained recognition in more recent years, although its origins are thought to be rooted in the oldest evolutionary designs in human existence: the vagus nerve, or our body's "freeze response" to perceived danger.

Fight, Flee, or Freeze: The Polyvagal Theory

We now have a much more nuanced understanding of our response and threat-detection systems, thanks to the research and writings of renowned neuroscientist Stephen Porges, a pioneer in the field of biological psychology.

His polyvagal theory dispenses with the older model of two systems—the SNS and PNS—that complement and oppose each other to achieve homeostasis. Instead, he postulates that there are *three* systems altogether to detect threat—the original conceptualization of the SNS (involuntary mobilization or the fight-or-flight response), with the PNS being split into two distinct subsystems or "complexes": the dorsal vagal complex (DVC) and the ventral vagal complex (VVC).

Each of these two complexes are associated with a branch of the vagus nerve (a nerve that runs from the brain to the face and thorax to the abdomen and regulates things like heart rate, blood pressure, sweating, digestion, and speaking), and has a particular reaction to a perceived threat.

The Vagus Nerve

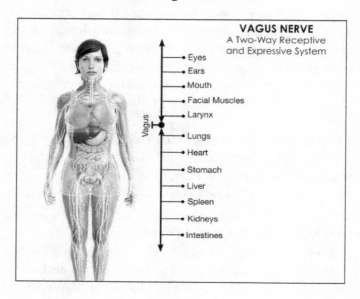

The Polyvagal Theory

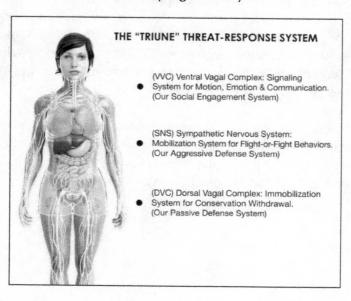

Here are the three components of Porges's polyvagal theory for threat-detection systems in humans and other mammals.

1. The SNS (in Porges's polyvagal theory): As stated above, the SNS directs the body's rapid involuntary response to dangerous or stressful situations. This response occurs so quickly that people often don't realize it's taking place. For instance, a person may steer out of the way of an oncoming car before they even cognitively register that there *is* a car in front of them.

According to Porges, the SNS provides protection in the form of involuntary mobilization that usually takes the form of aggression or avoidance ("fighting" or "fleeing"). When the human or animal in danger is able to navigate back to safety by successfully attacking or running away from the threat, they can immediately return to the comfort of the PNS. If the human or animal is unable to successfully navigate the threat and they *remain* in SNS activation, this part of the nervous system becomes dominant. This state is sometimes called hypervigilance, and it's in this mode of toxic SNS activation that all the distressing symptoms associated with stress are generated.

SNS dominance is not sustainable as a lifestyle, so Porges's polyvagal theory hypothesizes that people experiencing this toxic activation may then switch to the more primitive defense system in their PNS called the dorsal vagal complex (DVC), which causes the body to "shut down" or "freeze."

2. The dorsal vagal (DVC) complex: The DVC acts as a brake on the SNS, managing the "feed-and-breed system" and helping the body gently return from arousal to relaxation. It's also the most ancient threat-response system in our bodies, and one we share with reptiles and other mammals. Anatomically, the DVC consists of a nerve pathway that connects the brain stem to the organs situated below the diaphragm, especially those associated with digestion and reproduction and the muscles that anchor these organs in place.

The DVC first evolved in simple organisms that passively absorbed nutrients from the rich broth of dissolved organic compounds and gases found in the prehistoric ocean. Lacking organs and muscles for locomotion, these simple creatures never developed an SNS or the option to fight or flee. Instead, their defensive systems were focused entirely on preserving their energy reserves so they could recover as quickly as possible when the threat had ceased. For this reason, the DVC is sometimes referred to as the "passive defense system."

The DVC is now understood to control the third possible response to a perceived threat: freezing. We can see this survival strategy at work when we observe animals responding to danger by becoming immobilized. This is often described as the "deer-in-the-headlights phenomenon."

When we as humans perceive threat in certain instances or for too long at a time, the DVC will initiate an involuntary immobilization or "full-body shutdown" as a means of survival.

Consider the case of a driver trapped in his vehicle and unable to move after a car accident. His DVC immediately springs into action, slowing his heart rate, reducing his blood pressure, and preserving his energy resources for the key organ systems necessary for survival. If this inhibitory response is severe enough, though, the suppression of his heart and circulatory system may cause him to go into shock and lose consciousness. Our driver's amygdala may also respond by creating a powerful emotional memory of the accident and its aftermath. This memory will include all of the sensory impressions surrounding the accident, along with the signals of biological shutdown induced by DVC activation. Consequently, whenever the memory is triggered in the future, he may re-experience some of the classic physiological and psychological manifestations of the freeze response, including symptoms such as dissociation, paralysis of thought or action, or emotional numbing and psychological disengagement.

If the stress evoking the freeze response becomes chronic, the driver may attempt to manage these symptoms by self-medicating (i.e., drugs and alcohol), escapism (i.e., online surfing and videogames), self-soothing (i.e., overeating), or by distancing himself from others and avoiding activities he previously enjoyed.

3. The ventral vagal complex (VVC): The third component of our threat-response system according to Porges evolved most recently and is found only in humans. The VVC is the second branch of the PNS, and the one that most directly reflects our status as social beings with biological imperatives to form mutually beneficial relationships. Anatomically, the VVC connects the brain stem to the organs above the diaphragm (i.e., the heart, lungs, et cetera) and to the muscles of the face and head. As part of the PNS, the VVC has similar capabilities for relaxing our bodies and suppressing the fight-or-flight response generated by the SNS and the freeze response generated by the DVC. However, unlike either of these systems, it operates through the medium of face-to-face communications. For this reason, the VVC is sometimes referred to as the "social engagement system."

If the eyes are the portal to the soul, then our face is the window to the threat-response system (a "safe haven" of sorts), and our voices are the music of engagement or the source of rejection with those to whom we're connected. When the VVC is dominant, we feel safe, centered, and secure. We convey this through our facial muscles by smiling and maintaining appropriate eye contact. We do the same with our tone of voice, speaking in a relaxed and rhythmic way that eschews choppy or staccato phrases. Think of a mother singing a lullaby to her baby, or the sound of two lovers cooing their endearments. We hear differently too, focusing our attention on the person speaking to us and losing awareness of background noise. All of these stress-reduction responses are mediated by the VVC.

When we encounter stress, humans naturally turn to each other for comfort and support. If we see a friendly face, the VVC activates to calm us. If we encounter someone whose face and voice communicate anxiety or distress, we may become aroused and infected by their stress.

Our passive defense, social engagement, and fight-or-flight systems come online in a consistent, evolutionarily defined sequence. If we perceive danger, we look first to our fellow humans for support. If we find it, we relax. If not, our SNS takes over and we attempt to fight or flee. If we're prevented from fighting or fleeing, then our earliest evolved system takes control and we freeze up. This instinctual process occurs almost instantaneously, within a scant ten to fifteen milliseconds after the threat is first perceived.

The Road More Traveled = More Stress

As we've said before, the problem isn't brief SNS activation (if we recall the Yerkes-Dodson Law, short bursts of eustress are what make our lives vibrant and exciting). But when we encounter stress on an ongoing basis, our threat-response system can become dangerously overextended and sensitive. When this occurs, the SNS can get stuck in the "on" position, plunging us into a near-constant state of agitation and overarousal. Our bodies are like cars being driven with both the accelerator and brake pedals mashed to the floorboards. We spend our days "red-lined," going fast but getting nowhere as we burn out our engines—with the worst part being that it's a self-perpetuating cycle.

The Evolution of Reaction in the Polyvagal Theory

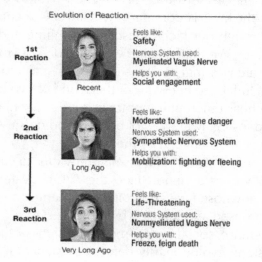

POLYVAGAL THEORY

Events trigger you to react. If your first reaction doesn't make you feel safe, you revert to the second, then the third:

Evolution of Reaction

1st Reaction

Recent

Feels like:
Safety
Nervous System used:
Myelinated Vagus Nerve
Helps you with:
Social engagement

2nd Reaction

Long Ago

Feels like:
Moderate to extreme danger
Nervous System used:
Sympathetic Nervous System
Helps you with:
Mobilization: fighting or fleeing

3rd Reaction

Very Long Ago

Feels like:
Life-Threatening
Nervous System used:
Nonmyelinated Vagus Nerve
Helps you with:
Freeze, feign death

Let us explain: If the SNS is "on" for too long—it's been perceiving danger continuously and/or frequently because of the amygdala's encoding of those experiences—our threat-perception system becomes enhanced, expanded, and attuned to possible threats from a larger pool of possibilities. The more these neural pathways are utilized, the stronger, faster, more automated, and more efficient they become. We might think of it as a road in the mountains; the trail starts small, but over time and with enough traffic, the path widens exponentially. Hypervigilance follows the same principle: the more times we perceive threat in the *now*, the easier it becomes for our system to perceive threat in the *future*.

Not only do the neural pathways of the brain become better developed, but the reaction speed shortens with repeated use. All the body needs is the *suggestion* of a threat to jump into overdrive, so that it's fully engaged almost immediately. This leads to impulsive and reactive behavior, all led by attributions and perceptions that have been repeatedly conditioned through this process of traumagenesis.

For example, most people find flowers relatively pleasant or at least neutral, but imagine that one day you encounter a flower that caused you to have a tremendous allergic reaction. Your reaction required an emergency trip to the hospital, a breathing treatment, and even a painful shot. Now, several years later, your perception of flowers is altered. Even though it was just the one flower that caused the reaction, your brain is going to forevermore perceive flowers—and possibly even items resembling weeds or plants—with an added threat factor that never existed before. Our painful learning experiences really do create a binary mindset: a black-and-white view of the world that is very difficult to ignore, even when logic says otherwise.

There's also an additional traumagenesis factor for educators: the schools *themselves*. These places of work are filled with many prior past learning experiences for us, because all adult educators once had experiences in classrooms as children. So unlike someone who grows up to become a lawyer and may have only had one or two occasions of being in a courtroom prior to it becoming a large part of their daily life, educators have spent most of their entire lives leading up to working in schools by being students in schools. Imagine the number of experiences ("flowers," you might say) that have already imprinted on our brains with the familiarity of desks, cafeterias, football fields, and more!

Tens of thousands of these experiences of traumagenesis throughout our lifetimes construct categories within our minds that are populated by painful learning—and this painful learning translates to hyper-attunement and hyperarousal to any other experience that remotely resembles the sensory experiences of the original traumatic event. It changes how we see the world and it influences our relationships, both at work and in our personal lives. Sometimes this can be to our benefit and safety (if you're deathly allergic to a certain kind of flower, you should probably avoid exposure to plants as much as possible), but in general, the chronic amount of SNS activation (i.e., stress) we are experiencing is neither necessary nor helpful—and is leading to unparalleled amounts of educator burnout and compassion fatigue.

The Breakdown of Tolerance and Memory That Can Lead to Traumatic Stress

As we detailed in the last chapter, trauma or painful past learning isn't necessarily one "big, bad event" (or even something that happens to you directly). It can also be a series of long-term interactions, witnessed events, and workplace factors that eventually dysregulate our physiological and emotional state enough to result in an overactive SNS. Every single human being has a range of tolerance and a range of adaption, one that's a moving target and is constantly changing with the state of our body.

Let's look at this concept a little further: Have you ever found that when you're sick, tired, or hungry, that you're not as nice to other people as usual? This is because as the state of your body is compromised, so is your tolerance level. Your range of tolerance is *always* going to be tied to your physical state, and as it fluctuates, so does your sensitivity to stressors.

Now imagine that this also applies to our brain-and-body system—when we're in fight-or-flight mode, we are stretched thin and taut like a wire, with far less flexibility if something (i.e., a stressor) were to tug on us. Rather than to bend or bounce back from the perceived threat, we are that much more susceptible to "breaking" from the effect of the perceived threat. This becomes another self-fulfilling cycle: When we perceive threat too much and/or too often, we remain in an overactive SNS. And when we are operating in an overactive SNS, we lack the immunity, tolerance, and resilience required to protect us from potential stressors.

Another component to the buildup of traumatic stress contributing to compassion fatigue is our own memory. Countless studies have found that our perceptions and recollections of memories often alter over time,[46] with various details forgotten or highlighted based on their relevancy to us. When we're referring to painful memories that are "lodged" in the amygdala—with *all* that sensorial detail catalogued and ready for reference at any time to keep us alive when the "threat" reappears—this can mean that the most disturbing parts of our painful memories become amplified and intensified, regardless of the reality of the remembered situation. While our memories continue to change and become increasingly unreliable,[47] they still end up constructing the reality that dictates the ways in which we move through our daily lives.

Furthermore, these embellishments and amplifications in our painful memories are problematic because they directly correlate with the magnitude and level of our physiological response to them. If we continue to recall a happy memory over time, our body will experience ever-increasing physiological reactions to the joy, contentment, and delight that the memory invokes. On the flip side, this means that every time we remember an experience that caused us pain, distress, aggravation, and hurt, the memory *grows* in intensity, with a subsequent reaction of body arousal that moves our focus from internal self-reflection and self-evaluation to an external focus of perceived threat.

There's one more factor that's worth exploring in terms of increased vulnerabilities to trauma and traumatic stress, especially when educators are working closely with children and have often experienced one or more of these events themselves growing up: adverse childhood experiences, colloquially known as ACEs.

Adverse Childhood Experiences (ACEs) and Traumatic Stress

In the mid-1980s, a physician and researcher named Vincent Felitti who was the director of Kaiser Permanente's Department of Preventive Medicine in San Diego had a problem. This department was renowned as one of the best preventative medicine facilities in the world, with Dr. Felitti—who was in his forties at the time—at an all-time high in his twenty-two-year-long medical career. He was well-regarded by his staff, regularly spoke at conferences, published papers, and was essentially a "rock star" of this budding new discipline of preventative medicine.

So what was his problem? *His obesity clinic*. He and his staff had developed a biopsychosocial treatment program that had been wildly effective in helping people who were morbidly obese (100 pounds or more overweight) to quickly lose weight *without* surgery. It was being used as a model for many other obesity treatment programs around the globe, but as the program matured, the data began to point toward two perplexing outcomes. The problems that arose were *dropout rates* and *recidivism* (a.k.a. the repetition of harmful or negative behaviors following attempts to cease the behavior), and Dr. Felitti found that many of the patients who were losing significant amounts of weight and seemingly on an accelerated path to health and wellness frequently dropped out of treatment right when they were doing so well.

Upon following up with these patients, he also found that a large percentage of the participants who'd discontinued their treatment had regained much of their weight—and quickly. This was a conundrum for Dr. Felitti and his staff, and they changed their program in an attempt to preempt these outcomes by addressing them in groups with his patients.

When asked why they'd regained the weight after working so hard to lose it, Dr. Felitti heard a common response from his patients: "We didn't deal with the underlying issues."

This "underlying issues" explanation continued to emerge as he questioned his patients, so he began to explore it—and in his preliminary investigations, he found that *all* of his patients had experienced some kind of trauma in their history. He also found that nearly every female obese patient he met with had had some kind of sexual and/or physical abuse in her childhood.

It started to become clear to Dr. Felitti that he was on to something that most of medicine *was not* addressing in the slightest—a patient's trauma history, and its significant impact on their current disorders and diseases. The more he learned of this correlation, the more motivated he became to produce quantifiable research that might demonstrate this phenomenon.

This goal was achieved in 1997 when Dr. Felitti met Dr. Robert Anda, an epidemiologist at the Centers for Disease Control and Prevention. They designed and launched the Adverse Childhood Experiences (ACE) study, one that queried 17,000 patients in the Kaiser Permanente health network to discover whether those patients had experienced any of ten significant childhood adverse experiences before the age of eighteen. Those ten traumatic experiences listed in the survey are as follows:

1. Childhood emotional abuse.
2. Childhood physical abuse.
3. Childhood sexual abuse.
4. Domestic violence in the home.
5. Alcohol abuse or drug abuse in the home.
6. Mental illness of a household member.
7. Parental separation or divorce.
8. Criminal activity or incarceration of a household member.
9. Childhood emotional neglect.
10. Childhood physical neglect.

(Note: You can locate and take this "Find Your ACE Score" self-assessment for free online, but we've also included it in Appendix II of this book for ease of reference.)

Since 1997, the work with ACEs has changed the landscape of healthcare and is making its way to the field of education. Perhaps you've heard the terms "trauma-informed care" or "trauma-informed education" at your school, which is a direct result of the ACEs research.

Having ACEs in our history means that we did not grow and mature in a consistently safe and nurturing environment. The more the fields of mental health and education learn about early childhood trauma, attachment, and the brain's early development, the more evidence emerges that these experiences of danger, abuse, neglect, and disruptions of attachment can have lasting (even lifelong) negative effects upon the physical, emotional, psychological, behavioral, relational, professional, and spiritual health of the survivors if not addressed.

Children growing up in environments where there is intermittent-to-constant danger develop a highly adaptive self-defense system that is powered by toxic hypervigilance—and based on statistical evidence, a certain percentage of your students are navigating these ACEs in their own lives right now. That's why it's so important to learn these five steps to professional resilience and self-regulation: You could be the *only* person in a child's life who feels safe to be around, and is modeling what it looks like to be regulated and at home in one's body no matter what's going on in their surroundings.

We've just gone over a lot of different concepts, and sometimes the best way to grasp these processes and behaviors is to see them "in action" for everyday people confronting situations similar to our own. We will now spend some time with our school secretary, Mrs. Stanbury, whose own traumagenesis and distress levels have breached her innate tolerance, leading to chronic SNS overactivation and even brain-and-body "shutdown" behaviors to cope.

A Day in the Life of Mrs. Stanbury

The phone rang on Jamie's desk, and as she reached for it, she noticed her hand was *still* shaking following the verbal altercation with that belligerent father who'd stormed in the office during lunch. Jamie answered with her standard secretary greeting, vaguely noticing how her body had tensed from head to toe at the mere thought of another shrieking parent on the other end. It ended up being a mundane, standard conversation and the caller was perfectly pleasant, but Jamie had a pit in her stomach once she'd hung up and gone to clean up the empty water bottle and empty fruit cup left behind by Freda Whitmore.

Jamie shook her head as she tossed the trash away, wondering what the young girl must've thought watching Jamie practically sprint away from the

71

dad while he was in the midst of yelling at her. It hadn't even been something she'd done on purpose; the moment she'd seen the large, hulking man stalk into the front office with his eyes bulging and his veins popping, her heart started galloping and her palms began to sweat. It wasn't the first time she'd been the recipient of a parent's wrath as the first point of contact in the school's front office—not by a long shot. Jamie was used to stressful situations in her daily work: sick kids vomiting on her in their search for the school nurse, unexpected increases in administrative tasks for enrolling new students, responding to the hundreds of emails that streamed into her inbox every day, and keeping the school running smoothly amidst an ever-changing litany of district-wide mandates and legislative changes, drills and additional trainings, and the personal and professional needs of the entire staff and student body.

Jamie had never actually *run away* from a parent in the middle of a conversation, though, and she was humiliated. How unprofessional, how *unlike* her; who was this person she'd become? Someone who immediately had trouble taking deep breaths and thinking straight the moment a parent or the principal came by to talk to her, even when it was something as simple as asking if she could check on a student's attendance history, or if she'd like a coffee from the breakroom? Someone who dreaded answering her office phone every time it rang, and spent her weekends counting down the hours until she'd have to return Monday morning? It was as if she was always on high alert, anticipating the next school emergency that would need fixing or indignant parent who'd need accommodating. Where she'd once thrived off the excitement and challenge of attending to these unforeseen events as a competent and quick-on-her-feet professional and had always been proud of her abilities to act as a neutral party on behalf of the students and teachers and provide support as their ally and confidant, she now felt frazzled all the time, frayed at the edges, and conditioned to always fear the worst.

This type of pessimistic thinking and hypervigilance had started to bleed into Jamie's personal life, too; her husband Perry had grown tired of what he called her "dramatics" regarding the health and wellbeing of their two young daughters, scolding her for worrying about every little thing. Sometimes Jamie had so many thoughts in her head at once she couldn't see straight, and when it got really bad, she'd mentally and even physically detach or shut down. Sometimes that meant a brain fog that hindered her significantly in running their household—she'd forget to pay bills on time or schedule routine checkups and dental appointments for their family, and on several occasions, she'd gotten the dates or times wrong for her daughters' dance recitals and sports' competitions. Other times it meant that after the girls were put to bed for the night and Perry was in their bedroom playing his videogames, she'd eat an entire half gallon of ice cream or box of cookies without even realizing it.

Jamie and Perry had always had a loving, passionate relationship, even with two kids under ten years old, but Jamie's overstimulation lately had her seeking to *leave* her bodily sensations as much as possible, rather than to revel in them. She'd stopped attending her Zumba and workout classes and didn't feel confident in the way her body looked, and never read for pleasure anymore, or partook in art shows and concerts like she and Perry had always enjoyed attending in their younger years.

Romance and extracurriculars she'd once indulged in required too much energy and brain power now, and Jamie was just trying to survive— not just her job, either, but her whole demanding life.

❖ ❖ ❖

Once we realize that traumatic stress, burnout, and compassion fatigue all come from *within* us and not outside of us, we're gifted with the ultimate power to make it all disappear. We no longer operate at the mercy of our classrooms and districts, our coworkers and students and their parents—instead, we are promised an existence in which we are empowered and *freely choosing* to pursue our mission of educating children every single day that we show up to school.

So, there's really only one question remaining: Are you ready to begin implementing the healing methods of Forward-Facing® professional resilience in your own life?

Forward-Facing® Reflection 4: Responses to Perceived Threat in Our Own Life

In this chapter we taught you that any time you're feeling stressed at work or home, you've actually perceived a threat and your body is responding exactly the way it's supposed to for survival (and as any other animal's would).

What are your thoughts on this?

_____

_____

_____

_____

_____

We also discussed how staying in this stressed state (the "threat response") can lead us to aggression, avoidance, or shutdown ("fight, flight, or freeze"). Can you identify some behavioral examples of these from your professional and/or personal life?

1. Aggression or "fight" (how do you attempt to change the environment and neutralize the perceived threat?):

_____

_____

_____

_____

_____

2. Avoidance or "flight" (how do you attempt to get away from or avoid the perceived threat?):

_____

_____

_____

_____

_____

3. Shutdown or "freeze" (what do you do when you get overwhelmed?):

_____

_____

_____

_____

_____

Can you identify any negative consequences of having remained in one or more of these states for long periods of time in your own life?

1. Physically?

_____

_____

_____

_____

_____

2. Emotionally?

_____

_____

_____

_____

_____

3. Professionally?

_____

_____

_____

_____

_____

4. Relationally?

_____

_____

_____

_____

_____

PART II:
THE SOLUTION FOR EDUCATORS

CHAPTER FIVE

FORWARD-FACING® FOR EDUCATORS

Between stimulus and response there is a space. In
that space is our power to choose our response. In
our response lies our growth and our freedom.

Viktor Frankl

AS WE'VE SEEN, the burnout and secondary traumatic stress symptoms that lead to compassion fatigue are not a ubiquitous feature of our school environment, or a heavy yoke imposed on us by parents, students, or colleagues. They are simply the result of our biological response to a perceived threat where there is little or no danger—a response we can learn to modulate, control, and gradually extinguish with practice.

We've traced the neural and hormonal pathways that collectively comprise our primitive threat-detection and response systems and shown how they operate largely outside of our conscious awareness. We've demonstrated how toxic amounts of stress—in the form of primary, secondary, and environmental trauma—can push these systems into dysregulated overfunctioning. We've explained why the near-constant overactivation of our fight, flight, and freeze responses can be so destructive to our work performance, physical and mental health, and overall life satisfaction, and we've delved into some of the challenges and shortcomings within the field of education that are unlikely to go away or be ameliorated any time soon.

If this were the end of the story, our prospects for a stress-free and resilient professional future would seem very bleak indeed. Fortunately, biology is not destiny. We can learn to overcome dysregulation and restore a healthy balance to our threat-detection systems, eliminating our vulnerability to burnout and compassion fatigue in the process.

As we emerge from our entrenched patterns of reflexive reactivity, we can become free to behave and work in ways that are consistent with the ethics, values, and aspirations we'll soon be designing for ourselves in the mission, vision, and code of honor that comprise our personal covenant. We can learn to reframe our perceptions of the demands placed upon us at work, becoming empowered by setting healthy boundaries and recognizing that we *always* have the ability to choose. We can find support and personal accountability from chosen others, while serving ourselves through dedicated nurturing and self-care. Increasingly, we can bring the full weight of our skills, intelligence, and creativity to bear in every sphere of our lives, facing hardships with new energy and confidence. In short, we can become our best selves, no longer reacting to the world based upon our painful pasts.

But what does it take to bring about such a fundamental transformation? What strategies and methods should we employ? How will we put them into practice?

Any meaningful approach to eliminating compassion fatigue at work and home must satisfy a number of critical requirements. First and foremost, it should employ methods that anyone can learn to apply with a little practice and dedication. Buddhist monks spend decades mastering advanced meditation techniques that enable them to control their heart rate, suppress their involuntary startle responses, and "light up" different parts of their brains at will. However, few of us possess the time or discipline to devote ourselves in this way. Our approach should empower us to reduce the impact of traumatic stress and burnout on our lives as quickly and efficiently as possible.

We know that the stress response operates along a continuum. Some of us are contending with the relatively mild levels of arousal associated with daily stressors, such as an unexpected assembly being called that interrupts our lesson plan for the week and pushes our entire unit plan into the next grading period, or an impromptu parent-teacher meeting that leaves us grading papers late into the night. At the other end of the spectrum, some of us— like our principal, Mrs. Burkhart, or our school secretary Mrs. Stanbury—are struggling with panic attacks and intrusive thoughts disturbing enough to potentially warrant a PTSD diagnosis. Therefore, the stress-reduction strategy we choose should work effectively for everyone, regardless of where we find ourselves on the stress continuum. It should also be applicable and deployable in every stage and aspect of our lives.

Of course, we cannot and should not ignore the painful past learning (traumagenesis) that has caused us to become dysregulated in the first place. However, we shouldn't have to excavate every trauma we've ever experienced in order to heal. Instead, our stress-elimination regimen should gently empower us to make choices today—in the present moment—that reflect our most cherished goals and aspirations for why we pursued a career in education in the first place. The techniques we use should help us move beyond discouragement and aggravation to a sense of pride and self-reliance. In short, rather than looking to the past riddled with its suffering and frustration, applying these five simple steps will allow us to be "forward-facing" toward a life defined by freedom, optimal living, and professional resilience in perpetuity.

The Five Steps of Forward-Facing® for Professional Resilience

Forward-Facing® for professional resilience represents a new way of eliminating our compassion fatigue and its negative, harmful effects on our minds, bodies, and professional and personal lives. The purpose of the Forward-Facing® approach is not to eradicate the stress and threat responses completely, but to teach you how to become aware of them, manage them, and calibrate them to lessen your distress, while optimizing your functioning and reaping the benefits and healing that self-care practices and support systems have been proven to offer. The Forward-Facing® approach for professional resilience is comprised of five simple steps to be performed in order (or at times interchangeably):

Forward-Facing® Step One: Self-Regulation: We can't just flip a switch and reboot our brains into a state of harmony and homeostasis. However, we *can* learn to consciously shift out of sympathetic nervous system (SNS) activation, a.k.a. our fight-or-flight response, whenever we sense it perceiving threat where there is little or no danger. We won't be able to entirely prevent this SNS activation (nor would we want to when confronted with a real threat to our safety), but we will be able to rein it in rapidly and effectively by sensing when it's begun to run amok. We *can* learn to regulate the frequency, intensity, and duration of the threat response through simple body-and-brain techniques, and we'll begin developing this foundational skill of self-regulation in chapter six.

Forward-Facing® Step Two: Intentionality: Intentionality is aligning our behavior with our values by mapping out our mission, vision, and code of honor—a.k.a. our personal covenant. In the throes of SNS dominance, we're much more likely to lose control and behave in ways that are, at

81

best, ineffective. At their worst, they are destructive to ourselves and others. Reducing the frequency and intensity of these episodes is certainly a worthwhile goal in itself. However, an equally important goal is learning to act in accordance with our ideals, values, and principles—to become intentional. The first step in achieving that goal is deciding who we are, who we want to be, and which principles define our own personal and professional morality. In chapter seven, we'll begin a process of self-exploration that culminates in the development of a written covenant to help us navigate the ups and downs of work and home life with intentionality, purpose, and a renewed sense of mission.

Forward-Facing® Step Three: Perceptual Maturation: Too many of us become discouraged by an underfunded, overextended education system that pays little heed to our needs and sets what we perceive to be unreasonable performance expectations. We have described compassion fatigue as being a perceptual problem, one that we ourselves—*not* the system that employs us—have control to change. In this chapter, we will focus on restarting the natural maturational processes that have become stalled by our secondary traumatic stress and reflexive reactivity. This begins with learning how to examine and change the ways we perceive ourselves and those around us. We will consider the difference between workplace choices and demands, examine how to focus on processes rather than outcomes, recognize and shed a sense of victimhood or entitlement to suffering, and discover how to maintain integrity in the face of workplace demands so we can bring our best selves to everything we do. We will learn to turn our locus of control away from that which we cannot control to that which we *can*: our perceptions and our responses.

Forward-Facing® Step Four: Support and Connection: Many of us retreat into isolation and despair when we become overwhelmed by stress and trauma. In this chapter, we'll consider the vital importance of cultivating a "resilience safety net." We will learn how our biologically-based social engagement systems function, and discover the restorative effects of sharing our experiences with colleagues, friends, and loved ones. We will also learn techniques for dismantling interpersonal barriers and enhancing our self-disclosure skills.

Forward-Facing® Step Five: Self-Care and Revitalization: As you gain mastery of the first four professional resilience skills, you are likely to find yourself recovering some of the energy and passion that originally attracted you to the education field. In this chapter, we will consider how to consolidate these gains with an ongoing plan that addresses your physical, psychological, emotional, spiritual, and professional needs.

We will conclude this second half of the book with the means to design your own self-directed Forward-Facing® professional resilience plan, using the Forward-Facing® worksheets, assessments, and end-of-chapter self-reflections as reference points. By your completion of this book and its exercises, we guarantee you'll have a structured, actionable plan for healing to be utilized for the rest of your career (and life!).

Are You Ready for Forward-Facing®?

The techniques you'll be applying toward Forward-Facing® professional resilience are simple and easy to learn and then master—but to become effective, you must decide to practice them diligently. This may seem a daunting prospect to those seeking a "magic bullet" solution to their problems. The Forward-Facing® approach should be viewed as a *process*, not an endpoint. It is a pathway to your best self with minimal distress and maximal quality of life. Its benefits are incalculable, but they require effort and dedication. If you're not ready to commit to change and growth, then this approach is not for you. If you are, then buckle your seatbelt!

The beneficial effects of Forward-Facing® accrue more quickly as you're able to adopt healthier strategies than the *over-adaptive* behaviors you may have previously employed to manage your stress and soothe your anxiety at work. With the five Forward-Facing® steps for professional resilience, we emphasize the importance of a healthy lifestyle in promoting growth and healing. That means getting plenty of sleep, eating a healthy diet, exercising regularly, and participating in a spiritual tradition or mindful practice that gives meaning to your life and connects you to your community. All of these are essential for healing from past painful learning and becoming your best self in the process. The exciting part about this is that as you diminish the ever-present threat response from your life, these healthy choices will become much more easily attainable because you're no longer needing to soothe your distress in unhealthy and compulsive ways.

Depending on your level of dysregulation, you may find that certain triggers are so powerful and primal that you're plunged into reactivity despite your best efforts to self-regulate. This is most often the result of traumatic learning that causes your fight-or-flight response to spike so quickly and intensely that the space between stimulus and response collapses. In these cases, treatment methods can be utilized by a skilled therapist to reduce the intensity of your triggers until they are no longer so overwhelming.[48] Once you've received professional support, the Forward-Facing® approach for professional resilience can resume.

While many of us will be able to employ this approach successfully without ever visiting a therapist's office, you *should not* engage in this process on your own if you're contending with severe depression, PTSD, an anxiety disorder, a substance use disorder, or if you're taking medications to treat these or any other mental health conditions. Instead, you should work with a trained professional who can coordinate your care and utilize appropriate evidence-based interventions to reduce the severity of your symptoms and help you stabilize. You can't practice Forward-Facing®'s steps productively when you're in crisis.

A few sources for immediate support and assistance in crisis:

- National Suicide Prevention Lifeline, available 24/7: 1-800-273-8255 (online chat also available 24/7 at: www.suicidepreventionlifeline. org/chat/).
- National Domestic Violence Hotline, available 24/7: 1-800-799-7233.
- Substance Abuse and Mental Health Services Administration (SAMHSA)'s National Helpline, available 24/7: 1-800-662-4357.
- Gay, Lesbian, Bisexual, and Transgender (GLBT) National Hotline: 888-843-4564.

A few resources to consider if professional mental health help is the best next step:

- Inquire with your insurance company for behavioral health resources and coverage options.
- Psychology Today's "Find a Therapist" database online.
- Talkspace online/virtual therapy with a licensed professional: www. talkspace.com.
- EMDR International Association: www.emdria.org.

We should also never overlook the possibility that your stress and any symptoms may have a medical/biological cause. Please consult with your physician to make sure you have a clean bill of health before starting the Forward-Facing® process. Keep in mind that while this approach cannot cure disease, it can play a major role in healing by enhancing your resilience and dissipating some of the stress you may be experiencing due to poor physical health.

As always, the first step in solving a problem is to admit there's something that needs solving. Let's take a moment now to take out a writing utensil and fill out the first Forward-Facing® worksheet, which is a self-evaluation of where your stress levels are at currently. If you'd prefer to write your answers on a sheet of paper or your notepad, feel free to do so.

Forward-Facing® Worksheet 1: Self-Evaluation

Answer YES or NO to the following ten questions by circling them here, or writing the answers down in your journal or notepad.

1. My life is so stressful that I often feel overwhelmed. YES or NO
2. I often behave in ways that I regret later. YES or NO
3. I frequently say and do things that hurt people I care about. YES or NO
4. There are situations and people that push my buttons and make me crazy, so I avoid them and keep to myself as much as possible. YES or NO
5. I feel empty and unsatisfied with my life. YES or NO
6. I've tried to change, but have found it impossible on my own. YES or NO
7. I feel controlled by other people. YES or NO
8. I would like to have more meaning in my life. YES or NO
9. I want to do a better job of being true to my principles and living with integrity. YES or NO
10. I think I may be suffering from primary, secondary, and/or environmental trauma. YES or NO

If you scored four or more "yes" answers above, then you are a prime candidate to begin implementing the Forward-Facing® approach for professional resilience in your life today. If your score was less than that, you will still be able to find wonderful insight, healing, and optimization for your future in education by adopting this five-step process in your daily activities.

✶ ✦ ✶

Compassion fatigue is a well-understood phenomenon that should and *can* be prevented before it causes the kind of suffering that can severely hinder many educators' careers and cause great personal pain. With Forward-Facing®, no educator has to live at the mercy of their body and brain's threat response to their work any longer.

Are you ready to escape the vicious, self-defeating cycle of stress, reactivity, and burnout that only leads to more stress, more reactivity, and more burnout? Are you ready to find new or revived meaning, joy, and fulfillment in your career? If so, it's time to embark on your journey from trauma to transformation. You're ready to begin practicing the Forward-Facing® approach to professional resilience with the first step: learning to overcome the reflexive activation of your fight-or-flight response through the act of self-regulation.

CHAPTER SIX

FORWARD-FACING® STEP ONE: SELF-REGULATION

We are both the Beast and its Rider.

Krishna Murti

WHEN WE'RE COMBATING compassion fatigue at school because of burnout and secondary traumatic stress, our bodies and brains have learned to perceive threat dozens of times each day. The strained, tremoring voice of an administrator over the intercom announcing a pre-planned practice lockdown still makes everyone's heart skip a beat as they leave their seats. The bustling hallways during classroom transitions or immediately following the lunch bell creates an environment of chaos that makes our pulse rise and our palms sweat. A social media challenge encouraging campus destruction and student violence against educators for online clout can leave us flinching whenever someone approaches too quickly. A parent who sends a strongly worded email because they don't like the district's recent mandate makes our muscles tense up whenever we check our inbox again.

In very few of these situations are we in actual, lethal danger (and when we are, it's all the more important that we learn to self-regulate to stay alert and make the safest decisions for ourselves and our students). As Eric often likes to say, "Perceived threat is usually ninety-eight percent about our ego, and just two percent about real physical harm."

Yet for any stimuli that reminds us even *remotely* of a painful past learning experience—even something as innocuous as a teasing comment from a coworker or a parent-teacher conference to discuss a student who's been struggling—our bodies and brains respond as though our very survival is at stake. When we chronically perceive threat where there is little or no danger, we live on a hair trigger, ready to explode or implode at the slightest provocation—but that's not how we are *designed* to be.

RELAXED JOYFULNESS: OUR Natural State of Being

The phrase "relaxed joyfulness" might feel like an unattainable or foreign mindset when we imagine ourselves on campus or in the busy classroom, but it's entirely possible—here's Eric with more.

> *Eric*: It's the spring of 1995, and I'm lying on the floor next to my then-wife Janet and fifty other couples. We're taking part in a guided meditation led by Dr. Harville Hendrix, cofounder of Imago Relationship Therapy (IRT) and author of the bestselling book, *Getting the Love You Want: A Guide for Couples*. I'm starting to feel a bit sleepy as he gently urges us in a sonorous voice to "picture yourself moving with relaxed joyfulness."
>
> I'm not exactly sure what he means, but I'm doing my best to cooperate until his next words send me bolt upright, confused and agitated to the point of near panic. "Relaxed joyfulness—*that* is our natural state," he has just told us. Looking around the room, I notice that everyone else is smiling in agreement. *Why am I the only one who finds his words so disturbing?*

For those of us whose careers and lives have been powerfully impacted by painful past learning and hypervigilance leading to burnout or all-out compassion fatigue, the claim that our natural state is "relaxed joyfulness" sounds like a cruel joke. We often distrust and dislike being in our bodies and thoughts, feeling that they've somehow betrayed us or make us suffer. *Our* natural state is one of tension and anxiety over what the next day will bring—the very antithesis of relaxed joyfulness. Our traumagenesis is evident in our chronically clenched muscles and rigid, inflexible joints, our racing pulses and quickened, uneven breathing. In biological terms, we are living in a near-constant state of fight-or-flight/SNS dominance.

Some twenty-five years later, I have come to understand that a state of relaxed joyfulness is not only possible, it's *inevitable* when we perfect the skills of self-regulation. In this chapter, you'll learn to pay attention to your body on a moment-to-moment basis so that you can instantly recognize and respond to the muscular constriction that signals fight-or-flight activation. You'll start to notice how intentionally relaxing those muscles can quickly return your body—and your mind—to the restful and healing state of PNS dominance.

While we can't always control what's happening around us at school, we *can* control the comfort levels in our body—and the reason this mindful muscle relaxation works so instantaneously and completely is due to a fact about our biology that was discovered more than sixty years ago: that stress *cannot* exist in a relaxed body.

Stress is Impossible in a Relaxed Body = Reciprocal Inhibition

A South African psychiatrist named Joseph Wolpe was studying people with anxiety disorders in 1958 when he discovered a process that has been truly revolutionary in the treatment of toxic levels of traumatic stress: that exposure to an anxiety-inducing stimulus *while in a relaxed body* will resolve the symptoms of anxiety. Wolpe called his theory "reciprocal inhibition," and described it in his book *Psychotherapy by Reciprocal Inhibition* as "a process of relearning whereby in the presence of a stimulus a non-anxiety-producing response is continually repeated until it extinguishes the old, undesirable response."[49]

Put another way: *When we confront our perceived threats/triggers from a self-regulated body, we extinguish our stress response to that trigger in the present moment and lessen our reactivity to it in the future.*

This is the evidence-based, scientifically supported concept of reciprocal inhibition—that the stress caused by our fight-or-flight response instantly dissipates when we relax our muscles, and that these triggers lose their activating power over time as we continuously confront them with a relaxed body.[50] This process has been so effective in reducing and resolving post-traumatic stress symptoms that it is now the primary foundational tool in the most effective treatments for PTSD to date.[51]

Another pioneer of this biological reflex of exposure + relaxation = extinguished stress is Dr. Herbert Benson, a cardiologist and researcher at Harvard Medical School and the founder of the Benson-Henry Institute for Mind Body Medicine. Dr. Benson's initial goal when he began to study our body's relaxation response was to ameliorate the physical symptoms of extreme stress that his patients were experiencing during the painful and often lengthy process of diagnosis and treatment. He published his seminal work, *The Relaxation Response*, in 1975, sharing the results of his research that revealed how intentional relaxation of our bodies successfully counteracted the fight-or-fight response, while helping the body to heal: "The relaxation response is a physical state of deep rest that changes the physical and emotional responses to stress...and [is] the opposite of the fight-or-flight response."[52]

Dr. Benson's core insight—that our bodies cannot simultaneously be relaxed and SNS-activated—explains why self-regulation is the cornerstone to healing our traumatic stress, burnout, and compassion fatigue by shifting our bodies out of SNS dominance in real time.

The Three Components of Self-Regulation

Self-regulation is a process of three primary components that give it the potency to gradually lessen our traumatic stress while returning us to a comfortable body and a calm, clear-thinking mind (both of which we want at all times in our schools!). These three components are neuroception, interoception (a.k.a. "bodyfulness"), and acute relaxation, with the first two being interchangeable when completing them in order.

1. or 2. Neuroception: Neuroception is the act of establishing our safety in a situation where we are perceiving threat (i.e., a stressful situation). We do this by asking ourselves, "Am I in real/empirical danger right now?" to which the answer will presumably be, "No, I am not." (Obviously this doesn't apply to an actual threatening situation in which we need to act with the survival and/or safety of ourselves and our students in mind.) While acknowledging the fact that we are "not in danger" during a stressful situation might seem somewhat inconsequential, it actually makes *all* the difference because of the physiological processes occurring beneath the surface of our consciousness at all times. This concept of neuroception was identified by Stephen Porges, the same neuroscientist who created the polyvagal theory. This is what he has to say about it:

> By processing information from the environment through the senses, the nervous system continually evaluates risk. I have coined the term neuroception to describe how neural circuits distinguish whether situations or people are safe, dangerous, or life-threatening. Because of our heritage as a species, neuroception takes place in primitive

parts of the brain, without our conscious awareness. The detection of a person as safe or dangerous triggers neurobiologically determined prosocial or defensive behaviors. Even though we may not be aware of danger on a cognitive level, on a neurophysiological level, our body has already started a sequence of neural processes that would facilitate adaptive defense behaviors such as fight, flight, or freeze. Neuroception describes how neural circuits distinguish whether situations or people are safe, dangerous, or life-threatening. Neuroception explains why a baby coos at a caregiver but cries at a stranger, or why a toddler enjoys a parent's embrace but views a hug from a stranger as an assault.[53]

This capacity to *intentionally determine* that we and our environment are presently safe—even when our body is already beginning to respond to a perceived threat—is essential for interrupting the fight-or-flight response and allowing us to learn (and eventually master) self-regulation.

1. or 2. Interoception or "bodyfulness": Interoception is the process of consciously shifting our attention away from the outside world or our thoughts to the inner world of our body in order to analyze our physical state. Colloquially referred to as "bodyfulness," interoception is quite different from mindfulness, which would be to simply observe our thoughts or sensations without judging or engaging them. With interoception, our goal is to become fluent in the silent but eloquent language of our bodies—to instantly recognize when we're becoming activated. Interoception can be done by monitoring our heart rate or breathing, but it's easiest and simplest to scan our bodies for muscle tension.

There's only one reason that muscles constrict and stay constricted: stress. They will constrict if we're doing manual labor or working out, but as soon as we're done with the job or the workout is completed, the muscles will relax. The reason muscles *remain* constricted is because we're perceiving a threat and our fight-or-flight response is engaged. As we're able to divert our attention away from our thoughts and environment and discover the tension in our muscles, then the last part of self-regulation—acute relaxation of these muscles—is relatively simple.

There is, however, a caveat to this when we're dealing with significant trauma or post-traumatic stress. For those of us experiencing ongoing trauma, or who have high ACE scores (traumas in our childhood), we've likely been in an active threat response for much of our waking life. When we've experienced frequent distress from the heightened energy of hypervigilance with no way to release it, we can become increasingly estranged from our own ongoing physiological processes. This condition is called "somatic dissociation," and many survivors of trauma suffer from it. They can look you in the eye and tell you that they feel no stress at all, while their leg is bouncing up and down in clear psychomotor agitation (a hallmark indicator of too much energy in the body).

So for those of us who don't possess a clear "felt sense" of our bodies, care should be taken to honor our own personal journey to recovering that competency—a journey that might best be aided by the guidance of a mental health professional in conjunction with the Forward-Facing® process. When dissociation from our bodily sensations was the way we survived during times of overwhelming distress and trauma, the incremental gains we make through interoception over time are to be recognized and celebrated.

With practice, anyone, even those who've historically been dissociated from their bodies, can learn to become aware of their bodily processes enough to know when they're experiencing a threat response, and which muscle group(s) are constricting. From there, it's an easy step to the final task of self-regulation: the *intentional* release of these constricted muscles with acute relaxation.

3. Acute relaxation, a.k.a. "invoking the relaxation response": This is where self-regulation differs from most therapeutic stress management or performance-enhancement strategies. When most of us think of relaxation, we think about taking a break and meditating, stretching, or leaning back in a chair and daydreaming about our next vacation.

Virtually all relaxation strategies require us to break away from the activities of our daily living—professional or personal—to practice and master these strategies. Guided visualization, progressive muscle relaxation, meditation, and many other approaches *have* demonstrated effectiveness in helping people lessen their traumatic stress, but each one involves an interruption of several seconds to several minutes in order to achieve this relaxation response.

For those with a schedule that allows them to engage in these deeper relaxation processes, by all means continue, as achieving this more profound relaxation throughout the day can enhance the ability to successfully self-regulate. These practices are not the same thing as self-regulation, however, which involves acute relaxation *while continuing to be* fully engaged in the activities and challenges of our day. We don't take a break to practice self-regulation. Instead, we establish our safety (neuroception), begin to develop an awareness of our body and when it's activated (interoception/"bodyfulness"), and interrupt our body's threat response in brief two- to three-second intervals throughout the day. We achieve this interruption by invoking our relaxation response via one (or more) of these five acute relaxation methods:

- Body scan, a.k.a. the "wet noodle."
- Pelvic floor relaxation.
- Peripheral vision.
- Diaphragmatic or regulated "belly" breathing.
- Soft palate relaxation.

(Read on for descriptions of these methods below, followed by step-by-step guidance for performing each one in Forward-Facing® Worksheet 2.)

4. Face-to-face contact with regulated others, a.k.a. co-regulation: There *is* a fourth method of regulating our bodies that's not solely "*self*"-regulation—engaging our ventral vagal complex, or VVC, by having face-to-face contact with other regulated human beings. This is called co-regulation, and can be very effective in a frenzied environment like a school, where our students are oftentimes experiencing high amounts of energy and frequent activation of their SNS.

If you'll recall from chapter four, this social engagement system is an ingrained part of our nervous systems that seeks out regulated (i.e., "relaxed") humans nearby and promotes our own physiological calm in response to theirs. We are herd animals, constantly gauging the perceived safety of our surroundings by observing other people and reacting in kind. So when we make eye contact with a smiling, relaxed person nearby, our VVC immediately engages to shift us out of an activated fight-or-flight response and into PNS dominance (a state of inner peace and calm).

To invoke this kind of regulation, the answer is simple: Have face-to-face contact with someone else who is relaxed. It could be a coworker you trust, your teaching assistant, or a student you have an especially good rapport with; just a few seconds' worth of eye contact will regulate your body, allowing for your brain to regain its highest levels of functioning so that you're optimized and thinking clearly and rationally. Relaxation—just like stress—is infectious, especially in a hectic environment like a busy classroom or hallway. This method is especially effective for not only regulating yourself during a chaotic time, but also helping your students become regulated since they're engaging their own VVCs while having face-to-face contact with *you*. A nice rule of thumb: The more we put ourselves in the presence of other relaxed people, the more our own lives improve, while theirs do too. A win for everyone!

When and How to Self-Regulate

The short answer to when we should self-regulate is every day, all throughout the day! Self-regulation is a brief, two- to three-second act in which we complete the steps of neuroception, interoception, and acute relaxation *without anyone noticing*. This is essential in meeting our goal of eliminating stress while interacting with our coworkers, students, and their parents, and in the variety of situations we encounter every school day. (If you have a bit more time, say, between classes or during a bathroom break, it can be especially beneficial to spend between ten and thirty seconds performing this self-regulation regime. The essential ingredient here is that you're *interrupting your threat response by releasing all constricted muscles*—this can be done in as little as one or two seconds, or more profoundly for ten to thirty seconds.)

In contrast, other relaxation techniques might require us to find a secluded space where we can sit quietly and practice mindfulness for ten to twenty minutes while using a "mental device" such as a repeated sound or mantra. We'd hardly expect to apply such methods while engaging with a room of thirty students or giving announcements during a school assembly!

Self-regulation is easy to learn, but difficult to master. You can see this for yourself by trying out one of the acute relaxation methods we'll be teaching you in Forward-Facing® Worksheet 2 right now: the **body scan, a.k.a. "the wet noodle."**

Sit down in a comfortable chair, close your eyes, ascertain your safety in the present moment, and begin focusing on the sensations within your body. Scan up and down from head to toe, searching for tense muscles. Pay close attention to tension hot spots, such as your neck, shoulders, jaw, and stomach. Whenever you find a tense muscle, consciously relax it until your whole body is as floppy and droopy as a wet noodle. Notice how calm, relaxed, and centered you feel. Congratulations! You've just performed your first official act of self-regulation (neuroception + interoception + acute relaxation). Biologically speaking, you've restored yourself to the healing state of PNS dominance.

Now while this illustrates just how easy it is to learn, the true power of self-regulation lies in our ability to apply it while remaining fully engaged in our daily lives. This is why we always emphasize that self-regulation is easy to learn, but difficult to master. It will never become an automatic, unconscious process like driving is. If you want to live stress-free, you'll have to perform it consciously and consistently for the rest of your life. However, you do have a good deal of flexibility when it comes to choosing an acute relaxation method that works best for you. Let's explore what we believe to be the most efficient method first.

As was described in chapter four, our muscles contract in preparation to fight, flee, or freeze when we perceive threat. When we're chronically activated by traumatic stress and a burned-out state, this creates a destructive feedback loop that keeps our stress response escalated long after the perceived danger has passed. Eventually, our threat-detection systems become set at the redline level of hypervigilance, leaving us in an unhealthy state of dysregulation.

One of the quickest and most efficient ways to overcome this SNS activation is to relax the core muscles connected to our vagus nerve (if you'll recall from chapter four, the vagus nerve runs through our entire body and is mainly responsible for "turning on" the threat response when we perceive threat). These core muscles are located between our pelvic and tailbones, thus this acute relaxation method is termed **pelvic floor relaxation**. When we do this, reciprocal inhibition forces the SNS to disengage, allowing for the PNS to rapidly restore dominance. This method of stimulating the relaxation response doesn't work right away for everyone, however. If we've spent considerable time in an environment of fear, shame, and threatened or actual violence, and/or are battling severe post-traumatic stress or PTSD, we've often learned to tune out the unpleasant sensations of stress we carry in our chronically constricted muscles. We might understand intellectually that we possess the same core muscles as everyone else, but are no longer able to feel or locate them easily.

Such was the case with Bailey (not her real name), a teacher and client of Eric's from years back. Here he is with more.

Eric: During our first session, I introduced Bailey to the core tenets of the Forward-Facing® approach for professional resilience, and explained the connection between the distressing symptoms she was experiencing at school and the dysregulation that was being created by her amped-up stress response. At the end of the session, she agreed to try relaxing her body whenever she encountered a perceived threat at work. Bailey left the session bright with hope that her life was about to change for the better.

But when Bailey arrived for our next session, I could see that she was depressed and irritable. Despite her best intentions, she had been so distracted by the moment-to-moment pressures of her classroom that she'd gone almost the entire week without checking in with her body and self-regulating. As a result, she'd spent the week "stressed out," indulging her tendencies to treat colleagues in a short-tempered and condescending manner. They'd retaliated in kind, ratcheting up her stress levels even higher as the vicious cycle repeated over and over again.

To solve this conundrum, I instructed Bailey to close her eyes and visualize several of the most stressful situations she'd encountered during the previous week. I then asked her, "What do you notice happening in your body *right now*?"

Bailey reported that she felt tightness in her abdominal and gluteus muscles. I asked her to clench these muscles as hard as she could for five seconds, and then release the tension to perform that specific method of acute relaxation (pelvic floor relaxation). I encouraged her to repeat this exercise five more times, until she was able to consistently "find" these muscles and relax them while visualizing stressful situations. By the end of the session, she'd completely regained her stability and mental composure. As homework, I asked her to continue practicing the three elements of self-regulation—neuroception or declaring "I am safe," bodyfulness, and the chosen acute relaxation method of pelvic floor relaxation—while noting down the school situations she found most stressful and considering what each of those "triggers" might have in common.

A week later, a very different Bailey entered my office. She proudly reported that she'd been able to keep her muscles relaxed in more than half of the stressful situations she had encountered the prior week. As a result, her interactions with coworkers and students had gone more smoothly, and her stress level at work had plummeted. Bailey now regarded her abdominal and gluteus muscles as a kind of friendly "early warning" system that allowed her to control her stress before it overwhelmed her. She expressed amazement that something as simple as purposefully relaxing her muscles could have such a rapid and decisive impact on her quality of life. She also felt far more hopeful about her prospects for continued improvement in the months to come.

Some of us may need to employ multiple acute relaxation methods to achieve self-regulation in our daily lives. This was the case with another one of Eric's clients named Amir (not his real name), a forty-two-year-old administrator at a large elementary school in a busy downtown district. Amir sought Eric for private counseling after a visit to the ER for heart palpitations revealed he was in the midst of a severe panic attack. Amir's home life was also suffering due to his angry outbursts and self-medicating with alcohol on the weekends, which upset his wife and children and left him feeling alienated and confused. As a result, he avoided family activities and kept to himself as much as possible. Eric will share more now about the steps they followed to address Amir's significant compassion fatigue symptoms.

My first session with Amir began the usual way. I outlined the roles of the SNS and PNS in regulating our responses to stress and explained how this process could go awry, especially for educators in charge of caring for hundreds of students and faculty every day. At that point I walked him through the same process I'd used with Bailey, and soon Amir was able to locate and then relax the muscles of his pelvic floor while visualizing some of the stressful events that had provoked his anxiety and anger. By the end of the session, he felt ready to apply self-regulation at work.

I saw Amir again about a month later during a follow-up visit. Overall, he said, things were getting better. His relationship with his wife and children had improved considerably and he was now taking greater pleasure in family activities. He seemed calmer and more centered, thanks to his practice of self-regulation at home. However, he was still struggling whenever he stepped foot on campus.

Much like Bailey, Amir was continually overwhelmed by the demands of his job. He was so busy he often forgot to eat lunch or go to the bathroom, much less take time to monitor and relax his muscles. He expressed disappointment and confusion that no matter how hard he tried, he was unable to apply the self-regulation he was using so successfully at home in his school environment.

Recognizing that Amir needed another "tool in his self-regulation toolbox," I taught him a second acute relaxation method to supplement the pelvic floor relaxation he'd already mastered. The **peripheral vision** method was first developed by the U.S. military to help snipers improve their shooting accuracy. Trainees would be instructed to attend to their peripheral vision for ten seconds before peering through the rifle scope at their target. This enabled them to relax their muscles, allowing for greater stability while inhibiting the micro-movements of arms and hands that can sharply degrade shooting accuracy. Amir mastered the technique on his first try, and resolved to put it into practice shortly thereafter.

Over the next few months of sessions, Amir transformed from a nervous, sleep-starved, underweight client to someone who was setting healthy boundaries between his work and "off" time, exercising and eating better, getting enough sleep, and spending quality time with his family in the evenings and on weekends.

Amir attributed his success to the peripheral vision relaxation method, which had enabled him to "get a lever into the space between stimulus and response." After diligently practicing the peripheral vision method for several weeks, he'd become increasingly attuned to his body while at work. Eventually, he was able to discard the peripheral vision method entirely and respond to stress by simply releasing the muscles in his pelvic floor. As a result, his stress level dropped precipitously, and he was able to derive a newfound sense of fulfillment and enjoyment from his career helping the staff and children at his school to feel their best.

Here are two more acute relaxation techniques to consider (and that we teach you how to perform in the following worksheet), with the first being **diaphragmatic or regulated "belly" breathing**. One of the effects of SNS activation is a dramatic change in our breathing patterns. As we prepare to fight or flee, we fuel our muscles with oxygen by breathing rapidly and shallowly, using our chest muscles rather than our diaphragms (which are nearer to our abdomens) to draw air in and out. The reverse is also true—when we engage in rapid chest breathing, our threat-detection systems may interpret this as a danger signal and react by setting off our fight-or-flight response. Diaphragmatic breathing acts as a counterweight to this SNS activation, utilizing reciprocal inhibition (stress cannot exist in a relaxed body) to trigger the relaxation response and return us to PNS dominance.

The final acute relaxation method we'll be instructing you to do is **soft palate relaxation**. Like pelvic floor relaxation, this technique directly counteracts vagus nerve stimulation to restore PNS dominance, but it does this by acting upon the branch of the vagal system that originates at the soft palate near the roof of the mouth rather than the branch that connects to the muscles of the pelvic floor.

Now it's time for you to try things out for yourself and see what happens. First we'll start by learning, step by step, how to perform each of the five acute relaxation methods described in Forward-Facing® Worksheet 2. We encourage you to experiment with all five of these acute relaxation methods (while pairing them with neuroception and interoception) to find the ones that work best for you.

Once you've identified which techniques are preferred or the easiest to master, we want you to begin practicing them while you're at work as directed in Forward-Facing® Worksheet 3. You'll be amazed to discover that a state of relaxed and joyful bliss can truly be yours with a little practice and persistence.

Lastly, we'll revisit a day in the life of our school principal, Mrs. Burkhart, to see how the technique of self-regulation has led to significant positive change in her career and personal life, as well as in the lives of the students and staff she interacts with.

FORWARD-FACING® WORKSHEET 2: THE METHODS OF INVOKING THE RELAXATION RESPONSE

The five methods listed below are arranged to begin with the "easiest" (least intensive) to apply, continuing toward those which require a bit more concentration and practice. They are all equally effective at the acute relaxation portion of self-regulation, and are designed to be performed multiple times a day (or more) as needed.

Method 1: Body scan, a.k.a. the "wet noodle"

This process is executed by simply becoming aware of all the muscles in your body and relaxing them. It can be completed while standing, sitting, or lying down, but we recommend sitting in a chair when you're just starting out.

1. Sit or recline somewhere.
2. Take five seconds and release all of your muscles from head to toe simultaneously, paying special attention to areas of increased tension (i.e., abdominal muscles, throat, chest, et cetera).

One, two, three, four, five.

That's it!

Method 2: Pelvic floor relaxation

As was explained earlier, our pelvic muscles are linked to our fight-or-flight response, and when we're SNS dominant, they are constricted. By releasing them, we initiate a potent and instinctual relaxation response. In this exercise, your goal is to locate and then relax the muscles in your core.

1. Sit down comfortably and place a hand under each side of your bottom.
2. Now feel for the pointed bones that you're sitting upon. These mark the lower boundary of your core.
3. Next, find and touch the two bony points just above your waist on the right and left sides of your body. These mark the upper boundary of your core.

4. Now that you've made a "touch memory" of these four points, imagine connecting them with lines to form a square that encircles your body. This is your core—the location where your vagal nerve connects to your pelvic floor muscles.

5. Next, take ten seconds and imagine allowing that square to expand in all four directions, so that there is no clenching anywhere in the middle of it. Completely soften that entire area of your body.

One, two, three, four, five, six, seven, eight, nine, ten.

6. For ten more seconds, focus on the muscles in the center of the square, opening and completely releasing them.

One, two, three, four, five, six, seven, eight, nine, ten.

Once you become adept at interoception (sensing your body becoming activated), you'll be able to practice this acute relaxation method while sitting or standing as part of your daily regimen of self-regulation.

Method 3: Peripheral vision

This method was originally developed by the U.S. military to train snipers. Fortunately, it works just as well for civilians.

1. Find a spot at eye level that's located five to ten feet in front of you.

2. Focus your eyes for five seconds on that spot.

One, two, three, four, five.

3. Now soften your focus until the spot becomes blurry. Hold that for five seconds.

One, two, three, four, five.

4. Still facing forward and without moving your eyes, shift your focus to your peripheral vision. Do this simultaneously with both eyes.

5. Maintain your peripheral focus for ten seconds.

One, two, three, four, five, six, seven, eight, nine, ten.

6. Repeat steps 1 through 5 five times.

Note: If you're having difficulty shifting your focus from the center to the periphery, try extending your arms straight out in front of you so that your hands touch, palms down. Slowly start to move them away from each other, keeping your eyes fixated forward, until each arm is held straight out on either side of your body, and you can still see them both in your peripheral vision. Now hold that peripheral focus for ten seconds.

This is one of the few methods of self-regulation that requires less, rather than more, interoception. While interoception/bodyfulness is still helpful at augmenting the effectiveness of this skill, it's not necessary to master a felt-sense awareness of your body to begin the practice of peripheral vision. We've found that this technique works especially well for individuals in service roles that require a lot of interaction with others. You can continue to look at someone, and without their knowledge briefly stop paying direct attention in order to focus on your periphery for a few seconds. Then you can immediately return to the interaction, but with a relaxed and regulated system.

Method 4: Diaphragmatic or regulated "belly" breathing

Also known as belly or abdominal breathing, this is the most common breathing exercise. With diaphragmatic breathing, you're training the body to let your diaphragm do all the work. Your goal here is to breathe through your nose and focus on how your belly fills up with air, and you can do this either sitting up or lying down.

1. Sit comfortably, with your knees bent and your shoulders, head, and neck relaxed.
2. Locate your diaphragm by placing one hand below your rib cage and the other on your upper chest. As you breathe, you will feel your diaphragm rising and falling.
3. Breathe in slowly through your nose so that your stomach moves outward against your hand. Count in your head and make sure the inward breath lasts at least five seconds, paying particular attention to the feeling of the air filling your lungs. The hand on your chest should remain as still as possible.

One, two, three, four, five.

4. Tighten your stomach muscles, letting them fall inward as you exhale through pursed lips. The hand on your upper chest must remain as still as possible.
5. Repeat steps 1 through 4 five times.

Another simple way to practice diaphragmatic breathing is to lace your fingers together and put them behind your head. Then lean back in your chair and pull your elbows back as far as is comfortable. You should notice that your abdominal muscles are now doing all the work to draw your breath.

Method 5: Soft palate relaxation

Here your goal is to locate and then relax your soft palate, a.k.a. the muscular part at the back of the roof of your mouth.

1. Sit down comfortably and shift your focus to the muscles along the roof of your mouth.
2. Release all the tension in this area.
3. Now expand your focus to include the muscles in your face and jaw.
4. Release the tension in these muscles too.
5. Next, with all of these muscles relaxed, silently say the letter "R" to yourself and try to gently maintain the subtle arch this creates in the roof of your mouth for five seconds.

One, two, three, four, five.

6. Repeat this exercise five times.

Forward-Facing® Worksheet 3: Self-Regulation Practice at Work

It's time to start practicing the skill of self-regulation in the work setting (and at home too). At this point, you should already have chosen the acute relaxation method or methods that are easiest for you to engage in. For the next three days (at least), perform self-regulation five to ten times a day as you go about your normal routine at school. On each occasion, use the log below to write down the level of tension you're feeling before and after self-regulating, which muscles were involved, and the method(s) you used to invoke the relaxation response. (You can also do this in your separate journal or notepad.)

Once the three days are up, you should be familiar with the three components of neuroception, interoception/bodyfulness, and acute relaxation that make up self-regulation, with the Forward-Facing® approach's step one growing to become a habitual part of your daily work and home activities for lasting professional resilience and optimization.

Self-Regulation Log Day 1 (five to ten occasions altogether)
**Occasion 1**
-Date and time: _____
-Muscle tension on a scale of 0 to 10 (0 = no tension, 10 = highest tension possible): _____
-Tension location (which muscles were tense):

_____

_____

-Acute relaxation method(s) used:

_____

_____

-Results of how you felt afterwards:

_____

_____

**Occasion 2**
-Date and time: _____
-Muscle tension on a scale of 0 to 10 (0 = no tension, 10 = highest tension possible): _____
-Tension location (which muscles were tense):

_____

_____

-Acute relaxation method(s) used:

_____

_____

-Results of how you felt afterwards:

_____

_____

Occasion 3

-Date and time: _____

-Muscle tension on a scale of 0 to 10 (0 = no tension, 10 = highest tension possible): _____

-Tension location (which muscles were tense):

_____

_____

-Acute relaxation method(s) used:

_____

_____

-Results of how you felt afterwards:

_____

_____

Occasion 4

-Date and time: _____

-Muscle tension on a scale of 0 to 10 (0 = no tension, 10 = highest tension possible): _____

-Tension location (which muscles were tense):

_____

_____

-Acute relaxation method(s) used:

_____

_____

-Results of how you felt afterwards:

_____

_____

Occasion 5
-Date and time: _____

-Muscle tension on a scale of 0 to 10 (0 = no tension, 10 = highest tension possible): _____

-Tension location (which muscles were tense):

_____

_____

-Acute relaxation method(s) used:

_____

_____

-Results of how you felt afterwards:

_____

_____

Self-Regulation Log Day 2 (five to ten occasions altogether)
Occasion 1
-Date and time: _____

-Muscle tension on a scale of 0 to 10 (0 = no tension, 10 = highest tension possible): _____

-Tension location (which muscles were tense):

_____

_____

-Acute relaxation method(s) used:

_____

_____

-Results of how you felt afterwards:

_____

_____

Occasion 2

-Date and time: _____

-Muscle tension on a scale of 0 to 10 (0 = no tension, 10 = highest tension possible): _____

-Tension location (which muscles were tense):

_____

_____

-Acute relaxation method(s) used:

_____

_____

-Results of how you felt afterwards:

_____

_____

Occasion 3

-Date and time: _____

-Muscle tension on a scale of 0 to 10 (0 = no tension, 10 = highest tension possible): _____

-Tension location (which muscles were tense):

_____

_____

-Acute relaxation method(s) used:

_____

_____

-Results of how you felt afterwards:

_____

_____

Occasion 4

-Date and time: _____

-Muscle tension on a scale of 0 to 10 (0 = no tension, 10 = highest tension possible): _____

-Tension location (which muscles were tense):

_____

_____

-Acute relaxation method(s) used:

_____

_____

-Results of how you felt afterwards:

_____

_____

Occasion 5

-Date and time: _____

-Muscle tension on a scale of 0 to 10 (0 = no tension, 10 = highest tension possible): _____

-Tension location (which muscles were tense):

_____

_____

-Acute relaxation method(s) used:

_____

_____

-Results of how you felt afterwards:

_____

_____

Self-Regulation Log Day 3 (five to ten occasions altogether)
Occasion 1
-Date and time: _____
-Muscle tension on a scale of 0 to 10 (0 = no tension, 10 = highest tension possible): _____
-Tension location (which muscles were tense):

_____
_____

-Acute relaxation method(s) used:

_____
_____

-Results of how you felt afterwards:

_____
_____

Occasion 2
-Date and time: _____
-Muscle tension on a scale of 0 to 10 (0 = no tension, 10 = highest tension possible): _____
-Tension location (which muscles were tense):

_____
_____

-Acute relaxation method(s) used:

_____
_____

-Results of how you felt afterwards:

_____
_____

Occasion 3

-Date and time: _____

-Muscle tension on a scale of 0 to 10 (0 = no tension, 10 = highest tension possible): _____

-Tension location (which muscles were tense):

_____

_____

-Acute relaxation method(s) used:

_____

_____

-Results of how you felt afterwards:

_____

_____

Occasion 4

-Date and time: _____

-Muscle tension on a scale of 0 to 10 (0 = no tension, 10 = highest tension possible): _____

-Tension location (which muscles were tense):

_____

_____

-Acute relaxation method(s) used:

_____

_____

-Results of how you felt afterwards:

_____

_____

Occasion 5

-Date and time: _____

-Muscle tension on a scale of 0 to 10 (0 = no tension, 10 = highest tension possible): _____

-Tension location (which muscles were tense):

_____

_____

-Acute relaxation method(s) used:

_____

_____

-Results of how you felt afterwards:

_____

_____

A Day in the Life of Mrs. Burkhart Revisited

Shannon settled into her office chair for another weekday morning of reading and answering emails, noting the immediate and familiar pit in her stomach and tightness in her chest as she turned her computer monitor on. After having attended a Forward-Facing® workshop available for the administrators in her district a month prior, Shannon didn't shy away from the sensation—in fact, she welcomed the opportunity to practice the first and most important skill she'd learned during the workshop called self-regulation.

Shannon now knew all about perceived threat from painful past learning and the stress response, and how over the years serving as a teacher and principal she'd developed fears and triggers to all sorts of activating situations with students, faculty, and *especially* parents. She could identify when she was beginning to shift into the fight-or-flight response on campus by that instant roiling in her gut, and had been utilizing her Forward-Facing® worksheets to practice the five methods of acute relaxation, as well as spending the last three days writing down the specific occasions when and where she experienced muscle tension, and which method she used to regulate herself.

Before Shannon opened the first unread email—this one from a parent with a snarky subject line that read "Why Was My Child's Cell Phone Taken

Away in Class?", which meant it wouldn't be a fun one to read—she started to engage the self-regulation process again.

"I'm not in danger," Shannon said aloud to the empty office, feeling a bit silly, but recognizing how important this first step of neuroception was. "I am completely safe; I am in no danger right now," she continued, feeling her pulse begin to slow right away, even with this simple statement. She then turned her focus inward to her body's sensations via interoception. Shannon scanned from her toes up to her head, noting the unsettled feeling in her stomach as well as significant tightness in her jaw and throat. She decided to practice her favorite acute relaxation technique so far—the soft palate relaxation method. She felt it was very effective for her because she seemed to frequently hold tension in her jaw, and consciously relaxing all of the muscles in the roof of her mouth while making a silent "R" and counting to five was something she could do throughout the day without anyone else noticing.

Shannon did five rounds of counting in that moment in her chair, closing her eyes and mindfully relaxing all the muscles in her face and neck while arching the muscles at the base of her throat to say a silent "R." The knot in her stomach loosened as she did so, and her heart rate slowed even more.

When she was done self-regulating, Shannon opened her eyes softly and began to read each email, engaging in the soft palate relaxation technique several times between answering them any time she felt like she was getting activated again. When she was done, Shannon retrieved one of the worksheets from a folder in her desk drawer to write in her self-regulation log for the day.

Self-Regulation Log Day 4
Occasion 1
- Date and time: September 25th, 7:05 a.m., anxiety before opening my unread morning emails.
- Muscle tension on a scale of 0 to 10 (0 = no tension, 10 = highest tension possible): 6.
- Tension location (which muscles were tense): My stomach felt tense/unsettled, my jaw was clenched, and my throat was very tight.
- Acute relaxation method(s) used: Soft palate relaxation five times before reading any emails, and once or twice more during responding to each one.

- *Results of how you felt afterwards: I felt much calmer and more clear-headed. I had patience in my responses to parents and faculty, and felt like I was better able to access my higher cognitive functioning to make the best and most rational decisions for my staff and students' needs.*

Not only had Shannon been able to keep herself better regulated on campus, but she was also able to help her teachers and students stay regulated through the face-to-face contact she knew was so important for maintaining a calm school environment. That month had been a particularly difficult one for everyone because of a social media trend encouraging school vandalism and theft, with one young teacher, Ms. Hernandez, having various items like trash bins, desks, and chairs going missing from the classroom earlier that week. When Alexandra had told Shannon about the missing items, she'd been in tears, afraid she'd have to pay for everything out of pocket.

While Shannon had been upset about the classroom items going missing (they were already overextended on everything and had very little funds allocated for anything new), she'd deployed the only acute relaxation technique she could think of in the moment: the body scan, or "wet noodle." As Alexandra shared who she thought had taken the items, and that part of the challenge was filming it so there might be video evidence for further action, Shannon focused on relaxing every single muscle in her body like a "wet noodle" for two seconds at a time, making sure to consciously loosen her jaw where she held so much of her tension.

"Alexandra, take a breath for me please," Shannon had said as the new teacher's voice rose higher in panic and tears ran down her cheeks. "It's going to be okay. I will handle this—you're not paying for anything yourself. Please just focus on doing some deep breathing with me for a bit, okay?"

They'd taken a few breaths together, with Alexandra mirroring Shannon's slow inhales through her nose and exhales out her mouth.

"Better?" Shannon had asked, with Alexandra nodding and seeming to mean it—she was no longer crying, and her whole demeanor had changed from frazzled to calm and collected.

It wasn't until Shannon was filling out her self-regulation log worksheet during the lunch period that she realized she'd used two techniques at once: the "wet noodle" *and* diaphragmatic breathing, which she'd then modeled for Alexandra via co-regulation with clear success in helping the teacher become more equipped to handle the situation. That was the moment Shannon had decided she couldn't be the only educator at their school to learn the Forward-Facing® approach for professional resilience firsthand.

A workshop training on campus was already scheduled for early next month, and Shannon was confident it would help her faculty tremendously. Since she'd begun self-regulating, her sleep had been better, her acid reflux was less severe, and several times when a panic attack had loomed, she'd been able to down-regulate herself before it worsened. She no longer felt like she wanted to leave her career and the life she'd built in a desperate escape plan—she could face whatever each hour brought forth, competent and reinvigorated about the mission that had first drawn her to education all those years ago. It was a freeing place to be, and Shannon looked forward to sharing that freedom with her staff so they could more comfortably and optimally achieve what they came to work every day to do: educate their students and foster positive, everlasting change in their communities.

You may find it hard to believe that something as simple as self-regulation has the power to transform your life in ways that are profoundly positive and far-reaching. However, after teaching this first step of the Forward-Facing® approach for professional resilience to thousands of educators over the years, we can assure you that it's true. The more you practice these simple skills, the more attuned you'll become to your body and its powerful distress signals. You'll be able to make increasingly fine, moment-to-moment adjustments to the level of energy you bring to each challenge in your professional life, until you are consistently operating within that optimal energy zone of eustress. Self-regulation will allow you to create the needed space between stimulus and response in which you're free to make rational, principled choices about how you want to respond at school and beyond.

With this newly acquired ability to stay calm and regulated no matter what comes your way, it's time to move into the second Forward-Facing® step of intentionality. This is a beautiful, soulful practice that involves crafting your current mission, vision for the future, and code of honor—altogether known as the personal covenant you wish to educate and live by.

CHAPTER SEVEN

FORWARD-FACING® STEP TWO: INTENTIONALITY

*My mission in life is to be kind, compassionate, caring, and
loving in order to find and feel the deepest joy in life.*

Debasish Mridha

MANY EDUCATORS WAKE up and make a solemn resolution similar to this one every workday: *Today I will succeed in my quest to be the best educator I can be. I will be patient with my students no matter what they say or do. I will be calm, rational, and flexible when managing whatever unexpected changes come my way. I will continue to stay focused on supporting my students and meeting their needs even when others with different priorities try to draw my attention away from my students. I won't get frustrated by things my coworkers or students' parents say, even if hostility or negativity are directed at me. I will stay regulated at all times so that my students can mirror that regulation, and I will not be "infected" by the chaotic and dysregulated environment around me, regardless of what occurs.*

No matter how prepared, well-intentioned, and principled we wish to be, on campus and off, compassion fatigue by its very nature makes this impossible. Burnout and post-traumatic stress go beyond just damaging our bodies, minds, and health through chronic dysregulation—they carve deep spiritual and moral wounds by shattering the essential, largely unstated assumptions we have about ourselves and the world that imbue our professional and personal lives with meaning and purpose. Instead of viewing the world as a fundamentally benevolent place, where right action reaps rewards and wrong actions are punished, we begin to perceive it as hostile and capricious. Instead of feeling empowered, optimistic, and free, we perceive ourselves as helpless victims. Ultimately, we lose every vestige of the hope and conviction of self-efficacy we all need to feel joy, connect with our students and coworkers, and pursue the passions and dreams that led us to education in the first place.

The damage is compounded when we lose control and act out, cursing out a fellow driver on the way to work, sending a sarcastic email reply to a parent, or bringing our frustrations home with us to our loved ones. How are we to make sense of our values if we rescind them every time we're overwhelmed by our compassion fatigue? How can we know or trust ourselves if we chronically breach our integrity by acting in ways that contradict our core beliefs?

In terms you now know apply to our daily battle with a chronic amount of workplace stress: How do we shift from an *external* locus of control to an *internal* one that empowers us to live in accordance with our morals and ethics? How do we capture and optimize that "space" between stimulus and response? In short—how do we move beyond our toxic entrenched reactivity to the state of relaxed joyfulness that allows us to be truly intentional at school and out of it?

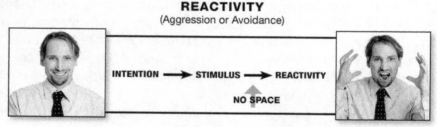

REACTIVITY
(Aggression or Avoidance)

INTENTION ➙ STIMULUS ➙ REACTIVITY

NO SPACE

Loss of Integrity Caused by ANS Dysregulation

Forward-Facing® for Educators provides an answer. It offers a moral antidote to toxic levels of traumatic stress and burnout that is deceptively simple but profound in its implications. To heal ourselves, we must make intentional use of that "space" that lies between stimulus—what sets us off—and our response to it. In that space, with a relaxed body and clarity of mind, we can consult our moral compass and allow the best within us to guide our actions.

Like self-regulation, the recipe for intentional living is simple but not easy. It takes practice, perseverance, and many rounds of revisions; but the effort is well worth it, because the resulting effects are immediate, enduring, and transformational. We believe this capacity—the ability to live with fidelity to our principles—is the state psychologist Abraham Maslow was referring to at the apex of his well-known hierarchy of needs. Living intentionally *is* self-actualization.

Every time we succeed in acting intentionally, we grow stronger and more resilient. Our moral wounds heal bit by bit as the hypervigilance of SNS dominance gives way to the relaxed awareness of a regulated ANS. Our fractured "spiritual skeleton" begins to mend itself organically, and the destructive symptoms of compassion fatigue and its aftermath lose their grip upon us. We begin to feel lighter and more optimistic. Small successes lead to greater, more far-reaching ones as this process evolves into a deep satisfaction with ourselves, our careers, and our lives.

The people around us sense this tectonic shift taking place within, and begin to treat us in new ways that reinforce the positive changes we make as we evolve. Our virtuous circle expands, building strength upon strength. As we learn to trust ourselves, we become increasingly confident, less reactive, and more capable of right action, loving-kindness, and patience for all, even when we don't agree. As our relationships improve, our social engagement system kicks in more frequently, soothing us when we're triggered and further enhancing our resilience. Gradually and inevitably, our psyche and soul align to make us whole again. When we apply Forward-Facing®'s second step of intentionality to our professional life, we facilitate a rebirth of our mission in education and a renewal of hope for the future. We become empowered and inspired to transform ourselves into the people we used to be (or sought to be) at the beginning of our careers, endowing our pursuits with deep meaning and a noble purpose.

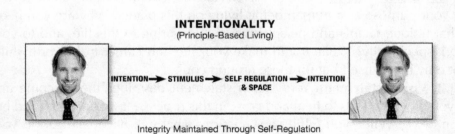

INTENTIONALITY
(Principle-Based Living)

INTENTION ➡ STIMULUS ➡ SELF REGULATION ➡ INTENTION
& SPACE

Integrity Maintained Through Self-Regulation

The Roadmap to Intentionality: Your Personal Covenant

For more than 2,000 years, navigators traversed the seas by looking to the North Star through a sextant (a pre-industrial GPS that measured the distance between two visible objects using stars in the night sky) to determine their location and the direction home, correcting their course nightly as needed. Without this celestial reference point, they might've been lost forever. In much the same way, we must orient ourselves to our own "moral true north" if we hope to successfully navigate the waters of everyday life at school. Thus, in Forward-Facing® we always begin our journey to intentionality by embarking upon a discernment process to identify our current mission, our vision for the future, and the core values and beliefs that will get us there.

Some of us may already have embraced a fully constructed moral framework that was passed down to us from our parents, teachers, or spiritual leaders. Others may have lost faith in their moral training or possess only vague intuitions of who they are or want to be in their career and personal life. Still others may have been so deeply wounded that they have embraced nihilism, rejecting all religious and moral principles entirely and adopting the cynical view that nothing, least of all their own behavior, has any real meaning or significance. Regardless, this fundamental quest for our "true north" principles is essential because it forces us to identify our often unspoken and unacknowledged moral assumptions, state them explicitly, and then align our behavior accordingly.

With Forward-Facing®'s step two, we complete this process of discernment and self-discovery by crafting three documents, or "roadmaps," for intentionality:

1. Mission statement: Your mission statement defines what you believe to be your purpose as a human being living on this planet. Why are you here? What unique talents and perspectives do you bring to this life, and to your work specifically? What would make your life and career truly worthwhile, not only for yourself but for those around you?

2. Vision statement: Your vision statement describes the outcome and payoff of your efforts to heal and grow in this process as an educator and human being. When you fulfill your mission, what will have changed in your life? Who will you be? What will you be doing professionally, personally, physically, and spiritually? Your vision statement must be so vivid and compelling that it energizes and sustains you throughout the arduous process of practicing ongoing self-regulation and intentionality in your daily work and home activities.

3. Code of honor: Your code of honor articulates the fundamental moral and ethical principles that will guide your behavior from this point forward, particularly when you're triggered. What constitutes right action for *you* personally? How should you choose between two actions when they appear to be morally equivalent? Your code of honor banishes all ambiguity and rationalizations, delineating clear guidelines about your personal character strengths to follow as you make sense of the world and your place within it.

Collectively, these three documents comprise the personal covenant that will guide you on your journey to intentional living, professional resilience, and personal optimization. Consider the metaphor of a train, with your mission statement constituting the engine and cars, your vision statement defining your destination, and your code of honor furnishing the tracks upon which the train is traveling. The longer you remain on track without derailing, the more quickly and easily you'll achieve your plan for a principled career and life.

It's time now to start crafting your own vision statement, mission statement, and code of honor by completing the next three Forward-Facing® worksheets below. Don't overthink this process or try to produce perfect prose. What's most important is to be honest with yourself, and to let the exercises guide you through the deeply personal process of self-exploration and self-definition. Don't be surprised if you find yourself changing or elaborating upon what you've written as time goes on—these documents are meant to be organic, and evolve in much the same way we do. The changing nature of our personal covenant is a sure sign that we're making meaningful progress toward becoming the fully realized educator and person we *choose* to be, rather than someone whose life continues to be disfigured by the wounds of our past.

This evolution is especially true in our own paths to intentionality—Eric has gone through ten different variations of his personal covenant so far, and will continue to revise it as the years go on. Here are summarized versions of our personal covenants to give you an idea of how one might look.

Cheryl's Personal Covenant

Writing and sharing my covenant has been a profound experience. I have not yet made the revisions over time that Eric has done. I recognize I desire to shorten my covenant, but have not yet been able to decipher which pieces I want to remove or change, and therefore I have left it alone until that feels comfortable. As a result, I will share only a few pieces of my covenant:

-When I live my best life, I use all of my actions and words to help others to live their best lives.

-I will live a positive life of gratitude and appreciation for the many gifts bestowed on me and I will use those gifts to help others.

-In my work, I will use my knowledge and skills to teach and support in every way I am equipped. I will use words that demonstrate kindness, empathy, and compassion. I will hold myself and those I work with to a high degree of moral and ethical integrity to better serve those in our care.

-My presence in the world will be guided by my loving heart. I choose to be friendly and respectful to every individual I am fortunate to meet. I will use my skills of empathy and compassion to value those who come to me with a different perspective or understanding of the world.

-I choose to treat myself with the same degree of compassion, acceptance, kindness, and love that I am more easily able to give to others. I will then take this love out into the world and help others to experience their best lives. I will live my life as recognition of the precious gift it is, and offer myself to others in service.

Rebecca's Personal Covenant

I believe my path is true. As I trust in my path, I will strive to be aligned with spirit. Actions that flow from this alignment will allow for courage, creation, and joy to be the dominant outcomes in my life. I strive to be present and hopeful in each and every interaction I have with others. While leading with kindness and grace, I will remember to presume positive intentions without assessing shame or judgment on others. I will remember that I have choice. I will look for that moment, in every situation, the allows for alignment with self and spirit.

Eric's Personal Covenant

I choose to live passionately and creatively as a servant leader. I promote healing, health, and maturation in both professional and personal contexts. I believe in myself and the indomitability of the human spirit. I am an instrument of love, peace, and hope. While I recognize that I will always be in confrontation with fear, I will live my life with courage and intention—never allowing fear to become my god.

I continue my path of healing. I will remain open and deferential to the direction I receive from a loving God. I will endeavor and continually realign to live in accordance with my principles that include faith, hope, courage, humility, and love. I will be the change I wish to see in the world. I believe.

At some point, you may feel confident enough to share these documents with a colleague, partner, or other trusted person so they can support you in your journey and help you get back on track when you veer into dysregulation—but for now, they're for your eyes only.

After you've completed your personal covenant, we'll touch base with our young teacher, Ms. Hernandez, to see how Forward-Facing®'s second step of intentionality has provided a framework to remind her of why she pursued teaching initially, as well as healthy practices for nurturing herself and collaborating with others at school and home.

FORWARD-FACING® WORKSHEET 4: CRAFTING YOUR MISSION STATEMENT

In this exercise, your goal is nothing short of defining your mission professionally and personally. Why are you here? Who is your "best self"—the person you could become if the shackles of fear, anger, frustration, and stress were forever banished from your life? How would you fully express your talents and creativity at work and home? What role would you play in helping others become *their* best selves—how would this manifest in school and elsewhere? Now's the time to get out your writing utensil if you haven't already, and your journal or notepad if you're using one.

PREPARATION FOR CRAFTING YOUR MISSION STATEMENT

There are two parts to this preparation portion, with the first one consisting of five questions. Try to come up with at least two good answers for each of the questions below. Keep them short and concise, spending no more than a total of fifteen minutes here.

Part 1

1. Why are you alive? What is your purpose for living on this planet?

_____

_____

2. What do you want to be when you "grow up"? (This can be a professional distinction or a more abstract, generalized description, i.e., "a happy human" or "a positive influence in my students' lives.")

_____

_____

3. What dreams do you have for yourself that are, as yet, unfulfilled?

_____

_____

4. What is _really_ important to you?

_____

_____

5. What are your greatest strengths?

_____

_____

Now circle three to five of the answers that feel the most meaningful and accurate to you, reflecting for a minute on what they tell you about yourself, and how your current life and career match up with them.

Part 2

Next, spend a minute or two answering each of the below prompts so that you can begin articulating the key elements of your mission statement.
It is my mission…

1. To live…

_____

_____

2. To work...

_____

_____

3. To continue...

_____

_____

4. To love...

_____

_____

5. To be...

_____

_____

6. To become...

_____

_____

7. To believe...

_____

_____

8. To promote...

_____

_____

9. To strive...

_____

_____

10. To seek...

_____

_____

Your Mission Statement

Referring to the insights listed above in parts 1 and 2, write a paragraph that most closely defines your current mission on this planet.

My Mission Statement

My mission is to…

_____

_____

_____

_____

_____

_____

_____

_____

_____

_____

FORWARD-FACING® WORKSHEET 5: CRAFTING YOUR VISION STATEMENT

Close your eyes and picture yourself attending your own retirement party. As you sit on the dais, each attendee stands up in turn to give a short speech honoring you for having achieved your vision. What is each guest saying about you? What qualities or accomplishments are they praising you for? Below are seven guidelines to keep in mind before you begin crafting your vision statement.

1. Your vision statement should consist of at least several sentences written in the present tense. For example, write, "I am financially secure with a stable plan for retirement" rather than, "I will achieve financial security and a stable plan for retirement."

2. State an overarching objective rather than a specific one. For example, write, "I am a well-respected and appreciated educator in my school district who's received multiple honors and distinctions in my career" rather than "I will be chosen as Teacher of the Year at least once."

3. Write in the first person (i.e., "I build long-lasting and supportive

relationships with my students, and they feel safe coming to me for assistance.").

4. Make sure your vision statement is compelling enough to keep you motivated and inspired when you encounter setbacks and challenges at school.

5. Remember that you're writing a vision for yourself, not for your spouse, students, colleagues, or anyone else. This is the time to think deeply about what *you* want out of your career and life.

6. Be bold. Don't limit your vision to what you can accomplish now. Consider who you *could* become, and what that person *could* accomplish if they no longer experienced compassion fatigue or burnout in their professional life. Reach for the stars.

7. Most importantly, have fun and recognize there is no "wrong" way to write a vision statement.

Okay, let's start writing!

Your Vision Statement

Referring to the guidelines above, write a paragraph below that most closely defines who you want to be once you've fulfilled (or are fulfilling) your mission. If you feel you need more space, consider writing it in your journal or notepad.

My Vision Statement

My vision is to...

_____

_____

_____

_____

_____

_____

_____

_____

_____

_____

FORWARD-FACING® WORKSHEET 6: CRAFTING YOUR CODE OF HONOR

This exercise will help you establish the moral foundation of an intentional, principle-based life. Your goal is to identify the ethical guidelines you'll be applying in the course of pursuing your mission and achieving your vision.

Preparation for Crafting Your Code of Honor

Start by choosing seven or more words from the list of traits below that most accurately reflect your moral and ethical convictions (or add your own!), and write them down in the spaces below. If you're using a journal or notepad, provide yourself with some empty space underneath each one.

Traits to Choose From

A leader; active; approach vs. avoidance; assertive; altruistic; committed; compassionate; courageous; creative; detailed; effective; efficient; ethical; facilitative; faithful; farsighted; fearless; frugal; generous; honest; hopeful; humorous; joyful; just; lively; loving; optimistic; outspoken; passionate; peaceable; powerful; productive; resilient; responsible; scientific; secure; self-confident; service-oriented; strong; tolerant; tenacious; valiant; warm; witty.

Your Code of Honor

Now write a declarative sentence next to each of the words you've chosen above that states your aspiration to abide by that rule without fail. If "honest" is the word you've chosen, for example, you might write, "I am always honest with myself and others." Of course, as fallible human beings, none of us can adhere to our morals and ethics as fully and faithfully as we might wish. But our goal for now is to set as high a bar as possible for our future behavior. As we continue to practice self-regulation over time, our code of honor and daily behavior will increasingly converge until we are consistently living in accordance with our deepest beliefs and convictions.

My Code of Honor

1. I am...

_____

_____

2. I am...

_____

_____

3. I am...

_____

_____

4. I am...

_____

_____

5. I am...

_____

_____

6. I am...

_____

_____

7. I am...

_____

_____

A Day in the Life of Ms. Hernandez Revisited

Alexandra smiled as she watched the last few students leave her classroom following the final bell, no longer surprised by the upbeat mood she'd sustained all day. After attending the Forward-Facing® training her principal had set up for the school's faculty and applying the steps for the last few weeks, she'd noticed a marked improvement in her mental wellbeing and her physical health.

Alexandra especially liked the second step of intentionality, and knew that recommitting to her mission of helping her students while implementing better boundaries with her time, finances, and during interactions with coworkers had led to much of the positive shift in her mindset. She no longer felt like she wanted to avoid everything that might "hurt" in her life—with the tools of self-regulation and a personal covenant for intentional living at her disposal, Alexandra wasn't afraid of what the workday might bring, viewing the unexpected as an opportunity to continue learning to be the best teacher and person possible.

Alexandra glanced down at her desk, unearthing the Forward-Facing® worksheets comprising her personal covenant from a stack of tests she'd need to grade the following day (this was one of the nights she set aside to not take work home). She liked to review the three documents once a week or so, especially before situations that would've previously been dysregulating, like interactions with her colleagues in the teachers' lounge or in the halls after school. She read over her mission statement first:

My Mission Statement

My purpose on this planet is to inspire my students by sharing fascinating and relevant lessons about our world, history, and the human experience. As a Social Studies teacher with a diverse background and upbringing, I believe in helping students connect with one another, especially those with different experiences than them—this builds empathy and compassion, which I believe are vital for our youth to flourish in this connected, global society. I wish to model these behaviors of patience and compassion to all I interact with, so that I can be an example of how I believe all my students should be treated, regardless of how they (or their parents) act. I also wish to enforce boundaries in the classroom—if my rules are broken there will be consequences, but I want to be a teacher who is self-regulated, respected, fair, and still a safe person my students can come to for anything they need.

In my personal life, I want to make the best choices for my budget so that I am financially secure and stable, and can pay for my monthly needs like rent, food, and other essentials, rather than stressing out after buying items for my classroom that I can't afford. I wish to set boundaries between my professional and personal time so that I sleep at least seven hours a night, eat healthfully, exercise three times a week, and spend time with family and friends on weekends. I want to check in with my mental health frequently, and if I find I'm struggling to get out of bed, eat, bathe, or complete other activities for daily living due to anxiety or depressive thoughts, I will reach out to a friend or family member or seek professional help. I understand that in order to serve my students every day in the classroom, I need to take good care of myself first.

Next she looked over her vision statement, detailed during the workshop as "at least a few sentences describing who she wanted to become as she fulfilled her mission" and written in first-person present tense:

My Vision Statement

I am known at my school as a teacher who has a solid and supportive relationship with all of my students. I recognize that while test scores and grades are important, the reason I am an educator is to inspire my kids to love learning while being good to themselves and one another, and I reflect those beliefs in all that I do. I make fiscally responsible choices, planning for my future with retirement savings, an emergency fund, and a budget that I consistently stick to. I am a good friend, daughter, colleague, and partner, and surround myself with people who add joy and meaning to my life and are emotionally healthy themselves. I am committed to growing as a person and educator, pursuing additional trainings and opportunities for academic and professional achievement, as well as in personal avenues with therapeutic tools for mental health, exercise for physical health, and social time with loved ones for a strong network of stable support.

Lastly, Alexandra referred to her third worksheet—the code of honor she'd outlined for herself. Out of the three Forward-Facing® documents this one was her favorite, because it had prompted her to really consider her strengths, as well as what was most important to her professionally and personally:

My Code of Honor

1. *I am receptive and flexible to the unique needs of my students, parents, and coworkers, adjusting my routines and behaviors accordingly (within reason).*
2. *I am responsible for my actions in the classroom, enforcing fair and*

consistent boundaries with my students so that everyone is respected and safe.

3. *I am empathetic to my students and the struggles they might be experiencing at home, recognizing that disruptive behavior is not a personal offense to me.*

4. *I am confident in my interactions with colleagues, standing up for what I think and believe in.*

5. *I am kind to everyone I interact with, treating others as I wish to be treated.*

6. *I approach conflicts calmly and confidently with students, parents, or anyone else when they arise. I handle them directly with polite but firm responses that respect my own boundaries and the boundaries of others.*

7. *I am resilient when issues arise in my workplace, and I handle the situation to the best of my abilities while learning from my mistakes.*

When she was done rereading her personal covenant, Alexandra gathered up her belongings to head home for the day. She had plans with her roommate for a movie marathon that evening, and wanted to hit the gym and the grocery store beforehand. On her way out she passed the sixth-grade History teacher, Mike Richardson, a coworker she used to try to avoid at all costs because of his pessimism and frequent negative comments about students.

"Alexandra, did you hear they located the students who took your desks and chairs?" Mike asked as she approached.

"They don't have confirmation on who it was," Alexandra answered, refraining from saying Kail Jensen's name because of the few remaining students standing nearby at their lockers.

"I think the video evidence is definitely confirmation," Mike retorted.

Alexandra's pulse ratcheted up immediately as she grew defensive of her student, noting her fight-or-flight response engaging. *I'm not in any danger,* she told herself as she engaged in neuroception, did a brief moment of bodyfulness to scan where the tension was (mostly in her chest), and self-regulated for a few seconds with a few deep, slow breaths into her diaphragm while the other teacher kept talking.

"Here's hoping he finally gets expelled," Mike continued, and Alexandra fought the urge to roll her eyes. The History teacher had been around for so many years that he was likely dealing with severe burnout and compassion fatigue that skewed his perceptions and reduced his patience, and she wanted to be cognizant of that.

"I'm sure whatever is best for everyone is what the administrators will do," Alexandra said, unwilling to participate in the gossip or negative discussion any further. "I hope you have a nice evening Mike," she said with a grin, genuinely meaning it. "See you later!"

The teacher frowned slightly, appearing a bit embarrassed. "Yeah, see you. Have a good night too."

Alexandra continued on, proud of the way she'd handled the situation. In the past she would've avoided the confrontation altogether or given in, complaining about a student or parent or the current workload only to feel significantly worse afterwards, but no more. She had a mission and a vision and a code to live and teach by, and she was going to stay loyal to them. She hoped the other educators at her school would follow suit, because if the improvements in her mood, physical and mental health, behaviors, and thoughts were any indication, the Forward-Facing® steps were a beneficial toolset available to any educator at any time—they just needed to get started.

※ ✣ ※

As we've seen, the biology of the stress response, our attitudes about our career, and our behavior toward others at work and home are inextricably linked. Every time we breach our integrity, we reopen the moral wounds caused by compassion fatigue, reinforcing our dysregulation and consigning ourselves to a life bereft of meaning and self-efficacy. However, the reverse is also true. Each time we act in accordance with our moral precepts, we take a significant step toward healing our moral wounds and knitting together the shards of our shattered "spiritual skeletons."

The more we live in harmony with our true and honest selves, the more people around us will respond in kind (coworkers, parents, and students alike), sustaining us in our journey and reinforcing our sense of personal worth and self-efficacy. Yet the entire process remains entirely within our own control, fully empowering us every step of the way.

Like self-regulation, the recipe for acting with intentionality is simple but not easy. Sometimes, you'll be so overwhelmed by the destructive effects of post-traumatic stress and burnout that you'll experience a setback. You'll act out and feel you've let yourself down. Don't believe it. The process of acquiring intentionality is like that of a baby learning to walk. We all fall down sometimes. But every time we get back on our feet and "walk the intentional walk," our balance improves and our steps become surer. We begin to achieve the moral and spiritual rebirth that is one of the main goals of the Forward-Facing® approach for professional resilience.

Remember those sailors we mentioned earlier in this chapter? Well, each night when they looked through the sextant they discovered they were off course—sometimes by only a few hundred yards, but other times by entire miles! Did they get discouraged, turning their ship around and heading home because they didn't end up where they'd envisioned for the day? Did they succumb to hopelessness because they failed to stay on course *every single day* of their months-long journey? Nope! They *readjusted* their course, sailing the next day on this corrected course only to find that they were off course again the next night...and the next night...and the next night...all the way until they reached their destination. They made it, trusting the process and readjusting as needed to get there.

You've already taken the essential first steps toward achieving wholeness, integrity, authenticity, and intentionality at school and everywhere else. Armed with your personal covenant, you have all of the tools you need to begin tapping into your unique gifts and realizing your full potential as an educator and human being. Now it's time to apply this newfound direction, purpose, and motivation to your everyday life, combining it with your daily self-regulation practices to start feeling good and living well.

In the next chapter, you'll learn how to identify and replace the negative misperceptions we hold about our careers and responsibilities with ones rooted in autonomy, empowerment, and appreciation. When we reframe our perceptions to recognize we have the choice to say yes or no to every request laid before us, we develop our capacities for positivity, resilience, and gratefulness for the opportunities that come our way.

CHAPTER EIGHT

FORWARD-FACING STEP THREE: PERCEPTUAL MATURATION

The kids that need the most love will ask for it in the most unloving way.

Unknown

IF THE LAST few years have taught us anything, it's that our work in schools is unpredictable. Technology is constantly evolving against the backdrop of pandemics, political shifts, and personal divisions, while persistent budget cuts, changes in curriculum expectations, and ever-changing federal and local mandates continue to create a world of unpredictability for educators and students alike.

You might remember that at the end of chapter three, we discussed the concept of burnout as defined by Eric and his colleagues in their work on treating compassion fatigue as such: Burnout is the chronic condition of *perceived* demands outweighing *perceived* resources. They were frustrated by many researchers' overwhelming focus on the environment as the cause of burnout, and the ways this conceptualization subtly made professionals the "victims" of their workplace. We have found that this updated definition of burnout shifts our perception, evolving the paradigm away from a 20th-century external locus of control to a 21st-century understanding that *empowers* educators and provides them with a vision of hope and autonomy in their careers.

When reading the above definition, you can see that one's perception of the workplace—not the workplace itself—is identified as a primary contributor to burnout and compassion fatigue. As long as an educator believes the cause of their distress is the external workplace, they're compelled to change that workplace before they can achieve any semblance of professional quality of life. When an educator understands and embraces the notion of their *perception* as the chief cause of their work-related stress, they find themselves able to significantly lessen their symptoms by evolving their automatic and instinctual perceptions of work into ones that are thoughtful, effectual, and promote comfort and stability (as well as safety if there *is* an actual threat).

In this chapter, we will demonstrate how the educator can decrease the toxicity of their workplace through the two facets of perceptual maturation: workplace detoxification and self-optimization. Before going forward, however, we'd like you to become aware of any resistance you might have to this concept of perceptual maturation material. In training many thousands of professionals suffering from compassion fatigue and treating hundreds more through his private practice, Eric has found that a high percentage of professionals suffered from a darkened, constricted, and distorted perception of their work and workplace. These distorted perceptions can gradually lead professionals to believe themselves victims of their work.

Early on in Eric's work, he thought that the simple act of pointing this out would facilitate a change for the attendees to his Forward-Facing® Professional Resilience workshops. He'd expected that they'd relinquish this stance of workplace suffering for a vision of hope, comfort, and prosperity. Instead, he encountered professionals who, despite suffering acutely from compassion fatigue, held fiercely to the distorted perception that it was their job that was directly responsible for their pain. In response to this initial resistance, Eric started to suggest to his workshop participants that while they were entitled to a little skepticism at first, to reserve any contempt or defensiveness until after they'd done some investigation and application with an open mind.

We encourage readers to experiment with these practices in their own lives—if they don't work, you can simply stop doing them! If, however, you find that your professional and personal quality of life *does* improve immediately, perhaps you'll want to continue incorporating these methods into your daily living.

We also wish to dedicate some time to helping readers gain insight into the secondary gains they may get from remaining a victim of their work and workplace. The most salient secondary gain is that as long as we believe someone or something else is to blame, we don't need to change anything. Additionally, educators may find that by unconsciously clinging to a victim stance, they're able to extract pity and/or respect from others, and have ready-made excuses for indulging themselves (i.e., "I worked hard today so I deserve a drink or two") or justifications for lessening their personal commitments and contributions to their work.

What we're saying is that even when presented with the evidence we have generated in this book, you might notice you experience some resistance to these concepts. We just want you to know that you are in good company, and we ask that you explore whether you are getting any secondary gains from being a "victim" of your work. If so, we invite you to exchange the cold comfort of this instinctual and unconscious coping strategy with an intentional strategy of perceptual maturation that provides real change and lifelong resilience.

Perceptual Maturation Part One: Workplace Detoxification

Now we would like to introduce you to some of the perceptual shifts that educators can adopt to immediately and significantly lessen their workplace distress and improve their quality of life. As you read along, we encourage you to think about the responses you'll write down yourself in the worksheet portion of this section.

1. Real danger versus perceived threat: By now you have an understanding that because of traumagenesis, we perceive threat far more often than we are actually in danger every day. Our bodies cannot tell the difference between the two, and their repeated activation of the SNS in response to a perceived threat leads to symptoms of compassion fatigue and burnout. The first step to interrupting this automated fight-or-flight response is by reducing what seems threatening in our environments, but not by *actually* changing our environment in any way. Allow Eric to explain this some more.

Eric: Recently I was asked to provide a professional resilience workshop to a group of educators at a large, urban school district. The educators who participated seemed to me to be very "crusty," clearly demonstrating some characteristics of burnout, and I wondered if my nontraditional approach would resonate with them (yes, I have my own perceptions of threat when standing before an audience).

A week after the workshop, I received an email from one of the administrators who'd attended. This is what he said: "I've been an educator for twenty years, and the last five days of work have felt completely different to me than any I've worked before. I was able to recognize whenever my body began tensing up, and would self-regulate with the pelvic floor relaxation and breathing techniques that I learned. And here's the really cool part…I was able to remind myself over and over again that even though I *felt* like I was in danger, I really wasn't! That change in my perception made a huge difference in my experience at school all week, and I just wanted to send you a message and tell you about it. So on behalf of my wife and children, I want to thank you for what I received from the workshop."

Just that small change of the administrator's perception that he was *not* in any real danger, regardless of what he felt, helped him to calm his body and completely shift his work environment from a warzone to a place where he was safe and possessed competency. This is neuroception, and it's incredibly potent (and easy to do!).

2. Demand versus choice: *Nothing is demanded of you*. What is your immediate response to this simple truism? Do you find yourself becoming reflexively dismissive or immediately taking the counterpoint? If so, this may point to the ways in which you have "learned" to perceive your workplace environment through your experiences, and that can generate a significant amount of stress. Many of us have had lifelong training—by our families, colleagues, universities, bosses, students and their parents, or the media—that a request from another is a demand on us. The more "demands" we encounter when moving through our workday, the more likely we are to perceive them as a threat. As demands morph into threats, they have the potential to activate our threat response and trigger the process (and its accompanying symptoms) we wish to suspend. Instead, we must shift from seeing all of our work-related tasks as demands placed upon us to understanding them as activities we *choose to do or not do*. When a principal or superintendent assigns us a work task, that is not a demand upon us. We can ask ourselves:

- What are the consequences of each?
- What are the positive outcomes of doing it?
- What do I choose to do?

These are good questions to begin with, all while remembering that we do not *have* to respond immediately or in the favor of the asker.

Failing to "choose" to engage in these activities and instead viewing them as demands is one of the most obvious ways in which we participate in the toxification of our work environment. As soon as we perceive a request from our principal, a parent, or colleague as a demand, then it is most likely that we will: 1) perceive that demand as a threat; 2) have feelings of dread and avoidant behaviors associated with this demand; and 3) utilize brute force (i.e., "stress") to complete these dreaded demands. We have found that *choosing* to engage in and complete work tasks, even the ones we don't want to do, produces significantly less stress in the workplace.

The difference for all involved can be attributed to the associated perception with each option—one is a choice that provides freedom, comfort, and acceptance regarding the decision, while the other is a demand that doesn't allow for any of those positive results.

3. Outcome-driven versus principle-based: Related to the above, many of us feel more and more responsibility for the *outcomes* of our work. Parents, coworkers, and administrators are usually happy to allow us to take on the responsibility of our students' classroom attendance, behavioral issues and general wellbeing, and even whether they're clothed and fed in some cases. When we examine this more closely, we see that we are not capable of managing all the mitigating components that go into a positive outcome for our students or in the eyes of our bosses. There are a myriad of intervening factors over which we have no control, and oftentimes *these* determine the outcome—despite our best efforts.

Many educators find that they allow their sense of worth to be determined by the outcomes of their work. These people run the risk of developing or exacerbating SNS dominance throughout their career. Those who demand from themselves certain outcomes over which they have little to no control are more likely to be stressed out when some event or person negatively affects these outcomes. A more holistic and healthy approach is to *simply do the best we can* in all contexts, while simultaneously relinquishing the outcomes. That does not mean that we don't target classroom goals and periodically reorient our ideal outcomes with our students and their parents, colleagues, and ourselves—but we understand that while in the process of actually working, we need only strive to do our best and maintain fidelity to our principles and personal covenant. We can certainly apply valuable learning experiences to future situations, but in the present, we can only do what we can do. Paradoxically, many educators report that they enjoy better outcomes as they focus upon them *less*.

4. Relinquishing entitlement and other secondary gains: A common characteristic of professionals who are burned out is that they seem to have developed a sense of entitlement—they believe that they have sacrificed for their work, and that they are owed something for this sacrifice. They have become comfortable in their "victim stance," and seeing themselves as victims of their work has afforded them some secondary, albeit dubious, gains. Some examples of these might include the belief that we are owed accolades from our work ("nobody appreciates the work that I do here") or permission to indulge ourselves ("I worked hard today, so I deserve junk food and alcohol"), and that we are better or more important than other members of our educating team ("I have been here longer than anyone else and *they* should be the ones to do the extra work, not me").

We sometimes forget that we studied, graduated, and applied to be in our current professional position—we are *not* victims of our work. We are choosing to work where and how we do. As we become aware of the ways in which we harbor this entitlement and other secondary gains (i.e., relishing having people feel sorry for us because of the difficulty of our work), we become empowered to relinquish victimhood.

When we give up the secondary gains from suffering, we can instead rediscover the mission and purpose in our work. Letting go of what is "owed to us" allows us to rekindle the passion that made us choose the field of education in the first place: a desire to serve children and nurture their futures! As we shift away from entitlement and toward the intention of maintaining personal integrity in all our interactions with parents, students, coworkers, supervisors, and ourselves, our work becomes a metaphoric gymnasium for self-discovery and improvement, a place that helps us to grow and mature instead of causing us harm, where we can practice skills that make us better educators and human beings—strong, resilient, and compassionate.

5. Acceptance of a chaotic system: All institutions that provide care to others can be anxious systems for the employed and the people they serve. School districts are inherently toxic work environments. The demands, the lack of resources, the ratio of children to adults, and the political and personal issues of the staff and community at large all combine to forge a heady brew of anxiety and distress.

Add to this that many of these institutions' true mission, no matter what it says on the mission statement posted in their foyer, is immortality. When the organization's primary purpose is to sustain itself into perpetuity, then the individuals who serve the organization are expendable and disposable. Your school, office, classroom, and district will, in most cases, go on working just fine without you. No matter how much we do for our institutions or our students, they are always going to demand more from us than we can give them.

These are all truisms of the current state of our schools. While they are slowly getting better in some areas, we predict that it will be decades—if ever—before these environments become truly ergonomic, supportive, and generative. Working in education is challenging, painful, and can make us sick if we do not grow our resilience and immunity to its toxicity.

As we mature in our professional careers, we must accept and embrace this phenomenon. We invite educators to stop expecting things to be different than they are. That does not mean that we stop advocating for and working toward a better system of educating, but resilience demands that we stop blaming the environment for the poor quality of our professional and personal lives.

We encourage you to stop fighting and instead start to develop the fortitude to: 1) advocate for yourself in a coworking space that doesn't lead to polarization with others; and 2) self-regulate while working in these high-demand situations. We need to develop these skills so that we can maintain fidelity to our principles, even while the systems in which we work are attempting to squeeze us into breaching our integrity. This becomes a hallmark of professional resiliency and maturation: Can you hold on to yourself and maintain your principles, all while your workplace demands more from you than you can give?

When we foster our capacity for self-regulation, intentionality, and perceptual maturation, amazing things happen. We find ourselves comfortable in our bodies most of the day at work. We discover self-esteem and self-efficacy in professional and personal contexts. We become intuitively graceful in relationships with our students, coworkers, friends, and family. And—perhaps most importantly—we become a potent catalyst for positive change and growth in our schools.

Perceptual Maturation Part Two: Self-Optimization

This second area of perceptual maturation focuses more on evolving our perceptions of *ourselves* than our environment. Much of the development of this section has been borrowed from the work of those who have brought mindfulness and positive psychology to the forefront of treatment and professional resiliency.

The concept and development of mindfulness is inherited from the Buddhist and Taoist traditions, and has been practiced for centuries in India and Asia. Mindfulness meditation has been described as a disciplined practice of "watching without engaging" with one's own internal processes—including thoughts and emotions.

These ancient principles were adopted by psychologists in the 1990s to assist medical patients in both lessening their anxiety and restructuring their negative cognitions about themselves and the world. Over the next twenty years, mindfulness became a central focus of many psychotherapies and treatment approaches for a variety of disorders and had a great deal of success—especially with patients who'd previously been very difficult to treat. These principles and practices have found their way into business and industry as a way of developing and maintaining inspiration, creativity, and satisfaction (i.e., resilience). In recent years, mindfulness practices are also being taught in schools and classrooms, with children learning mindfulness skills alongside their academic studies.

Mindfulness usually involves practicing two skills simultaneously: calming the body and noticing (without engaging with) our thoughts. Calming the body, in many mindfulness practices, is achieved by developing disciplined breathing practices. It can involve belly breathing, regulated breathing, or breath counting. Any of these disciplines that help a person to become intentional about their breathing will result in lessened anxiety. Once the body is calm and self-regulated the brain regains optimal functioning, and we can much more efficiently notice, control, and shift our thoughts.

Mindfulness is a collection of skills often utilized simultaneously, all of which require diligent practice. The skills are briefly described below:

1. Awareness: One skill of mindfulness is learning how to focus your attention on one thing at a time (research has shown that multitasking is not an efficient way of working and can elevate stress levels). This includes being aware of and able to recognize all the things that are going on around you (sights and sounds, for instance), as well as all the things that are going on inside you (your thoughts and physiological state).

2. Nonjudgmental/nonevaluative observation: This skill is focused on looking at your experiences in a nonjudgmental way—that is, simply viewing things in an objective way as opposed to labeling them as either "good" or "bad." An important part of this skill is self-compassion.

3. Being in the present moment: Part of mindfulness is being in touch with the present moment as opposed to being caught up in thoughts about the past (also called rumination) or the future (i.e., worry). An aspect of this skill is being an *active participant* in experiences instead of just going through the motions or being stuck on autopilot.

4. Beginner's mind: This skill of mindfulness focuses on being open to new possibilities. It also refers to observing or looking at things as they truly are, as opposed to what we *think they are* or evaluate them to be. For example, going into a situation with a preconceived notion of how things will turn out can influence your experience, preventing you from getting in touch with the truth of it.

Mindfulness takes practice. Some people may put aside time to practice mindful awareness of their breath or thoughts, but the good thing is that you can practice it at any point throughout your day. For example, you can bring mindful awareness to a number of activities that you often do without thinking, such as eating, walking through campus, driving in the car, or relaxing at home.

Another perceptual shift is in regard to positive psychology or, colloquially, the "science of happiness." Happiness is defined as: "…a mental or emotional state of wellbeing characterized by positive or pleasant emotions ranging from contentment to intense joy."[54]

In recent years, many psychologists and researchers have begun to look at the science of happiness and have generated some interesting findings. In his book *The Happiness Advantage*, Shawn Achor points out that many people have a tendency to postpone happiness, making statements like "I'll be happy when I retire," "I'll be happy when it's summer break," or "I'll be happy when I get more classroom support." Dr. Kirk Schneider, another happiness researcher, mentioned in a 2011 article: "perhaps genuine happiness is not something you aim at, but is…a by-product of a life well lived…"[55]

The "science of happiness" understands that human beings evolved to develop a "negativity bias" as a coping strategy. The brain preferentially looks for, reacts to, stores, and then recalls negative information before it recalls positive information to help us survive—"don't eat the red berry," "watch out for what lurks behind the lichen-covered, jagged boulder," and so on. This is all in service to survival of our species and better acumen toward dangers, but these thoughts are frequently intrusive, self-critical, and unwanted.

Now for the good news: If you reverse the order of the formula, you end up with greater happiness and greater success. People who are able to train their brains and internal dialogue to focus upon positive thoughts are significantly happier than those who do not. Happiness is an advantage, and the precursor to greater success. Relationships, professional endeavors, and educational outcomes improve when the brain is positive *first*. If you cultivate happiness while in the midst of your struggles at work and home, you increase your chances of attaining all the goals you are pursuing...including happiness.

According to psychologist and author John Gottman, it takes at least five positive interactions to make up for just one negative one. Rick Hanson states in his book *Hardwiring Happiness* that we can overcome our brain's natural "negativity bias" and learn to internalize positive experiences more deeply, all while minimizing the harmful physical and psychological effects of dwelling on the negative.[56] All kinds of good things happen in our daily lives that we hardly notice—we have all experienced this when someone pays us an unexpected compliment. Yet because of all the criticisms we have endured throughout our lives, we find ourselves dismissing or deflecting the compliment, thus reducing its value and potency. Positive psychology seeks to help our brains learn how to tolerate and *embrace* happiness by allowing ourselves a few seconds to a few moments to "encode" positive experiences.

Achor has developed a very practical "nuts and bolts" approach to practicing this skill of encoding, and shared it on Psychology Today's website in 2011.[57] He listed five easy "happiness habits" to apply to our work lives, encouraging readers to select one and try it out for twenty-one days in a row:

1. Spend two minutes a day describing a positive experience from the last twenty-four hours. This tactic transforms your thinking from task-based to meaning-based, and promotes a viewpoint that is engaged and focused instead of searching for the next thing to do.

2. Exercise for ten minutes a day; not only is it physically beneficial, but trains your brain to believe your behavior and choices are important and impactful for the rest of your day.
3. Write down three things you are grateful for every day in a journal, on your phone, or anywhere you can refer to later. Research says this will greatly increase your optimism and success rates.
4. Take two minutes to meditate and focus on your breathing, fully disengaging from any multitasking you may have been doing. This decreases your stress and resets your brain so that you can address each task one at a time, with optimized neocortical functioning.
5. Write one short email when you wake up in the morning to a colleague, friend, or family member praising them and what they have been doing. A study Achor conducted at Harvard found that this type of social support was the largest predictor of happiness in students.

It is not a surprise to learn that happiness is closely intertwined with resilience—trying times stretch and challenge us, and many people find meaning and purpose in overcoming adversity. When we have strong social supports and fulfilling relationships, we can experience contentment and joy even as we are faced with hardships.

We can view happiness not as the absence of negative emotions altogether, but as positive emotions *outweighing* the negative emotions a person feels. Happy people can experience just as many negative emotions as individuals who say they are unhappy, but the difference lies in perception—is this a trial you can grow from, learning and evolving to become a better, wiser version of yourself? Reframing your perspective has almost everything to do with experiencing happiness daily and during challenging situations, much like physician, author, and Holocaust survivor Viktor Frankl demonstrated in his book *Man's Search for Meaning*—it is this intentional reframing, this *diligent* pursuit of comfort and balance among difficulty, that fosters resilience and paves the way for a happy life.

If we think about it, positive emotions are not allowed to occur unless we become vulnerable, which is often a result of negative emotions. There would be no compassion or forgiveness if we had not been wronged in some way beforehand. The creative process is rife with rejection and initial failure that leads to new ideas, innovative design, and heartfelt music, art, and books.

The act of generosity, financially or otherwise, requires us to acknowledge another's needs and sometimes put aside our own in the meantime.

As we stated earlier, happiness does not mean never feeling negative emotions. Psychologists Jack Bauer and George Bonanno examined this very concept in their research with individuals who had lost a spouse six months prior. When they followed up two years afterwards, it was discovered that those who spoke only negatively about the situation were not doing well—but neither were those with only positive responses. The most well-adjusted spouses made about five positive comments to one negative one, acknowledging the tragedy of what they had gone through while not being consumed by it.[58]

The "upward spiral" toward better wellbeing and happiness through resilience was explored by psychologist Barbara Fredrickson and her colleagues in 2001, who discovered that positive emotions are one of the main providers of fuel for long-lasting resilience. Frederickson stated: "...to the extent that positive emotions broaden the scopes of attention and cognition, enabling flexible and creative thinking, they should also augment people's enduring coping resources."[59] Positive emotions and their results—joy, amusement, creativity, inspiration, gratitude, and many more—provide a well of strength and fortitude from which we can draw during stressful situations. As said by researchers in a 2011 study on life satisfaction and building resilience, "...happy people become more satisfied not simply because they feel better, but because they develop resources for living well."[60]

The last area of self-optimization we will explore is the concept of moving from other-validation to self-validation. Here's Eric to share his own experiences and expertise on this.

Eric: This subtle but far-reaching area of personal optimization is one I discovered while treating hundreds of educators and care providers who were suffering from compassion fatigue symptoms. As I listened to their stories, many of them thematically complained that they were no longer getting joy from their work. When I queried them about what gave them the most joy from their work, many cited things like "appreciation from their students/patients," "recognition from coworkers," and "accolades from their bosses and supervisors." In short, they liked hearing from others that their work was meaningful and helpful.

I have spent most of my nearly forty-year career as a psychotherapist working with trauma—especially developmental trauma. I have learned how the effects of negligent, anxious, and/or aggressive parenting with children can severely disrupt adolescent and adult development, frequently causing these survivors of attachment trauma to feel anxious and awkward around others later in their lives.

One of the ways that children learn to cope with parents who are frequently dysregulated, unattuned, or aggressive is by becoming "exquisitely attuned" to their parents' moods. They frequently interrupt their activities to "check in on" their parents, and if the parents are distressed (angry, depressed, anxious, etc.), then the child will often engage in behaviors attempting to assist the parents. This unconscious and instinctual adaptation is a competency on the part of a child whose parents fail to provide them with safety, comfort, and/or connection. This is also a frequent coping strategy for children who have alcoholic or addicted (i.e., drugs, food, sex, money, power) parents.

By the time these children are launched into adolescence, they have become highly skilled providers of care to others, albeit unconsciously. They frequently find that they feel uncomfortable around others and believe themselves to be less than their peers, think that they're somehow missing the social competency their peers seem to innately possess, and/or believe themselves to be inadequate, deficient, damaged, or afflicted. To offset this social anxiety and sense of diminished worth, many adolescents find this well-honed skill of helping others as a bridge to gain competency, worth, and status with their peers. They become compulsively helpful to others as a way to deflect potential criticism or rejection, channeling their anxiety into prosocial activities in order to gain power in relationships with their peers. As these adolescents transition into young adulthood and begin to consider career decisions, many find themselves gravitating toward the caregiving field. They embark upon paths to become educators, counselors, nurses, and other care providers, so that they might continue to utilize the competency and comfort that comes from being of service to others.

This sounds like a story with a happy ending, right? I think that for a few it is, however, for most the happy ending doesn't come until these five steps of professional resilience have been implemented. Many clients I've helped heal from the effects of early childhood trauma are, indeed, professional caregivers. They find early in their careers that they love the work of being a professional caregiver. They have competence. They get to assist others in excelling and/or healing. They find a sense of worth and value that has eluded them for much of their lives. Others have referred to this as the "zealot" or "honeymoon" period of a professional caregiver's career trajectory...but what happens to the zealot when, after a year or two, they find themselves confronting the realities of an overburdened education or care delivery system with high demands and a lack of proper resources? Or frequently encountering students with behavioral issues? Or angry parents? Or unsupportive coworkers? What happens when they find that they are unable, even with super-human dedication and effort, to affect change in others' lives? Many become overwhelmed, demoralized, and disillusioned with their career choice—and that's what we call burnout or compassion fatigue.

A subtle but powerful protective factor for compassion fatigue is addressing this issue of other- versus self-validation in the life of the educator. When our worth is determined by someone other than ourselves, then we are in danger of losing it if that person does not approve of or appreciate us.

For those of us who've developed this adaptation as a way to navigate and survive chaotic home lives as children, other-validation almost always becomes a liability as we mature into adulthood. If we perceive every human interaction as a threat that has to be managed by gaining approval and appreciation from that other person, it is easy to see how quickly the process can become exhausting and debilitating. Other-validation makes intimacy nearly impossible. The better we know someone and the more important they are to us, the better they know *us*—and if our worth rests in the hands of these other people, we cannot tolerate when they begin to see our shortcomings and flaws. People who are other-validated are very adept at quickly developing relationships with deep emotional bonds, but it is a strenuous challenge for many of them to maintain and grow these relationships into true intimacy—the ability to fully share ourselves with another human being. What this means for educators who are in this other-validated stance is that work is truly an emotional minefield that has to be carefully navigated each day. Other-validated professionals are volatile and fragile. They become easily derailed from their mission, intentions, and good mood with the slightest snub or jab from a coworker, administrator, or even student.

Understanding all the subtle ways in which we seek validation from others—our supervisors, our significant others, our children, our students—is a difficult, challenging, and sometimes painful lifelong process. The more we require acknowledgment from another, the more threat we perceive in social contexts. Other-validation makes us hypersensitive and reactive in social and intimate settings—it becomes nearly impossible to simply be ourselves around others. For those of us who are other-validated, we find ourselves engaging in a host of reactive behaviors, including competing for attention, polarizing with others, sabotaging peers, being contemptuous of others, self-aggrandizing, and/or completely isolating ourselves, in an attempt to avoid this perceived threat.

Once we begin to understand the matrix of perceived threats that are embedded in an other-validated stance, we can begin to "make sense" of these reactive behaviors. They are all driven by the SNS and have one of two goals: fight or flight. When we "fight" we are attempting to neutralize the threat, and these fight behaviors can be seen in those who become rigid, controlling, and aggressive in social situations. Conversely, the "flight" behaviors—attempting to get away from the perceived threat—can be seen when we attempt to ingratiate ourselves with or pander to others, when we do not speak up for what is right and true for us, or when we isolate ourselves.

There *is* an antidote for other-validation: self-regulation, as well as beginning to appreciate and support ourselves through positive internal language without indulgence. Self-validation begins when we can tell ourselves things like, "I believe you can do this," "you have lots of strength, and even though this might be challenging, you are going to get through this," and "your work is good enough even when it's not perfect." The shift to self-validation and away from the approval of others as the goal of our actions allows us to lead optimized professional and personal lives that are marked by graceful, intentional, and resilient behavior.

Now we'd like to invite you to complete the next two worksheets and begin to apply both parts of perceptual maturation to your thoughts and behaviors for the future. Following those is a narrative that revisits our veteran (and severely suffering) teacher, Mr. Richardson, as he endeavors to apply perceptual maturation to his professional life and in his relationships with his wife and daughter, his students and colleagues, and himself. It's a story of significant healing and rejuvenation for a skilled educator who is able to reconnect to all he was once passionate about, and we hope it provides some hope and positive expectancy for your own journey.

FORWARD-FACING® WORKSHEET 7: WORKPLACE DETOXIFICATION

Below is a list of all four perceptual shifts that lead to maturation and detoxification of the workplace spoken of earlier. Read each and follow the recommended exercise for a better understanding of what your perceptions look like currently, and to better enable yourself for professional resilience.

1. Real Danger versus Perceived Threat

While at work, ask yourself several times a day: "Am I really in danger right now?" (This is neuroception in the self-regulation process.) If the answer is "no," then dial down the arousal in your body by relaxing the tension in your muscles through one or more of the acute relaxation techniques detailed in chapter six.

If the answer is "yes," then it is even more important that you relax your way back to peak cognitive and motor functioning. (Remember, you are stronger, faster and smarter in a regulated nervous system.)

What percentage of the time do you currently feel you are in *real* danger while at work? _____%

Are there methods that could be deployed to reduce any instances of real danger at work?

Example: "Carrying a radio on me at all times to stay connected with other staff," or "Strengthening my relationships with students to create a supportive and safe environment for myself and everyone else." Write them down below or in a notepad.

_____

_____

_____

_____
_____
_____

2. Demand versus Choice

Notice how frequently you say to yourself or out loud "I have to..." at work. When you begin to shift your perception from which tasks are demanded of you to what you can choose to do or not do, this diminishes much of the stress you experience while at work. What are some work tasks that you currently see as demands?

_____
_____
_____
_____
_____

Do a cost/benefit analysis. How might you change the way in which you view these tasks so that they are no longer demands, and rather necessary facets of the job you've chosen to pursue?

Example: "I choose to grade these tests during my lunch hour while I eat so I can leave right at the end of school today, because in the end, grading is a part of being a teacher."

I choose to _____

because _____

I choose to _____

because _____

Example: "I choose to be at my duty station every afternoon because I don't want my students to experience an unsafe situation and not have an adult immediately available to help them."

I choose to _____

because _____

I choose to _____

because _____

3. Outcome-Driven versus Principle-Based

Write down several ways you currently make yourself responsible for outcomes that are *beyond* your control:

Example: "I will ensure every student gets a passing grade in my class," or "I will be sure I have one hundred percent of my parents participate in parent-teacher conferences this fall."

_____

_____

_____

_____

_____

Now, see if you can rewrite these to articulate an intention that is *within* your control:

Example: "I will provide support for passing grades for all of my students to the best of my abilities."

_____

_____

_____

_____

_____

4. Relinquishing Entitlement and Other Secondary Gains

Can you identify any entitlements you secretly hold on to because of the "sacrifice" that you make in educating others?

Example: "Because I am so busy and stressed, I expect my friends and family to understand that I can't attend social engagements or communicate with them as much as they'd like me to."

_____
_____
_____
_____
_____

What unconscious "secondary gains" have you received from being a victim of your work?

Example: "My spouse should understand all that I go through and take care of the problems of the household. Those issues are more than I should have to handle."

_____
_____
_____
_____

How are these entitlements and secondary gains improving your quality of life?

_____
_____
_____
_____

Are you prepared to relinquish them?
Yes _____ No _____

5. Acceptance of a Chaotic System

Identify one way in which you find yourself struggling with your work system. How do you allow your unmet expectations of your work system to cause you distress?

Example: "The school should hire more staff members so I don't have to keep adding kids to my classroom when there aren't enough supplies, desks, or chairs for them. I am bothered by this every day I go in to work. What is the district thinking?"

_____

_____

_____

_____

_____

Now try accepting that this is the way that systems behave—they demand more from you than you can give, and they are rarely appreciative of what you *do* give. Relax knowing that you are in no danger when more is demanded of you than you can give. How might you shift your perception in this context toward identifying what *is* within your control to complete effectively?

Example: "I am doing the best with what I have—if I need to find an extra chair or desk unexpectedly, I will try my best. If I can't find exactly what I need, I have the skillset to get creative about a short-term solution until something else can be arranged."

_____

_____

_____

_____

_____

FORWARD-FACING® WORKSHEET 8: SELF-OPTIMIZATION

This next set of exercises are built off mindfulness techniques to help you identify specific areas of stress in your own professional and personal life, so that you can work toward resolving your negative perceptions and strive for happiness and resilience in all situations.

1. Awareness

Identify three situations that cause you stress and practice relaxing and disengaging from the intensity of the situation. Practice "noticing" everything you can about the situation (your thoughts, your body's reaction, how others are acting, etc.) without engaging in the drama.

Example: "I get so frustrated when a parent challenges my decisions about their child. I get so caught up in it, wanting to prove that I'm right and they're wrong. When I think about what is best for the student, I find that I am most effective."

1. _____
_____
_____
_____
_____

2. _____
_____
_____
_____

3. _____
_____
_____
_____

2. Nonjudgmental/Nonevaluative Observation

Notice your thoughts when you are anxious. What are some of the involuntary and patterned thoughts you think during these times? Write them down.

Example: "This stress has caused me to overeat and gain weight, which hasn't made me feel good about myself. I don't like looking or feeling this way, but I don't know how to stop."

_____
_____
_____
_____
_____

How are these negative thoughts predicated on the instinctual desire to help you "survive" the threat (hint: fight, flight, or freeze)? Can you make "good sense" of how your negative/critical thoughts are actually attempting to protect you from perceived threats?

Example: "I know I should eat better and exercise, but I've had a good reason not to—I don't have enough time in the day!"

_____
_____

_____

_____

_____

Practice letting these thoughts go on by, or through you, without engaging with them. Recognize that they are old neural patterns meant to help you through an experience that is being perceived as a threat, but that you now know isn't one. Write down any noticeable changes or shifts in your thinking when you adopt this "observant," nonjudgmental perspective to the negative thoughts.

_____

_____

_____

_____

_____

3. Being in the Present Moment

Notice times when you are anxious. What is the correlation between those times and when your focus has gone to past or future situations? Practice re-orienting yourself to the here and now. Now identify a situation at work when you can devote time to being present without any demands being put upon you—a moment to just *be*.

_____

_____

_____

_____

_____

4. Beginner's Mind

Use fewer "I know" statements and allow yourself to approach life with curiosity and a fresh perspective. Identify a situation at work where you can change your "knowing" into curiosity and open-mindedness.

Example: "How can I improve myself in this situation? What can I do better? How can I make things better for others around me? What is there to learn here?"

_____

A Day in the Life of Mr. Richardson Revisited

Mike stood at the front of his classroom as he finished the lesson for the day, noting with satisfaction that his students seemed riveted by the material throughout the hour-long period. It was a new series of lesson plans he'd begun recently that interwove the nation's history with current events that his kids were most interested in (namely social media, but also global movements and youth-led activism), and Mike could see how his sixth-graders were drawn in by the content's relevancy to their own lives.

"That's it for today," he said as the bell rang to dismiss everyone and his students dispersed. "No homework over fall break! Except maybe to spend some time outside *without* a screen!"

That elicited a cheer from his students as they grabbed their backpacks and rushed out, ready for the week-long respite from school. Mike was ready for a little time away as well, but not for the reasons he'd normally felt in years past. In the last few months since learning about the Forward-Facing® path to professional resilience and adhering to the five steps, he was genuinely a new (or more, appropriately, a *renewed*) teacher, husband, father, and human being. He planned to spend the next week continuing to work on his relationship with his wife Bianca, and putting together more new material for his students for the first time in years—and was excited to do both.

Initially following the Forward-Facing® workshop all the faculty had attended earlier on in the school year, Mike had been defensive about the steps—especially the third one, perceptual maturation, that required him to really examine his own role in his descent into compassion fatigue and the profound personal and professional suffering he'd been experiencing. Mike had been on the brink of quitting just before attending the workshop, even meeting with the principal to discuss his options.

"Just stay until winter break," Shannon had practically begged him that day. "I have a training planned for everyone that will make a huge difference. It's helped me to cope a lot better in just a few weeks, and I think it can for you too." Shannon had shared with Mike about her own struggles with anxiety and panic attacks then, and how the Forward-Facing® method had relieved her symptoms significantly. "I know you're hurting right now," Shannon went on, validating Mike's pain both in the classroom and at home with his interpersonal relationships. "Just try it, okay? If it doesn't help at all, you can leave in December."

Mike had reluctantly agreed, having worked with Shannon for over a decade and considering her not only a boss, but a close friend. He didn't want to leave the school in the lurch after twenty-five years there, nor did he want to give up on his career just yet. It had given Mike the smallest sliver of hope for a better life, and he'd been desperate enough to grasp it.

Now here he was a few months onward, using self-regulation as a daily tool for managing his fight-or-flight response everywhere he went. He no longer viewed his students' rule-breaking or attention-seeking behaviors as a personal affront—he understood that they were kids testing the boundaries for a myriad of reasons that weren't in his control or his responsibility, and that he was in little to no danger during those times, even if his nervous system was perceiving a threat. He no longer felt disrespected at school, because his students weren't his enemies—they were *children*. Mike had evolved his perceptions to acknowledge that they were just kids who could choose to listen and appreciate him or not, without him becoming dysregulated and behaving in ways *he* wasn't proud of.

This recognition had been the foundation for his shift in mindset, alongside the second step of intentionality that had allowed him to reconnect and recommit to his mission to help children—why he'd wanted to be a teacher in the first place—and to act in alignment with the beliefs, principles, and morals he'd once held very dear. These first two tools had provided Mike with the "mental space" and reduced defensiveness he'd needed to incorporate the third step of perceptual maturation into his daily work and home activities.

Evolving his perceptions to recognize the responsibilities that were his choice rather than uncomfortable or irritating demands placed upon him had made a huge impact in every aspect of his life. He didn't have to make new lesson plans to inspire his students—he *wanted* to be a great and memorable teacher. He didn't have to go back to counseling with Bianca to work on better communication skills so that she felt fulfilled and cherished in their marriage—he *wanted* to be a good husband and father who fought to keep the family together. He didn't have to go church or Bible studies or out with friends—he *wanted* to receive support, accountability, and the space for spiritual growth that those people and environment offered.

With Bianca moved back in, Mike was eating more healthfully, sleeping better, adding fitness into his weekly routine, and was trying to titrate off several medications while incorporating a more holistic, natural approach to treating his diabetes and high blood pressure diagnoses. He spent ten minutes in the mornings in meditation and mindfulness practices with breathing exercises before going to work, and most evenings made it a point to write down three things he was grateful for in his phone's notetaking app. He'd even gotten Bianca and his daughter to join in with this practice, and they often shared their responses around the dinner table when their daughter came home from college on the weekends.

Mike struggled with his old patterns of defensiveness or entitlement sometimes—he was still unlearning these entrenched patterns of thinking, and school districts had been under a lot of stress in a post-COVID world—but he understood that his slip-ups were a part of the perceptual maturation process as well. He observed them, he learned from them (and was thankful for the opportunity to grow), and he endeavored to do better next time. It was all he could do, and for the first time ever, Mike realized it was all he *needed* to do. He was free—free to stay curious and open to becoming his best self even through the hard times, to enjoy his professional pursuits and meaningful personal relationships, and most importantly, to leave behind a legacy of students who'd been changed for the better because Mike had been their teacher once. It was a beautiful existence, and Mike was so grateful he'd been given the opportunity to truly see it that way.

Here at the end of step three of the Forward-Facing® approach to professional resilience, we've learned many things—among them being that we *can* overcome the reflexive activation of our threat-response systems and learn to bring them under conscious control. We know that when we encounter challenging situations at school, we can view them from a mature, choice-over-demand perspective and respond with intelligence, good judgment, and creativity. We can feel comfort in our bodies as we think and act with maximum efficiency—and once we do this, we can begin to eliminate the negative effects of compassion fatigue, optimize our health and wellbeing, and live productive, satisfying lives infused with intentionality, inspiration, and meaning. When we master the skills of self-regulation, intentionality, and perceptual maturation, transformation is within our grasp—but these tools become all the more effective when we incorporate the fourth Forward-Facing® step into our healing process: connection, accountability, and support from trusted others.

CHAPTER NINE

FORWARD-FACING STEP FOUR: SUPPORT AND CONNECTION

In everyone's life, at some time, our inner fire goes out. It is then burst into flame by an encounter with another human being. We should all be thankful for those people who rekindle the inner spirit.

Albert Schweitzer

WE ARE *ALL* affected by our workplace, and isolation or hardened self-reliance does not equal resilience in the school system. Our work with students, colleagues, and the community at large is relational, and to be effective and well-adjusted in our career as educators, we must learn to function interconnectedly. A part of healthy professional maturation is the development and utilization of a support network to which we can turn for honest and caring feedback.

Such a safety net not only provides us with support, but confronts us when we're becoming symptomatic. It's important to utilize our network of support to share the difficult, painful, and traumatic aspects of our work so that we're diluting the effects of secondary (witnessed) traumatic stress in our lives. Additionally, we can use our network as a source of accountability in our efforts to move toward more principle-based, intentional interactions with our students, parents, and coworkers in the workplace.

Should such networks be designed as a function of our organizational structures, or left to us personally to create? The answer is both, but the *primary responsibility remains our own as individuals*. Healthy, stable socialization facilitates not only emotional support for us, but also opportunities to consider personal perceptions and reactions in a broader community context.

Human beings are "wired" to thrive relationally. We are herd animals and, as we illuminated earlier in chapter three during the section on traumagenesis, when one of the herd is frightened, this fear is likely to elicit a threat response among the others in their periphery. This is a survival competency for our species. Anxiety is contagious, and we believe working in environments where professionals remain chronically anxious contributes greatly to work-related symptoms, and is a primary reason why those in educational environments are so often combating burnout, traumatic stress, and compassion fatigue.

There is some silver inside of this gray cloud, however. As we're able to engage anxious people in our anxious environment with a regulated nervous system and relaxed body through co-regulation (two people sharing face-to-face contact) and collective regulation, we facilitate a relaxation response in all those we encounter—at no cost to us. When *we* remain relaxed in our bodies, we become a catalyst for health and resilience in a toxic school environment for *others*.

As was discussed in previous chapters, all human beings are affected by exposure to trauma. Remember that the effects of exposure to big-T traumas such as natural disasters or life-threatening emergencies are often felt immediately, while the effects of little-t traumas on educators (aggressive or threatening emails from parents, behavioral issues in the classroom, growing workload for reduced compensation, et cetera) are more insidious, gradual, and cumulative. We've learned that if we're able to consistently interrupt our fight-or-flight response with self-regulation, we're able to heal our existing compassion fatigue and protect ourselves from accruing more negative effects from these exposures. In the course of educating others, however, we will never be 100 percent effective in preventing the symptoms of secondary traumatic stress from infecting us. The effects of exposure to anxious or traumatized students, parents, or coworkers and in our chaotic school environments accumulate within us over time. We gradually become symptomatic, often without our own awareness, and it's often our family members, friends, or colleagues who notice the changes in us before we realize they've appeared.

Building A Support System

The goal of developing a network of trusted others with whom we can connect and share support is four-fold:

1. To be our eyes and ears, assisting us in monitoring ourselves and noti-fying us when we begin to show early signs of burnout or compassion fatigue. We intentionally empower these people to "call us out" and confront us during these times.
2. To hold us more personally accountable for our behaviors and actions.
3. To facilitate the safe resolution of our accumulated secondary trau-matic experiences.
4. To provide social support.

The benefits of peer support are well documented, yet not all educators avail themselves of these benefits. We know that therapists routinely establish relationships with other therapists or supervisors. Why is this? Essentially for the same benefits that we've articulated for this resilience skill: to have some-one else monitor their emotional/behavioral environment, create some peer pressure that will enhance their sense of personal accountability, and to offer the opportunity of relief from the traumas that they experience as a result of their work.

A common practice among many schools has been to assign a "mentor" teacher to beginning teachers in their first few years of teaching, with institu-tions recognizing the need for connection, support, and shared wisdom that such a mentorship offers. When this mentorship ends, however, it may imply to all involved that we no longer need that kind of direct support and com-munity for the rest of our careers. In reality, no matter how long we've had our jobs, we can all benefit from specific relationships and connections to others, and it's often our own responsibility to cultivate these relationships with intention and purpose.

For this reason, we suggest you pick two or three people you may wish to build a support network with. This may or may not be your spouse or someone you're related to. Once you've chosen these individuals, the initial conversation with them could sound something like this:

My friend/coworker/partner,

I've learned that I have a high likelihood of experiencing the effects of compassion fatigue. (With what you've learned from this book, you may wish to explain the term.) I've learned that being able to connect with others would help me to ameliorate the effects of compassion fatigue.

My request is that you be part of my support network. If you agree, I'm asking that if you notice that I'm acting in ways that are inconsistent with how you understand that I want to be as a person and a professional, that you let me know this, as I may not always see it myself.

Also, I'd like to create some opportunities to speak with you to share certain specifics about my work experiences. I promise that I will not stop you in the hall, or call you randomly on the phone to talk. Rather, I'll contact you and request a convenient time for both of us where we can share these things, perhaps over a meal or a cup of coffee. During these encounters, I ask that you simply listen. I'm not looking for you to fix me or solve my problems. Rather, I understand the therapeutic value of just being able to relate my experience to another person. In return, I offer myself to be a similar resource for you.

By appointing another or others to watch our backs, two important benefits result:

1. We have an ally who will let us know that we are exhibiting some signs of work-related stress or compassion fatigue symptoms before we may be aware of it ourselves.
2. Knowing that someone else is keeping an eye on us naturally motivates us to be even more accountable to ourselves. We will likely pay extra attention to what is happening in our bodies at school each day, turning to our learned skills in order to dial down our reactiveness and striving to act in alignment with our personal covenant.

You will have a chance to try writing out your "script" for recruiting trusted members to your support network in the worksheet below.

Connection through Narrative

Another objective for setting up a support system is to provide an opportunity to share our stories with others. Why is this important?

Ask yourself this: Do you know of any containers or vessels in this universe that have an infinite capacity to take on contents without spilling over or breaking or exploding?

You'd be hard-pressed to find such an example. We know that every vessel has a maximum capacity to contain whatever it is designed or fated to hold, and anything beyond that is bound to spill over.

Sharing narratives with our trusted network is a mechanism that allows us to "unload" the effects of previously experienced trauma leading to compassion fatigue. We refer to the story of a painful situation as a "narrative." One's narrative about an event should be detailed, because we may not be aware of which specific component of our experience acted as the trigger for our fight-or-flight response and the resulting generation of symptoms. Keep in mind that the retelling of one's experience must be done *with a relaxed body*, so as not to induce more SNS activation. This is how painful past experiences become just another memory, no longer capable of producing further stimulation and hurt.

As the treatment of trauma has moved out of the twentieth and into the twenty-first century, researchers have discovered some important truths about treating this insidious condition. The most important is that the treatment of traumatic stress is simple—not easy, but simple. As exploration into effective treatments has matured, it's been found that *all* effective treatments for post-traumatic stress and PTSD share three common factors: 1) stable therapeutic relationships; 2) relaxation/self-regulation; and 3) exposure + narrative.[61]

When we're able to build solid therapeutic relationships and feel safe confronting our traumatic memories/stories by sharing them with others *while in a relaxed body*, we extinguish the threat response associated with the experience (if you'll recall Joseph Wolpe's work, this is the basis for his concept of reciprocal inhibition from chapter six). Let's look at it this way:

**Good relationship + relaxed body +
sharing story of experience(s) that caused
fight-or-flight response activation =
resolution of secondary traumatic stress symptoms**.

While some educators might consider cultivating this relationship with a therapist or other mental health professional, this formal relationship is helpful in some cases but not necessary—the process can work just as effectively in a peer-to-peer context.

It is important to note that the individual listening to someone's narrative should *also* have competency in self-regulation. They should be regularly relaxing their muscles to dial down their SNS response so as not to become infected by the details of the sharer's story. The listener's primary job is to be present while in a relaxed body, possibly offering encouragement for the sharer to speak freely. The listener is not expected to offer solutions or advice, and the person sharing their narrative is not broken, weak, damaged, or sick. They are simply filled with secondary traumatic stress, which needs to be released so that they can become desensitized while the stress is diluted.

One of the primary purposes of this resilience skill is to develop a mechanism that allows us to unload the effects of previously experienced trauma—an opportunity to empty some of the contents of our vessel before it cracks or explodes. Doing so will enable us to continue to function and thrive as we carry out our mission and purpose to educate. We cannot avoid all future exposure to secondary trauma, but by taking advantage of peer support experiences, establishing our own support networks, and utilizing this resilience skill of sharing our narratives, we increase our capacity to better tolerate and even flourish in our workplace.

It's time now to fill out the next two worksheets for building your network of trusted others, followed by an opportunity to write about any dysregulating or traumatic work-related memories that may need processing and that you'd like to share with your support system. Please do remember that while you spend time journaling about any situations that invoke an emotional response, that you consistently self-regulate throughout the process—this is also an effective exposure method for extinguishing your reactivity to the situation *without* the presence of someone else.

Afterwards, we'll read about our school counselor, Ms. Waite, as she replaces her workaholism and isolating behaviors with the acceptance of support and accountability from her loved ones and coworkers, processing her childhood trauma and realizing she doesn't have to "muscle" through each day to save her students—she can and should lean on others, just as her students lean on her.

FORWARD-FACING® WORKSHEET 9: ESTABLISHING YOUR SUPPORT NETWORK

We stated earlier how important it is to have a stable support network in place to connect and share your thoughts and experiences with. Feel free to list a few people who you might consider contacting to ask if they'd be interested in filling this role for you—they can be colleagues, mental health professionals, or close friends or family, but they should all be trusted individuals you feel safe with.

_____
_____
_____
_____
_____
_____

Below is a chance to organize your thoughts and craft a "script" for inquiring with someone about whether they are able to be a part of your trusted network of support and accountability partners. Be sure to include a description of self-regulation to share with them so that they can understand what this role would look like. Not only does this protect them from any secondary traumatic stress in listening to your narrative, but it also provides them with the first Forward-Facing® tool for professional resilience in their own life—a win-win!

_____
_____
_____
_____
_____
_____

FORWARD-FACING® WORKSHEET 10: SHARING YOUR STORY

This is a place for you to write down your experiences before sharing them with your network. (You might wish to make this a regular activity in your journal or notepad.) These memories can focus on current or past work-related issues, but if they involve any significantly traumatic material such as physical or emotional abuse, grief and loss, and/or anything that remains significantly disturbing from childhood, it's recommended that you connect with a mental health professional to work through these memories together. Save this space for journaling about those workplace experiences that remain in your consciousness and are mildly to moderately dysregulating, practicing self-regulation as you write.

_____

_____

_____

_____

_____

_____

_____

_____

_____

_____

_____

_____

_____

A Day in the Life of Ms. Waite Revisited

Holly thanked her student Kail at the end of their counseling appointment and walked him out, returning his smile before he ducked into the throng of kids outside her office heading to their next class.

She waved and said hello to a couple of the kids she saw regularly, before closing her office door and returning to her desk. She currently had thirty minutes off between appointments, and had been steadfastly sticking to this break once a day (in addition to her thirty-minute lunchtime) since earlier in the school year—which was new for her as a self-identified workaholic. The catalyst for Holly making this intentional change, among many others, had been attending the Forward-Facing® workshop organized by Ms. Burkhart for all staff members in September. It was there that Holly had been forced to confront the reality of her unsustainable workload, isolating behaviors, and persistent traumagenesis resulting from the untreated childhood trauma surrounding her brother's death.

Holly had gone at the workshop during a span of several weeks of extreme mental discomfort, when she'd nearly broken up with her partner James because she was under so much stress and was self-medicating with food and alcohol in the evenings while ignoring him and everyone else who contacted her. Upon reading the descriptions of secondary traumatic stress, compassion fatigue, and diagnosable PTSD during the Forward-Facing® workshop, she'd seen too many similarities to her own dissociative behaviors and self-isolation to ignore the pain she was in anymore. She'd realized that if she wanted to keep helping the students she so deeply cared for, she needed to get well herself first.

Holly had sought a therapist the following day, and after an intake session with someone she hadn't really clicked with, she'd found a wonderfully supportive clinician named Eileen who she was still seeing regularly for therapy to process her primary trauma from adolescence.

The fourth step of the Forward-Facing® approach to professional resilience had really resonated with Holly, who recognized that she was not utilizing the offered support or connection of those close people in her life. She'd endeavored to do things differently, starting with her partner James. After a conversation in which Holly had read off her script detailing her compassion fatigue and asking if he'd commit to being part of her support system and an accountability partner if she started to exhibit unhealthy behaviors like self-isolation or "zoning out" instead of seeking his help and staying present, he'd happily agreed. They were now in the midst of moving in together—Holly's lease was up at the end of the month, and they'd been dating for over a year and were very much in love. Living in the same place would not only help them both financially, but it would offer more opportunities to spend meaningful time together as Holly healed from her past and James showed her that he was someone she could consistently rely on.

Through her therapy with Eileen, Holly had identified the multitude of methods she'd employed through the years to maintain distance between herself and friends or romantic partners; not wanting to be a burden to anyone, she'd "put on a brave face" with fake smiles and chipper text messages, and when she hadn't been able to keep it up any longer, she'd disconnected from everyone completely to recharge. Holly was working to replace these habitual coping practices with ones that sought and nurtured connection—which was what she was doing now during this break in her workday.

Holly had asked her close friend on campus, fourth-grade teacher Sierra, if she'd be willing to act as another member of her support network, with Sierra requesting the same thing of Holly (Sierra had also attended the Forward-Facing® workshop, which was handy since they both understood the concepts of self-regulation and compassion fatigue now).

Holly and Sierra now tried to meet once every two weeks or so to go over any upsetting or dysregulating experiences they'd journaled about in the preceding days. They'd practice their acute relaxation techniques like pelvic floor relaxation, peripheral vision, or soft palate relaxation as they each took turns narrating their thoughts, feelings, and physical sensations during the re-called experience. Holly loved that Sierra was such a wonderful listener, and tried her best to reciprocate—it wasn't about getting or giving advice to one another, but more an opportunity to share, commiserate, and when appropri-ate, brainstorm a possible solution to use in the future. They'd oftentimes refer to their personal covenants as a "map" of sorts, so that they could make sure to behave in ways that aligned with their respective moral codes and missions as educators.

For the first time in as long as Holly could remember, she felt *energized* when she went to work and during her time off. She'd begun setting healthier boundaries between her work and "off" hours, seeking out resources and other specialists for her students with special requests and needs so that she wasn't trying to handle an entire school population's issues by herself.

She'd also started going to a yoga studio right before the school's fall break, and was enjoying the classes immensely. Holly had already befriend-ed several of the instructors and students, finding that their warm and wel-coming demeanors were extremely calming for her to be around after a busy workday.

Between her regular therapy sessions with Eileen, yoga and meditation classes, meetups with Sierra, and increased time together and soon-to-be-shared home with James, Holly was surrounded by stable, trusted others who made her feel cared for and connected with the world around her. With this newfound network of people in whom she could share some of the load, Holly now had an infinite capacity for providing her students with the com-petent, successful, well-regulated encouragement and support she'd always envisioned as a school counselor and educator of children.

All human beings are wired to manage difficulty relationally. This capac-ity is innate, and functions quite well once a person engages its power. By sharing openly and honestly with supportive others, we reset our nervous systems and regain a sense of wellbeing and belonging. This is in contrast to the isolation and lack of support that compassion fatigue leads to for so many educators, and is essential to personal healing and professional resilience.

An interconnected and interdependent community is a model for education that is sustainable both for the individual educator and for the institution as a whole, offering resiliency, longevity, and an exceptional quality of life to all.

Which leads us to the fifth and final step in the Forward-Facing® approach for professional resilience—self-care and revitalization. Because while we absolutely *do* need others for a rich and vibrant career and personal life, the path to total healing begins, and ultimately concludes, with our own efforts.

CHAPTER TEN

FORWARD-FACING® STEP FIVE: SELF-CARE AND REVITALIZATION

That which is to give light must endure burning.

Victor Frankl

THE QUOTE ABOVE from Holocaust survivor and physician Viktor Frankl can be regarded as an unavoidable truth for all educators—that there are some aspects of living a life of service that will unavoidably cause some pain. We hope that at this point you now understand the underlying cause of this distress, and have already begun to adopt some of the Forward-Facing® techniques to reduce its impact and minimize such occurrences as you go forward in serving others in your school and beyond.

We bring this quotation forward now as a prescription, a subtle command from Dr. Frankl to all of us who seek to remain resilient in the pursuit of our mission to educate. To tease out this prescription, we want to pose to you a question: What does anything require to burn, and—more importantly—to *continue* burning?

Fuel.

That's right, fuel. Fuel to power ourselves through our challenging day and fuel at the conclusion of that day to repair and restore our stamina, hope, and goodwill. In order to keep performing optimally, we need to find ways to refuel ourselves that are not self-destructive. Without developing healthy ways to re-energize, we will deplete our stores of natural energy. When that happens, we both metaphorically and literally burn out.

This chapter discusses how we as educators can restore our reserves of bright light and energy for our students, families, and communities in perpetuity. It's intentionally brief, because unlike other material in this book (much of which is groundbreaking and that you might not have encountered before), the content of this chapter is generally understood by most and written about extensively elsewhere.

An essential part of the maturational process for an educator is to intentionally acquire what is needed to maintain physical, emotional, psychological, and spiritual stamina. How much fuel do we need? While this will be different for each person, we can agree that it needs to be enough so that we can return to work each day with a sense of buoyancy and optimism. We will need more when we encounter significantly painful or difficult events in our professional or personal lives.

When weighing the potentially devastating effects of compassion fatigue in the educator's life, we understand that discipline around self-care and revitalization is as important as attending trainings and updating school curriculums and technology to stay current. With our positions being so heavily reliant on their relational aspects—with our students and their parents, our colleagues and other faculty, and the community at large—a dedication to self-care becomes even more important to our sustainability and success.

Self-Care: Promoting Resilience and Revitalization

What activities constitute self-care? Indulgent activities that comfort us immediately, like a hot bath or a bar of chocolate are examples of archetypal ideas that people in the helping fields often consider to be "self-care." The most effective methods of self-care often involve engagement in activities we don't necessarily *want* to do on the front end, however, but that make us feel better and more accomplished on the back end. Following effective self-care activities, we should have more energy, stamina, buoyancy, and a greater ability to withstand challenges. We should have a sense of strength, self-efficacy, and empowerment following these activities—not just comfort. That is why we've called this important resilience skill self-care *and* revitalization. This truism is often met with some dread and avoidance by those whose primary means of self-care have been sedentary and/or isolatory, but the revitalization component of self-care activities is essential.

Regular exercise has emerged in resiliency research and literature as the *single most important* and potent self-care activity available to us. In fact, we believe that regular aerobic (minimum of three times per week, twenty minutes per episode) activity is required for resiliency and for the healthy practice of educating others. Benefits such as better mood, fewer sick days, job satisfaction, contentment with life, longevity, and improved cognitive and motor performance are all correlated with the regular practice of aerobic activities. There is little else you can do, with the possible exception of self-regulation, that will provide more value to your resilience, physical health, and mental wellbeing than exercise.

In addition to exercise, activities like regular checkups, dental care, maintaining a good diet, spiritual/religious practices, intellectual pursuits, writing/journaling, developing mastery in activities outside of education, art/music, financial planning, and social activities can all be part of an effective self-care plan for professional resilience.

In the final Forward-Facing® worksheet below, we've divided the resilience skill of self-care and revitalization into five primary categories: physical, psychological, emotional, spiritual, and professional. The following exercise will help you assess your participation in common self-care activities for each of these five categories, before identifying those you wish to spend more time doing.

Following this exercise, we will revisit with our school secretary, Mrs. Stanbury, to see how this step of self-care and revitalization has transformed her physical and mental wellbeing, relationship with her husband and children, and professional life for the better. By making a concerted effort to return to the activities that once gave her so much joy while nurturing her health and basic needs, Mrs. Stanbury soon finds that she has the energy and confidence to return to her office every day with zeal, ready to take on each unexpected situation as it comes.

FORWARD-FACING® WORKSHEET 11:
SELF-CARE AND REVITALIZATION ASSESSMENT

Under each of the five sections below or in your separate notebook, we ask that you rate your current frequency with that particular activity using the scale provided (0 = never; 4 = frequently). After you've scored the items listed for each category, go back through all of them and pick one that you will intentionally focus on over the coming month, with the goal of raising your score by one more point on the scale.

Scale
0 = Never; 1 = Rarely; 2 = Occasionally; 3 = Moderately; 4 = Frequently

1. Physical Self-Care and Revitalization

This area focuses upon developing and maintaining a healthy body. It's all about moving toward (instead of away from) health and fitness. You don't need to eat a solely plant-based diet or participate in high-intensity boot camps multiple times each week to reap the benefits of intentional and gradual engagement in physical activity—but a good bit of attention applied to this area produces significant benefits.

_____ 1. Mild aerobic activity (<110 heartbeats per minute). Strolling, golfing, bicycling (<10 miles per hour), et cetera, for less than twenty minutes less than three times per week.
_____ 2. Moderate aerobic activity (110 – 140 heartbeats per minute). Walking (3.5+ miles per hours), jogging, bicycling (15 – 20 miles per hour), tennis, team sport games, etc., for more than twenty minutes three times per week.
_____ 3. Eating regularly (three times per day; no more than 2,400 calories).
_____ 4. Eating healthily (balanced diet, lowered carbs, fiber, fruits and vegetables, et cetera).
_____ 5. Anaerobic exercise (toning muscles, gym workout, carrying weights while walking, etc., one or more times per week).
_____ 6. Wellness checkups and preventative medicine.
_____ 7. Massage.
_____ 8. Outdoor recreation.
_____ 9. Sexual engagement.
_____ 10. Getting enough sleep.
11. Other: _____
12. Other: _____

2. Psychological Self-Care and Revitalization

This area of self-care is focused upon enhancing and optimizing psychological health and cognitive functioning. Clarity, better memory, quick wit, goodwill, being slow to anger, and having peace of mind are all results of a well-maintained psychological system. Focusing a little effort in this area can make life much easier and more satisfying for educators.

_____ 1. Intentionally facing (instead of avoiding) perceived threats with relaxed muscles.

_____ 2. Reading literature unrelated to work.

_____ 3. Puzzles (crosswords, Sudoku, word puzzles, et cetera), neural feedback practice (brain games and training on websites like Lumosity), videogames, et cetera.

_____ 4. Adult education activities.

_____ 5. Journaling (formal classes or informal).

_____ 6. Psychotherapy/life-coaching.

_____ 7. Meditation/mindfulness (formal or informal).

_____ 8. Self-regulating/relaxing muscles and refocusing when you find yourself perseverating or obsessing about something.

_____ 9. Reading self-help books/manuals.

10. Other: _____

11. Other: _____

3. Emotional Self-Care and Revitalization

Educators of all kinds spend a lot of time in chaotic—and thus traumatizing—environments, oftentimes around others who are anxious or traumatized as well. It's important to counter-balance the intensity of this environment with activities and surroundings that soothe and revive us emotionally.

_____ 1. Spending time in nature and/or gardening.

_____ 2. Connecting with positive people who support you.

_____ 3. Doing something new and exciting.

_____ 4. Engaging in financial planning, budgeting, and other activities for a stable financial future.

_____ 5. Building something.

_____ 6. Scheduling trips (day or extended) and activities that you enjoy regularly.

_____ 7. Anonymously being of service to someone.

_____ 8. Intentionally cultivating deeper and more fulfilling relationships with your partner and/or your support network.

_____ 9. Attending a support group.

_____ 10. Playing—with an animal or pet, kids, games with friends, or online with others.

11. Other: _____
12. Other: _____

Spiritual Self-Care and Revitalization

Spiritual self-care and revitalization is the process of discovering and deepening meaning, security, hope, faith, belief, and joy in your life. This can be done through formalized processes (such as attending church, synagogue, or yoga practice) or informal processes (such as walking meditation, prayer/meditation, or writing). Anything that enhances your connection to something greater than yourself and provides purpose and meaning to your life could be considered spiritual self-care.

_____ 1. Attending religious or spiritual services.

_____ 2. Yoga classes (also a powerful tool for developing interoception/bodyfulness and self-regulation).

_____ 3. Qigong, tai chi, or other martial arts training.

_____ 4. Prayer/meditation.

_____ 5. Listening to and/or playing music.

_____ 6. Taking a class in spiritual methods (i.e., mindfulness, Transcendental Meditation, Gnosticism, philosophy, et cetera).

_____ 7. Practicing gratitude (i.e., daily list of five things for which you are grateful as a discipline of cultivating happiness).

_____ 8. Practicing humility.

_____ 9. Reading books that feed your soul.

_____ 10. Watching films that feed your soul.

11. Other: _____
12. Other: _____

Professional Self-Care and Revitalization

There are a variety of simple steps to take and healthy boundaries to set in a professional space to make it work *for* us rather than against us. With continued education and self-development efforts and genuine feedback shared with those who make decisions in our institutional systems, you can feel confident and supported in your chosen career.

_____ 1. Identifying professional development training that will make your work easier and provide you with greater competence and confidence.

_____ 2. Scheduling training in one or more of these skill areas over the next year.

_____ 3. Seeking out professional and/or peer supervision, consultation, and/or support.

_____ 4. Discussing with administration (collaboratively and non-reactively) ways to improve ergonomics and climate of your school district.

_____ 5. Becoming a resource in your district for positive, solution-focused, and resilient action.

_____ 6. Scheduling and utilizing breaks throughout the day (i.e., regularly making time for lunch, planning periods, bathroom breaks, et cetera).

_____ 7. Interviewing coworkers who are competent and resilient. Discovering what they have done to become and remain successful.

_____ 8. Organizing a consortium of coworkers to explore ways to make your professional environment more resilient and able to provide better education to students.

_____ 9. Organizing and arranging your workspace so that it is comfortable and conducive for you.

_____ 10. Identifying books and research articles that will enhance your skills and knowledge and making time to read a little each month.

11. Other: _____

12. Other: _____

A Day in the Life of Mrs. Stanbury Revisited

Jamie stepped away from her desk during a lull in the activity of the front office, noting how thirsty she was and that a cup of tea and a healthy snack would be a nice way to gear up for what was sure to be a busy second half of the day.

Jamie nodded to the other faculty members she passed on her way to the lounge—Holly Waite, the school counselor, and Mike Richardson, the sixth-grade History teacher. They both returned her smile with genuine ones of their own, and Jamie wondered whether the shift in so many of the staff had to do with the workshop they'd all attended at the beginning of the school year. Jamie knew that the five Forward-Facing® steps for professional resilience had made a significant difference in all aspects of *her* life, and felt so confident about the workshop's positive effects for her so far that she'd already discussed scheduling another one with the principal for the start of the new year.

With the winter holidays approaching—a time when Jamie would normally be drowning in stress and anxiety because of her own hectic family schedule as well as the busyness on the school's campus—she found herself leaning into the fifth step of self-care and revitalization so she didn't become caught up in attending to everyone else's needs instead of her own.

Back in September following her attendance to the workshop, Jamie had felt a bit "called out" during the teachings about burnout and compassion fatigue symptoms. With sadness and some disappointment at first, Jamie had recognized how she'd withdrawn from so many of the activities that had previously given her pleasure, purpose, and joy—romance and spontaneity with her husband Perry, art exhibits and musical concerts that moved and inspired her, and regular exercise classes for wellness and good sleep. She hadn't been putting her health and physical and emotional needs first, and it showed in her low self-esteem about the way she looked, as well as her dissociative feelings and behaviors surrounding food and intimacy with Perry. Their marriage had been suffering for a while, and Jamie could see that it was due to the severe pain and discomfort in her own body while being at school—pain that was bleeding into the other areas of her life.

Right then and there at the end of the workshop, she'd resolved to heal the traumatic stress accrued from her work using self-regulation, so that she could restore total comfort to her body and mind and no longer need to "escape her life," whether by physically running away from a belligerent parent or by "leaving" her bodily sensations with hours of mindless TV, junk food, or other numbing activities.

For the last three months Jamie had incorporated the five steps into her daily routine, especially the self-care and revitalization methods from the final Forward-Facing® worksheet. She'd found that the easiest acute relaxation technique for her was intentionally releasing every muscle from head to toe like a "wet noodle," which she could do easily at her desk and during phone calls or conversations with parents or faculty. Other times when she had a quiet moment in the lounge or was walking between school buildings, she'd take a few breaths deep into her diaphragm and practice mindfulness and bodily awareness. She'd shift her concentration to her body in that present moment, noting all the physical sensations she felt, like the warmth of the bright morning sun on her skin, the fresh air that streamed cold into her nostrils and at the back of her throat as she inhaled, and the taste of the hot, flavorful coffee she sipped on her tongue.

These self-regulation and mindfulness/bodyfulness methods had already done wonders for Jamie, reducing her stress levels significantly. She was back to her capable and skillful self, navigating any number of unplanned issues occurring at the school every day with grace, confidence, quick-witted planning, and intentionality. When an angry parent sent an unkind email or a stressed coworker took out their frustrations on Jamie, she received it all in stride, reminding herself that it wasn't a personal attack on her character or worth, and that she was doing the best she could with the resources she had. Her highest cognitive functioning remained at her disposal all throughout her workday, and she handled each situation with access to the wealth of knowledge she'd gathered and maturity she'd cultivated for many years.

At home, Jamie's life flourished. She had mental clarity, remaining organized and remembering appointments and her daughters' school recitals and extracurricular plans with ease. She had joined a virtual women's book club that met online once a month, and was enjoying the books assigned and the journaling prompts that helped her to turn inward, as well as the insightful and supportive conversations she got to share with the other club attendees.

With a few tweaks to her schedule and scheduling a healthy meal delivery service for the family so she didn't have to do the grocery shopping herself, Jamie was able to return to her Zumba workout classes two or three times a week. She'd also spoken with Perry and they agreed to every-other-week date nights, hiring a babysitter and going out to a nice dinner followed by a local show or concert happening in their city. They'd also been striving to incorporate fun, flirtation, and romance into their relationship again, and even had plans for a New Year's Eve celebration with just the two of them at a nice hotel, with Jamie's mom agreeing to stay overnight at the house to watch their daughters.

Jamie felt revitalized in every sense of the word—physically, emotionally, spiritually, and in her professional career. She was in charge of taking care of herself, and had applied her efforts to doing just that. It had enabled her to be the best wife, mother, friend, and school secretary she could be, and she was thankful and appreciative for the many new opportunities ahead—ones she'd have the resilience, courage, and capacity to face head-on.

⊷ ✢ ⊶

Just like any other system in nature, we must renew our energy source in order to keep burning as we strive toward our mission and goals in educating. We hope that you will utilize this chapter to assess how you are currently doing with this skill, and to provide a framework of ways you can replenish your supply of energy while enhancing your resilience.

Here at the end of our chapters detailing the five Forward-Facing® steps for professional resilience, we recognize and honor your process of learning and relearning what compassion fatigue is and where it really comes from, and how to heal and protect yourself for the rest of your life. While these five simple methods are ones you can begin immediately, the true test comes next time you're activated at school, during meetings and trainings, or at home in your personal life. They often say that the best defense is a good offense, and we've found that this "defensive measure" can be constructed easily with a plan in place ahead of time: your self-directed Forward-Facing® professional resilience plan.

CHAPTER ELEVEN

FORWARD-FACING FOR EDUCATORS' PROFESSIONAL RESILIENCE PLAN

Start where you are. Use what you have. Do what you can.

Arthur Ashe

IF YOU'VE DECIDED by this point in the book that you're ready for more satisfaction from your work as an educator and have had enough suffering in this pursuit, then the next few pages are for you. This chapter provides you with the opportunity to formulate a self-directed "roadmap" for implementing the five Forward-Facing® professional resilience skills into your life—*starting today*. Before we embark on crafting your plan, let's briefly review what we've discussed so far about the true nature of compassion fatigue and how to heal from it.

First, you learned the difference between perceiving threat and being in real danger. Due to the sheer volume of painful past learning experiences we have at school, most of us perceive threat constantly throughout our workday. Encountering each of these perceived threats as though they're real dangers leads to an instinctual and habitual engagement of our fight-or-flight response, and this activation of the sympathetic nervous system (SNS) where there is little or no danger is the cause of all the stress-related symptoms in our lives.

This is in stark contrast to what many advance-degreed professionals believe—*that the environment is the cause of our stress, burnout, and compassion fatigue*. Once a person digests that it is not the environment that causes our distress, but instead what happens inside our bodies when we encounter the myriad of perceived threats embedded in that environment, things can change significantly and immediately. The tunnel in which we've been slogging through with brute force opens to a brand-new world, one where self-regulation paired with intention is all we need to successfully navigate our day without generating symptoms.

We invited you to practice neuroception by asking yourself a question multiple times as you made your way through the twists and turns of the haunted house of perceived threats you encountered each day: *Am I really in danger right now?* As you began to discover the answer to this question was oftentimes *no*, you likely discovered that your threat response was diminished, you were restored to some comfort in your body, your thinking was clearer, and you were able to discern the right action for yourself and your students in those situations.

Once you started to add to this changed perception the intentional and deliberate use of interoception/bodyfulness (i.e., scanning your body for muscle tension) and simply releasing the tension in those muscles, you engaged the core skill of resilience: **self-regulation**. You saw that no matter what was happening in the outside world—disruptive kids, a lack of resources in the classroom, active shooter drills, or antagonistic parents or coworkers—you were immediately able to restore comfort, motor functions, cognitive acuity, and intentional behavior each and every time you practiced this important skill.

Self-regulation is the centerpiece and cornerstone of professional resilience, and all other advances flow from gaining some mastery of this skill through practice. The more you engage it, the better your quality of life. How free from stress and strife do you want to be?

As you practiced self-regulation and read onward in this book, you also discovered that your behavior and thoughts became more aligned with your intentions. If self-regulation is the *heart* of this professional resilience program, then **intentionality** is its *soul*. While reading, you learned that all of your breaches of integrity—large or small—are the end result of a dysregulated autonomic nervous system (ANS). You realized that compulsivity, impulsivity, aggression, and avoidance are not a moral failing, but rather the outcomes of a hyperactive threat-response system. As you interrupted this threat response by releasing the tension in your muscles multiple times each day through self-regulation, not only were you less stressed and more comfortable, but you also found yourself walking through situations with your integrity intact. With your mission, vision, and code of honor (your personal covenant) put down in clear written terms, you were able to go where you aimed yourself, behave the way you envisioned, and say what you meant with grace and diplomacy. You are fast becoming the person you *choose* to be instead of what your past painful experiences have *programmed* you to be.

Building this capacity for intentionality can become a lifelong practice that transforms your workplace from what it used to be—a toxic environment that made you sick—to a crucible where you practice living with intention and integrity. By accepting this challenge and evolving this perception, your workplace is now *making you a better person*. You are growing stronger, more resilient, and more aligned with your principles. You are also likely to find that you are more present in your relationships, and more empathetic and patient with your coworkers, students, and family members. Finally, you are also likely to discover improved performance in your work. Not only are work-related compassion fatigue symptoms significantly dissipating by this practice of intentionality, but there is also an emerging sense of professional and personal wellbeing.

Perceptual maturation, the third resilience skill, first focuses upon helping educators to examine the ways in which they perceive their work, their professional environment, coworkers, and themselves. We started with challenging you to understand that it was the *perception* of the environment (i.e., perceived threat) that was causing the distress associated with your work. The upshot of this perceptual shift was simply this: It is the perception of our work and work environment and *not the work or workplace itself* that is causing all of our symptoms. With this perception shifted, the detoxification of our workplace can begin. You will remember that we separated perceptual maturation into two categories—workplace detoxification and personal optimization.

Workplace detoxification begins the moment that each educator understands that it is the *perception of their work* causing all of their stress symptoms. This shift of our attention and energy from an external causation and locus of control to an internal one we *do* have power and influence over— namely our perceptions and the muscle tension in our bodies—is the foundation of the Forward-Facing® approach for professional resilience. Once you understand that your perceptions govern your distress level—not the things you encounter or what is actually happening in your environment—you are free to begin to make additional changes in work-related perceptions. Intentional change in some of these perceptions will reward you with a less toxic workplace, less work-related stress, and a more satisfying professional quality of life.

Some other perceptual changes discussed in the workplace detoxification section of chapter eight were:

1. Real danger versus perceived threats.
2. Demand versus choice.
3. Outcome-driven versus principle-based.
4. Relinquishing entitlement and other secondary gains.
5. Acceptance of a chaotic system.

Each of these areas represent an invitation to the educator to examine and evolve their perceptions away from what they've learned from years of painful practice in a toxic environment. Instead, we challenged you to replace these intrusive perceptions (i.e., "no one understands how hard it is to be a teacher"; "there's too much work and not enough resources"; "they should appreciate me more"; "they don't pay me enough for this"; "nobody else works as hard as I do") with intentional, more ergonomic ones (i.e., "I always have a choice. I am not forced to do anything"; "when unexpected things happen all I can do is my best with what I've been given"; "I am not entitled to special treatment from my coworkers and/or family members because of my chosen profession"; "I sought out this opportunity and competed to work here"; "I will stop comparing myself with others and focus upon doing my personal best for myself today"). Maturing your perceptions in these areas will gradually reduce the toxicity of your workplace so that eventually its inevitable challenges no longer cause you to suffer. You will no longer dread your work, and even find that you have genuine joy in getting to be of service to others, which was likely the reason you pursued a profession in education in the first place.

Personal optimization is the second category of perceptual maturation. As educators learn that by changing the way they look at things (i.e., their work and workplace), the things they look at change, they willingly instigate these perceptual shifts in other areas of their lives. This perceptual maturation process often begins as an experiment about whether or not a change in perceptions will actually yield any positive effects, and once educators find that it indeed *does* lessen symptoms and enhance quality of life, they become more open to turning this experiment into an intentional and disciplined lifestyle.

In chapter eight we presented specific resources and methods you can utilize to evolve your perceptions, and the skills you should practice in order to experience a better life through that perceptual change. Some of these included:

1. Mindfulness.
2. Positive psychology or the "science of happiness."
3. Other-validation to self-validation.

These three areas represent invitations to engage in and master lifelong practices designed and demonstrated to improve your quality of life in both professional and personal contexts.

In chapter nine, we discussed the fourth resilience skill, entitled **support and connection**. In this chapter you learned that one of the most potent "medicines" educators can administer to ameliorate their work-related stress symptoms is utilizing peer support from trusted others. You also learned that the more we suffer from the symptoms of compassion fatigue, the more difficult it is to utilize and sustain these connections. Compassion fatigue can deteriorate our stamina, self-efficacy, and positive outlook and replace it with fatigue, shame, hopelessness, and isolation. Engaging, repairing, and optimizing a network of supportive peers, loved ones, and mental health professionals goes a long way toward both lessening work-related symptoms as well as keeping us resilient to their negative effects.

We discussed four ways in which support networks can be most helpful. First, we suggested that you empower one or more people in your life to become your "safety net." Compassion fatigue symptoms, especially those associated with secondary traumatic stress (intrusion, avoidance, negative alterations in perception and mood, arousal and reactivity, et cetera), have a gradual and subtle onset. Because of the insidious nature of these symptoms, they can significantly disrupt functioning in an educator's life before the individual becomes aware of them. Though initially not apparent to the professional, these symptoms are frequently noticed by close friends, coworkers, and family members first. Having several people that you trust and have previously empowered to monitor and confront you if they do witness you undergoing significant changes in your behavior, emotions, or appearance can mean the difference between catching compassion fatigue before it progresses and allowing it to fester and even derail a professional career. Additionally, knowing that the people you have empowered to monitor you are doing so will likely result in your increased self-awareness and willingness to address issues before they become overt.

Secondly, having a few people with whom you can "tell on yourself" about breaches of your intention and integrity—people who will support you in implementing and maintaining fidelity to your mission, vision, and code of honor—is instrumental in shifting away from reactivity to an intentional lifestyle. Cultivating a group of supportive peers or trusted others you can share your transgressions with and who will help you normalize and accept your shortcomings goes a long way in both lessening shame and helping you to redirect to your original path.

Thirdly, we can use supportive peers to share narratives of painful work experiences with, so that these experiences do not metastasize into secondary traumatic stress (one half of the "burnout + secondary traumatic stress = compassion fatigue" equation). By sharing these narratives while maintaining a relaxed body, we integrate and desensitize the experiences so that they are relegated into long-term memory instead of becoming intrusive traumatic stress symptoms that can elevate our arousal and lessen our professional effectiveness.

Finally, the majority of us benefit from a social support system. We need people we can recreate, revitalize, and share fun experiences with. Human beings are hardwired to resolve their threat response relationally in connection with other human beings. Even for introverts, it is important that all of us engage in regular social activities such as team sports, hiking, dining, travel, hobbies, adult learning activities, and/or support groups. By intentionally adding and enhancing our support and connection activities, we lessen the negative effects of our work and prevent others from finding purchase in an ongoing resilient professional lifestyle.

Self-care and revitalization is the final resilience skill in the Forward-Facing® approach for professional resilience. We used Viktor Frankl's quote, "That which is to give light must endure burning," as one of the influencing cornerstones of this fifth step, positing in chapter ten that if we've chosen to be a "giver of light" to others and "endure burning" in the process, we must engage in "intentional refueling" so that we burn this *fuel* and not *ourselves*.

This process of intentional refueling is what many of us refer to as "self-care." However, we also stated that the best examples of self-care are not those that are immediately gratifying, such as eating sweets or drinking a double scotch. Rather, the best self-care options involve those activities that we do not much want to do at the onset, but that provide us with stamina, buoyancy, and positive expectancy when we've completed them. Regular aerobic activity that burns off excess energy, increases metabolic efficiency, and increases mood and stamina is one of the most important activities in this resilience skill area. It would be difficult to achieve and maintain resilience while living a sedentary lifestyle; even minimal exercise (three twenty-minute sessions per week) is correlated with many positive outcomes.

Other important self-care and revitalizing activities that are easy to disregard but that are essential include preventative medical care, maintaining a balanced and nutritious diet, enforcing good sleep hygiene, and pursuing hobbies outside of work.

In the previous chapter, we presented you with a self-care and revitalization assessment (Forward-Facing® Worksheet 11). In this assessment, we asked you to rate yourself on the frequency of engagement in activities in five different categories of self-care and revitalization. These categories were:

1. Physical.
2. Psychological.
3. Emotional.
4. Spiritual.
5. Professional.

If you did not complete that assessment then, we suggest that you go back and fill it out in preparation for completing your self-directed Forward-Facing® professional resilience plan now.

Before you begin, we wish to note that this approach probably represents a big change in how you lead your life from here on out. We know that there will be huge benefits for you as you move through this material, and we also know that there's a lot to do in this chapter. We suggest you go slowly as you develop and practice these skills, referring back to the reflections and worksheets you've completed from parts I and II of this book for deeper exploration.

Self-regulate routinely, noticing your responses as you read over the exercises that are described here. Remind yourself that you are just perceiving threat, and that there is no danger. There is a lot here for you to digest. Do those steps which you want to, and do not do those that you prefer to skip. This is a self-directed protocol—go through this at your own pace, in your own way, working with what intrigues you first and then sampling other exercises to find what works best for you.

YOUR FORWARD-FACING® PROFESSIONAL RESILIENCE PLAN

1. Self-Regulation.

Self-regulation is the ability to monitor and regulate your ANS, activating only the amount of energy necessary for the task. This process requires three activities—neuroception, interoception, and acute relaxation—done within a few-second window while remaining fully engaged in professional, personal, and all other activities of daily living. Releasing tension in your core muscles is an excellent method to quickly achieve this, but becoming aware of and releasing the tension in *all* muscles of your body is successfully practicing self-regulation. You cannot experience stress with relaxed muscles, as proven by reciprocal inhibition.

Identify five situations in your personal and/or professional life in which you are habitually dysregulated, and make a commitment to confront these situations with intentionally relaxed muscles over the next month. (Example: "When I get an email from a parent or coworker and my pulse rises.") Feel free to refer to your answers from Forward-Facing® Worksheet 3 for ideas.

1. _____

   _____

2. _____

   _____

3. _____

   _____

4. _____

   _____

5. _____

   _____

2. Intentionality.

Intentionality is the ability to follow your personal covenant while maintaining integrity across the landscape of your life, both professionally and personally. It is shifting away from reactivity and impulsive behaviors toward chosen and intentional behaviors.

Identify two situations where you habitually respond reactively and find yourself derailed from your mission, vision, and code of honor while breaching your integrity (one professional and one personal). Make the commitment to self-regulate during the confrontation with the perceived threat(s) embedded in these situations to replace reactivity with intentionality. You can refer to your personal covenant documents in Forward-Facing® Worksheets 4, 5, and 6 for direction.

1. Describe a specific **professional** behavior (usually aggression or avoidance) that constitutes the breach of your integrity. (Example: "I become impatient and angry with a student.")

_____

_____

_____

What is the trigger/perceived threat(s)? (Example: "The student disregarded my request to put their phone away during class.")

_____

_____

_____

What is your intentional behavior in this situation? (Example: "I strive to have patience with my students and understand that they are children first and foremost, per my code of honor. If they are disregarding my politely voiced request to put their phone away after I've asked already, I will follow the class rules I've set out ahead of time of taking their phone for the rest of the period without getting dysregulated or allowing it to derail me from that day's lesson.")

_____

_____

_____

2. Describe a specific **personal** behavior (usually aggression or avoidance) that constitutes the breach of your integrity.

_____

_____

_____

What is the trigger/perceived threat(s):

_____

_____

_____

What is your intentional behavior in this situation:

_____

_____

_____

3. Perceptual Maturation.

Your workplace is not the cause of your stress. Instead, it is your perception of your workplace and the happenings therein that cause your stress. It is difficult to get workplaces to change to meet your specifications; it is much simpler to change your perceptions to more satisfying and ergonomic ways of seeing. You can significantly lessen the toxicity of your work by changing some of your perceptions and meanings by answering the questions below. Look back at the exercises in chapter eight as well as your responses to Forward-Facing® Worksheets 7 and 8 for reference if needed.

WORKPLACE DETOXIFICATION

1. Real Danger versus Perceived Threat. How often during each day do you encounter a real and present danger? How often during the day do you perceive threat? What is the ratio of real dangers to perceived threats? When you stop to consider these questions, it becomes clear that you perceive threat *much* more frequently than you encounter real danger. Reminding yourself that this is true is a good beginning for evolving and detoxifying your perception of the environment.

Ask yourself several times each day during the next month: *Am I really in danger right now?*

How does asking and answering this question impact your stress levels in those situations? Describe:

_____

_____

2. Demand versus Choice. What is demanded of you in your work? Answer: *nothing!* You retain choice in every single situation for the rest of your life. Your ability to move away from perceiving tasks at work, requests from your boss, or added trainings as a demand upon you and instead perceiving them as opportunities to evaluate the costs/benefits of doing or not doing the them before going forward, will significantly lessen the effects of a toxic workplace upon you.

You can begin to develop this skill by replacing language like "I have to…" with "I choose to…" This simple shift frees you from conscription and bondage where you are forced, against your will, to complete tasks to a voluntary action that enriches your quality of life. This works especially for the tasks you do *not* want to complete.

Name five tasks at work that you very much dislike doing but that you do anyway.

1. _____

2. _____

3. _____

4. _____

5. _____

For the next week try **choosing** to do these tasks while keeping a relaxed body and positive attitude. What is different when you choose to do them?

_____

_____

Next, identify five tasks that you catch yourself saying "I have to..."
1. _____
   _____
2. _____
   _____
3. _____
   _____
4. _____
   _____
5. _____
   _____

For the next week try **choosing** to do these tasks while keeping a relaxed body and positive attitude. What is different when you choose to do them?
_____
_____
_____

3. Outcome-Driven versus Principle-Based. There are very few outcomes that you are able, by an act of will, to make happen in the complex world of educating. Outcomes—good or bad—are influenced by a myriad of factors all beyond your ability to predict or control. When you make yourself responsible for outcomes in others' lives or even in your own life, you will find yourself having threat responses each time you encounter something that jeopardizes the wished-for outcome. The ability to relinquish outcomes in favor of embracing a commitment to bring your personal best—skills, attention, compassion, willingness—to a situation can significantly lessen the level of stress created by the need to have a situation turn out any particular way.

Identify five situations in your work where you find yourself preoccupied or obsessed with achieving a particular outcome (i.e., students' test scores, parent-teacher conferences, recognition from others, et cetera).
1. _____
   _____
2. _____
   _____

3. _____
_____

4. _____
_____

5. _____
_____

For the next week practice re-attenuating your focus away from outcomes like these, identifying five principle-based behaviors you can practice instead.

1. _____
_____

2. _____
_____

3. _____
_____

4. _____
_____

5. _____
_____

What impact does this change have upon your quality of life?

_____
_____

4. Relinquishing Entitlement and Secondary Gains. Professionals impaired by work-related stress can develop diminished functioning of the neocortical areas of their brains. This impairment can gradually and increasingly result in educators perceiving themselves to be victims of their work, and from this perspective to develop a sense of entitlement, believing they should be given more than they are getting from their work. They believe that their workplace owes them certain self-perceived things, like a less stressful environment, more pay, more time off, fewer students, and/or more resources to get their jobs done.

While it is true that we should expect our leadership to work toward enhancing operations and resources at our places of work, the holding of embittered entitlement and the perception of being a victim saps stamina, positive outlook, and resilience. Letting go of the entitlements and the underlying victim stance that supports them can immediately enhance resilience and quality of life.

Entitlement

Write down a list of all the things your work as an educator entitles you to that you are not getting from your workplace. (Example: "With my degree, I shouldn't have to do many of the menial tasks that I am expected to do.")

1. _____
_____
2. _____
_____
3. _____
_____
4. _____
_____
5. _____
_____
6. _____
_____
7. _____
_____
8. _____
_____

Which of these are you willing to let go of for the next week?

1. _____
_____
2. _____
_____
3. _____
_____
4. _____
_____
5. _____
_____

For the next week, practice going to your workplace as a place where nothing is owed to you. Where you are there because you have chosen to be there. Where your workplace is not responsible for your quality of life. What impact does this make?

_____

_____

Indulgences
What self-harmful indulgences do you allow yourself because of your "stressful" work?

1. _____

2. _____

3. _____

4. _____

5. _____

Which of these are you willing to relinquish and substitute with a healthy alternative? (See chapter ten for self-care and revitalization techniques and ideas.)

1. _____

2. _____

3. _____

4. _____

5. _____

5. Acceptance of a Chaotic System. Human systems, especially in education, are chaotic, anxious, and demanding. It has always been and will likely remain this way. Educators who have not yet matured into a resilient professional lifestyle often perceive the demands, anxiety, lack of appreciation, and system politics as a personal affront. As educators evolve into resilience, they find that they can stop fighting what is and begin to accept—just for today— that this is the way things are, while at the same time continuing to advocate and work toward positive change in their environments.

Make a quick list of all the happenings in your workplace that anger, frustrate, irritate, distress, or bother you in any way. (Example: "I become annoyed when I spend so much time planning out really good lessons and then unexpected situations like fire drills or assemblies disrupt my entire plan.")

1. _____
_____
2. _____
_____
3. _____
_____
4. _____
_____
5. _____
_____
6. _____
_____
7. _____
_____
8. _____
_____

Which of these are you willing to practice acceptance with—just for that day—instead of struggling and continuing to hold distress in your body while those things are not changing?

1. _____
_____
2. _____

3. _____
   _____
   _____

Identify three concrete actions—no matter how small—you can make over the next week to improve the quality of life in your workplace for both you and others.

1. _____
   _____
2. _____
   _____
3. _____
   _____

PERSONAL OPTIMIZATION

Mindfulness

List three recent situations when you intentionally engaged in mindfulness practice—whether that was returning to your breath and the current moment, approaching things with a "beginner's mind" of curiosity and positivity, practicing nonjudgmental observation of yourself or others, or something else.

1. _____
   _____
2. _____
   _____
3. _____
   _____

The Science of Happiness

Spend two minutes a day describing a positive experience from the last twenty-four hours. This tactic transforms your thinking from task-based to meaning-based, and promotes a viewpoint that is engaged and focused instead of searching for the next thing to do. Write one down here to practice if you would like.

_____

_____

_____

Exercise at least three times a week for twenty minutes; not only is it physically beneficial, but it trains your brain to believe your behavior and choices are important and impactful for the rest of your day. List below the days and types of exercise you chose.

1. _____
   _____

2. _____
   _____

3. _____
   _____

Write down three things you are grateful for every day in a journal, on your phone, or anywhere you can refer to later. Research says this will greatly increase your optimism and success rates. Practice below if you would like.

1. _____
   _____

2. _____
   _____

3. _____
   _____

Take two minutes to meditate and focus on your breathing, fully disengaging from any multitasking you may have been doing. This decreases your stress and resets your brain so that you can address each task one at a time, with optimized neocortical functioning.

Write one short email when you wake up in the morning to a colleague, friend, or family member praising them and what they have been doing.

FROM OTHER-VALIDATED TO SELF-VALIDATED CAREGIVING

A subtle, but powerful, protective factor for burnout and compassion fatigue is addressing this issue of other- versus self-validation in the life of the educator. When our worth is determined by someone other than ourselves, we are in danger of losing it if that person does not approve of or appreciate us.

Identify four situations where you perceive threat from another person's judgment or potential criticism.

1. _____
_____
2. _____
_____
3. _____
_____
4. _____
_____

Identify in which of the above situations you find yourself changing your behavior to avoid or lessen the potential risk of judgment or criticism.

1. _____
_____
2. _____
_____
3. _____
_____

If you were to become intentional and self-validated in these situations, what would you have to say to yourself?

_____
_____
_____

Write a letter to yourself from the voice of "the Great Administrator" telling you all that you have wished to hear from some external source. Provide yourself with all the validation for which you have ever longed. No criticisms—just identifying all of the positive things you have done and do regularly. Provide yourself with the support that you wish you had. Once done, put it in an envelope and mail it to yourself. When it is delivered back to you, read it with a relaxed body and an attitude of compassion and curiosity.

4. Support and Connection.
Throughout this book we have discussed the importance of developing, maintaining, and utilizing a support network. Now it is time to put it into action, using your answers to the Forward-Facing® Worksheets 9 and 10 for reference.

1. Safety Net. Identify one person who knows you well, cares about you, sees you regularly, and—maybe most importantly—is resilient themselves. Seek this person out over the next couple of weeks and invite them to be your "safety net." You may wish to use the following as a guide:

"Hey, I recently learned that I am at high risk for compassion fatigue and work-related stress. I learned that it is important to have at least one person who knows me well watching my back. Of all the people I know who could do this, your name was at the top of my list. Because the effects are hard to detect in ourselves, I am asking you to just passively notice if you see me starting to become symptomatic. That might be things like irritability, anger, complaining a lot, jittery, obsessed with something—anything that looks like stress. The symptoms can go the other way also, like withdrawal, isolation, depression, chronic fatigue, or disengagement. If you see me consistently— over a few weeks or months—displaying these negative effects, I ask that you would confront me. Chances are if I am in one of those places, I will not be very open to hearing your confrontation. I ask that you remind me of this conversation and do not give up confronting me until I commit to do something about it. Even though it may strain the ties of our friendship/relationship, you may save my life. I will gladly do the same for you, if you like."

Identify the one person to seek out to be your safety net:
1. _____

_____

2. Sharing Narratives. In chapter three we discussed secondary traumatic stress—the post-traumatic stress that comes from witnessing the trauma and/ or suffering of others. If you have frequent exposure to students (or their families) who are experiencing one or both of these, then you are high-risk for secondary traumatic stress. The bad news is that this type of traumatization can produce a wide array of symptoms, many of which can be debilitating.

The good news is that it is easily resolved by sharing the narratives of these painful encounters with peers (or a hired professional) while retaining a relaxed-muscle body. By doing this, the memories of the painful experiences are desensitized and generate fewer symptoms. You may wish to use the following script as a template to guide your conversation:

"Hey, I just learned that I might be high-risk for compassion fatigue, and that preventing compassion fatigue requires that I regularly share my narratives with another person. I'd like for you to be that person. If you are willing, I'd like to show you this thing I learned about how to keep your body relaxed while you are listening to me so that you don't get sick from my stories [teach self-regulation: neuroception + interoception/bodyfulness + acute relaxation technique]. I promise you I will always ask permission from you and allow you time to prepare yourself before I start talking with you about these issues—I won't hijack you. I would ask that you make yourself available sometime within seventy-two hours after I initially reach out, either in person or by telephone. When we meet, I will have everything I need to share organized into a twenty-minute narrative. I ask that you just listen and do not interrupt. If you have insights, comments, or suggestions I would love to hear them after I have completed my narrative. If you are willing to do this for me, I am more than happy to reciprocate. I will offer the same thing—I only ask that you ask me first, and I will make myself available to you within seventy-two hours as well."

Identify three peers or professionals (i.e., mental health) who you will seek out to fill this role:

1. _____

_____

2. _____

_____

3. _____

_____

3. Accountability. This important asset is developed and utilized to support you through your implementation and maintenance of intentionality. It is nearly impossible to live an intentional, principle-based life in isolation. We need support. Utilizing this support to celebrate our successful confrontations with situations where we have previously been out of alignment with our integrity is important, as it facilitates our continued progress. It is also equally (if not more so) important to have a cadre of safe and supportive individuals to whom we can turn when we are in breach of our integrity. We have discovered that this practice of "telling on ourselves" is an integral part of living an intentional life.

Identify three people you will recruit to fill this role (note—these may be some of the same people you are utilizing in other roles).

1. _____
   _____

2. _____
   _____

3. _____
   _____

4. Social Support. These are the people that you wish to include as part of your wider-reaching social support network. These should be people you feel safe and comfortable around, and share a camaraderie with. After spending time with the people you identify in this group, you should feel revitalized, hopeful, cared about, and joyful.

Identify three to five people who fit these requirements with whom you will seek to deepen connection.

1. _____
   _____

2. _____
   _____

3. _____
   _____

4. _____
   _____

5. _____
   _____

5. Self-Care and Revitalization.

We must intentionally refuel our bodies, minds, and spirits so that we can confront the rigors of our work. By regularly engaging these activities, you should find that you are able to burn a bright light that shines into the lives of others who are suffering and never burns out. Looking back to chapter ten's self-care and revitalization self-assessment, we ask that you identify one activity from each of the five categories that you will intentionally increase your engagement in over the next month.

Physical self-care and revitalization.
1. _____
_____

Psychological self-care and revitalization.
1. _____
_____

Emotional self-care and revitalization.
1. _____
_____

Spiritual self-care and revitalization.
1. _____
_____

Professional self-care and revitalization.
1. _____
_____

⁘ ✚ ⁘

Congratulations! Here at the end of your reflections, worksheets, and your Forward-Facing® professional resilience plan, you are well on your way to implementing an evidence-based protocol that lessens compassion fatigue symptoms, enhances resilience, and improves quality of life. We are so proud of you for having the courage and strength to help heal yourself and foster lasting resilience in order to stay true to your mission and passion for helping children and their families.

In the final chapter, we wish to speak a little bit about our Forward-Facing® vision for the institution of education—ways that the system can better serve educators, students, and communities, and how to possibly play a role in this process. Lastly, we'll leave you with an encouraging revisitation to a day in the life of our sixth-grade student Freda, showcasing what it's like for her now that she attends a school where the faculty have all mastered their self-regulation, intentionality, and perceptual maturation, and have support systems and self-care activities in place. We hope it leaves you with a vision of what could be at your own school—and what *will* be for you now that you've learned the five Forward-Facing® steps for professional resilience.

CHAPTER TWELVE

FORWARD-FACING® IN SCHOOLS: A VISION FOR THE FUTURE

*Everyone should have an opportunity to learn in a
positive environment, to enjoy the learning process,
and to feel comfortable and content within it.*

Barry Saide

WE HAVE ROUNDED the last turn of our journey together. In this chapter we invite you to envision with us how our commitment to personal resilience, once it has been manifested in our professional and personal lives, can begin to evolve the effectiveness and heal the toxicity of educational environments. We would like for you to imagine a workplace where *all* members are self-regulated, intentional, connected, and supportive—and not on a fictional 1970s television show, but here, in the twenty-first century. We believe that it is our responsibility to leave our educational environments significantly better for the next generation than it was for us, and in many ways, that has been the mission and legacy of all our work around Forward-Facing® professional resilience in education.

The introduction of this book presented what we called "a critical question"—the answer to which, we promised, would be addressed again in this final chapter: *Where does the responsibility to reduce our suffering and assure our professional fulfillment lie?* Does it belong to our leadership/institutions, or with each of us as individuals?

We declared in that section that the answer to this fundamental question was "a resounding *both*." The majority of this book is aimed at what you as the reader and educator have current and complete control over: *your own personal resilience.* We hope that you are now able to embrace the concepts and implement the skills that we have described, and that you have begun to reap the benefits of doing so. It is our individual responsibility to interrupt the hundreds of threat-response instances that erupt in our bodies throughout the school day and return to a regulated state. We all must be capable of navigating our way through the chaos and difficulty of our work every time we show up to provide education to our students, while walking the balance beam of our own integrity. It is our mantle to start to evolve our perceptions and make our schools less toxic. We recruit and utilize our own support systems to enhance our functioning and lessen our burden, but recognize that no one else is going to revitalize and refuel us; that is our own encumbrance. We—with the support of our peers—build our own resilience. There is little to nothing you can do to effectively change your external environment while navigating your students' ever-changing needs and behaviors, communicating with hundreds of parents, or getting through a day in your office or classroom. By focusing on maintaining your resilience each day, you will minimize your work's effect upon you while also enabling yourself to perform at your best, regardless of the task at hand.

And here is where we might all extend an olive branch to the leadership of the institutions in the education system. We promise that we will use what we have learned over the course of our lives (including this material) to do our personal best whenever we step into our roles as professional educators. We will focus on the care of the student and the performance of our staff (and of course the state of our muscles and perceptions), and not be distracted by the character of the workplace. This is our covenant: We will provide our best care and service to our students and communities, we will be the best team players, and we will give our best to advancing the mission of the institution each and every moment we are on the job. Each of us will be responsible for maintaining our resilience *today*.

In exchange, we request that leadership itself begins to understand the impacts of compassion fatigue, burnout, and environmental trauma and their effects on the educating workforce. We ask that those in leadership engage and partner with us to optimize the workplace for both the students we serve and for us—the educators. To phrase "the deal" we are offering into one sentence: If each of us is responsible for *today*, then you—the leadership in education—must take on the responsibility for helping to create a healthier, more ergonomic, more humane, and less chaotic workplace *tomorrow*.

We are here to assist everyone in stepping up to this responsibility by offering multiple options in training and supporting districts and individual schools in these practices. Just as we have individually developed our own professional resilience plans, we will continue to work with educational institutions to develop a roadmap for sharing these skills with all educators in a format that meets the individual needs of each school and district.

For example, to provide an opportunity to learn and practice these skills over time, many districts are choosing a "book study" model that has multiple opportunities to come together and share successes and challenges in implementing these skills before moving on to learning next steps, until the process feels comfortable and secure for all the learners.

Additionally, some districts are choosing to develop a cadre of people who become well versed and prepared in Forward-Facing® professional resilience skills and are then tasked with engaging others in their schools and districts. Conversely, some educators are using our resources to develop the skills of all employees across their schools and districts. No matter the roadmap we develop with you, our commitment remains the same: to teach these skills to as many educators as possible, knowing that all students deserve an opportunity to arrive in our schools each day with a building full of regulated, vision-focused, and collaboratively supported adults. Our covenant demands us to remain focused on a world where education as an institution is transformed by the power of professionally resilient adults within every single school and central office building.

In these pages we've set forth a clear path to achieve individual resilience and believe it to be essential for the next millennia of educators, and are offering additional Forward-Facing® trainings and programs to larger groups we connect with—but agree that this is still not enough. Institutions must ensure that the culture is supportive of educators' wellness. The health, morale, engagement, and retention of educators must become central to the institution's mission and daily administration (and budget). We call upon educational leaders (and funders) to make meaningful changes in procedure, policy, and resources that improve the efficiency of education. This is a win-win-win proposition—better care for educators, better care for students, and a healthier and more vibrant community resulting from supported school districts.

You are now empowered to go forward in your career with a stress-free body, maximally functioning brain, and a principle-based lifestyle. We have been able to demonstrate, with these evidence-based and empirically supported skills, that the majority of those who engage the five Forward-Facing®

steps illustrated in this book lower their work-related stress symptoms and significantly enhance their professional quality of life.

That is your responsibility for today, and you have now been equipped with the skills to successfully achieve this goal. However, institutions and their leadership teams have an important role to play in the future designs of our education system so that they can become more efficient, supportive, and sustainable. These results will only be enhanced by the relief and resilience fostered individually among us as educators.

Compassion fatigue is a real and debilitating issue faced by educators around the world who are performing some of the most strenuous mental and emotional work in our society today. It is not something to be ashamed of, nor is it something to keep buried within yourself until the pain is too great to bear. You are not alone, you are not defective, and this is not a permanent struggle from which you have no escape. We are extending to you an invitation for healing, satisfaction, and resilience that you can carry on for the duration of your career—and in doing so, you will also find that these skills apply to all other areas of your personal and professional life. Join us in this journey toward renewed strength, zeal, empathy, and the compassion that drew you to the education field when you first envisioned a mission serving the children of our future in countless ways.

We will leave you now with a vision of hope by returning to a day in the life of our student, Freda Whitmore, as she spends time among educators who feel and behave much differently than they did at the beginning of this book. This group of mission-driven educators are regulated, intentional, empathetic, supportive and supported, and—perhaps most evident of all—*resilient*.

A Day in the Life of Freda Revisited

The holiday cheer was infectious when Freda got to school on their last day before the winter break, and she couldn't help but reflect the smiles of the other kids and adults. After giving her little sister Devon a hug goodbye and promising to meet her by the corner to take the bus home together that afternoon, Freda followed the crowd of boisterous students toward the sixth-grade building that passed by the double doors of the front office.

Freda spotted the school's principal, Mrs. Burkhart, standing outside the doors and greeting many children by name as they walked on. The principal's gaze met Freda's and she grinned warmly, and Freda wove her way closer to the principal to say hello. It was nice to see one another for a reason other than Freda's unsigned behavior contracts—which she'd been getting a lot fewer of in recent months, especially from Mr. Richardson.

"Good morning, Freda!" Mrs. Burkhart said. "Haven't seen you in a while. How are you and your sister doing? How's your mom? Any fun plans for the break?"

Freda nodded enthusiastically, meeting the principal's excitement with her own. "Yeah, we'll be spending half the break with my mom and half at my dad's house."

"Oh, very nice. Will your mom be working at the hospital over the holiday weekend?"

Freda shook her head no, a bit surprised that the principal remembered that her mom was a nurse. She had so many other students and parents to keep track of, but whenever they saw each other, she genuinely seemed to care about Freda's life outside of school. It was a really nice feeling. "She took the days off to spend the time with us."

"Good honey, I'm glad to hear that," Mrs. Burkhart said, squeezing Freda's shoulder gently. As she did so, a concerned-looking parent rushed over and pushed her way between the two of them.

"Shannon, I need to talk to you about Kail, *now*," the woman said, blatantly ignoring Freda's presence and seeming to vibrate with rage. Freda was pretty sure she was Kail Jensen's mom, and if so, Freda could understand where Kail might be getting his extreme emotions and tendencies to act out from.

"Morning Denise, good to see you as always," Mrs. Burkhart said calmly, winking at Freda before ushering the angry mother through the front office's doors. "I'm gonna ask you to take a few deep breaths with me as we go to my office...I promise this'll all get worked out..."

Freda shrugged and readjusted her backpack as she watched the two women disappear down a hallway. She didn't know how the principal remained so pleasant with the parents who frequently seemed to show up yelling or upset about something day after day, but maybe that's why she held such an important job at the school. Either way, Freda thought she was really good at it and hoped the principal would have a nice rest over the holiday.

A few minutes later in Ms. Hernandez's Social Studies class, Freda considered mentioning to Kail that she'd seen his mom earlier, but decided against it because he was clearly in a mood.

"Everyone, please get in your seats!" Ms. Hernandez directed the class, with all the kids except for Kail and his friend Xander listening right away. They ignored the teacher, kicking a soccer ball back and forth between their desks and hitting the other students' ankles and chairs along the way. Freda watched raptly and didn't make a sound; she knew what the young teacher was going to do, just like Kail and Xander and every other sixth-grader did. Ms. Hernandez might've been a pushover earlier in the year, but she didn't play around anymore when it came to bad behavior.

"One more chance," Ms. Hernandez said evenly as she stared at both boys, the rest of the class watching silently. Freda's heartbeat increased with the tension in the room, but Ms. Hernandez didn't budge—she just continued to watch the boys with a frighteningly serious, confident expression.

Xander stopped then and flopped into his chair before digging in his backpack for his homework, but Kail remained standing.

"Hey Ms. Hernandez, why don't you bring us candy anymore?" Kail said, shifting his soccer ball between his hands. Even *he* seemed nervous, and Freda wasn't sure why he felt the nerve to keep pushing. "Not even for the holiday?"

Ms. Hernandez ignored the question and calmly went to her desk, opening up the top drawer which everyone knew contained her stack of behavior contracts, ready to be filled out with any rule-breakers' info and signed by their parents. "Kail, come here please," she said, and he sighed theatrically.

"Ms. Hernandez, come on!"

"Come. Here. Please. *Now*."

Freda felt like cheering as Kail went over and snatched the behavior contract from Ms. Hernandez's outstretched hand before sitting in his chair with a pout. She didn't know why Kail kept trying to mess with the teacher instead of learning his lesson—everyone else had, including Freda herself. Ms. Hernandez might've been young, and she was always really nice to everyone, but she was *not* afraid of discipline. It made Freda want to listen to her a lot more, actually, and she hoped for Kail's own sake that he'd figure it out too.

Freda's next class with Mr. Richardson had *also* changed noticeably in the way it was run over the past few months, but in the opposite direction. Instead of punishing kids all the time and seeming to make a sport out of seeing if he could make them cry, Mr. Richardson had lightened up considerably since the beginning of the school year. His History lessons were a lot more interesting, too—so much so that Freda hustled to get there on time every day.

"Hi Jonathan, hi Valerie, hi Freda!" Mr. Richardson said as they filed in that morning for class. Freda waved in response, and smiled when she saw that on her desk and everyone else's was a candy cane and a big piece of silver-wrapped chocolate tied together with red ribbon.

"Candy!" echoed several of the students as they sat down, most of them obediently waiting to unwrap the treat until Mr. Richardson gave permission, Freda included.

"Go ahead, eat! These are for you to enjoy," Mr. Richardson said, encouraging some of the kids in the front row to unwrap their candy canes and chocolate if they wanted. "Or you can wait until after lunch. Up to you guys."

Freda ate her chocolate as Mr. Richardson began his lesson, enjoying the flavor and feeling thankful for the snack, since she'd be spending that day's lunch period with Ms. Waite for their monthly counseling visit.

"Are you going to have any?" asked Freda's classmate Valerie between bites.

"Oh no," Mr. Richardson said from the smart board, patting his midsection. "Gotta watch my figure these days! There only needs to be one Santa around our town, I think."

Freda joined in on the other students' laughter and munched away. Mr. Richardson definitely looked healthier—less like Santa than she could remember at any other point that year. His face wasn't as red or puffy as it used to be, and he did seem to have lost some weight. Whatever he'd been doing, Freda hoped it continued, because he was clearly happier, which made History class a lot better for everyone.

When Freda went to Ms. Waite's office for their scheduled visit, the school counselor was waiting for her with a big smile.

"How are you Freda?" Ms. Waite asked once they were seated, folding her hands on a desk that was no longer piled up high with messy stacks of paper. The counselor seemed to be more organized these days, or maybe she just had less work to do? Freda wasn't sure, but Ms. Waite had been really good with scheduling their monthly appointments and asking Freda to stick to them (unless there was an emergency, in which case they could meet sooner).

"I'm good," Freda answered, going over her holiday plans with the counselor before they discussed what Freda had been assigned to work on for the past month—different ways for handling her stress and any bad thoughts she had, things she'd journaled about, how her sister and parents were doing, and other stuff like that.

When their session was done, Freda asked Ms. Waite what her plans over the break were.

"I'll be spending a lot of time with my boyfriend," Ms. Waite said, "have a few big dinners planned with family and friends...I've been trying to be a lot better about that. It's important to spend time with people who care about you. Which is why I want to remind you that *I* care about you, Freda. You and your family will be in my thoughts this holiday season. I look forward to seeing you when everyone gets back and hearing how things went."

Freda thanked the counselor and gave her a quick hug before leaving. She did feel cared about by the counselor and a few of the other teachers recently, but it was always nice to hear it out loud.

On her way to her first class of the afternoon, she heard her name being called and spun around toward the front office where the voice had come from.

"Freda! Hi Freda!" said the school secretary, Mrs. Stanbury, waving from the open doors of the front office. "I have something for you! Got a minute?"

"For me?" Freda asked, following Mrs. Stanbury inside the front office building. It was decorated and festive inside, with hanging bits of tinsel and twinkling, colored lights strung on the fake plant Freda used to sit next to during those lunch hours when she was being reprimanded for not getting her behavior contracts signed by her mom.

"Yep. For you," Mrs. Stanbury said, striding over to her desk and snatching a small plastic bag from a basket on the counter. "I hope you like homemade Christmas cookies."

Freda's eyes widened, instantly salivating. "I *love* homemade cookies." She took the bag from Mrs. Stanbury, admiring the big ones topped with M&M's and the smaller ones with Hershey's Kisses pushed into the middle.

"Those ones with chocolate in the middle are peanut-butter flavored," Mrs. Stanbury explained. "They're my daughters' favorite—we made them this past weekend."

"Oh wow," Freda said, already debating whether she'd share them with Devon (she would, of course, but a little begrudgingly). "Thank you so much, Mrs. Stanbury."

"Of course," the school secretary said, her eyes crinkling with a grin. "I know your mom is doing such important work as a nurse and sometimes she's a little busy, and I had the extra time and wanted you and some of the other kids to have something homemade this holiday. Take care honey, and I'll see you *next year!*"

"Okay. See you next year," Freda said with a chuckle, clutching the bag of cookies to her chest as she left the front office and headed toward her next class. She was smiling so hard her cheeks were beginning to hurt. What a wonderful way to end the semester—one that Freda honestly didn't want to be over. She couldn't wait to come back the following January, and looked forward to being reunited with everyone at school who she really liked, and who made *her* feel special and liked too.

As you move forward on your individual paths toward creating school environments where staff successfully relate to colleagues and students with regulated bodies, clear and committed covenants, and habits of self-care and peer support, please remember that we are always available to help you in your personal and professional transformation. We honor your courage and wisdom in looking inward, knowing that the greatest gift of education is what we learn within ourselves and take out into the world to be shared through experiences of compassion, joy, and love for ourselves and one another. We are Forward-Facing® educators, all on a collective journey to live our best lives and help others do the same.

APPENDIX I:

FORWARD-FACING° WORKSHEETS 1-11 AND PROFESSIONAL RESILIENCE PLAN

FORWARD-FACING® WORKSHEET 1: SELF-EVALUATION

Answer YES or NO to the following ten questions by circling them here, or writing the answers down in your journal or notepad.

1. My life is so stressful that I often feel overwhelmed. YES or NO
2. I often behave in ways that I regret later. YES or NO
3. I frequently say and do things that hurt people I care about. YES or NO
4. There are situations and people that push my buttons and make me crazy, so I avoid them and keep to myself as much as possible. YES or NO
5. I feel empty and unsatisfied with my life. YES or NO
6. I've tried to change, but have found it impossible on my own. YES or NO
7. I feel controlled by other people. YES or NO
8. I would like to have more meaning in my life. YES or NO
9. I want to do a better job of being true to my principles and living with integrity. YES or NO
10. I think I may be suffering from primary, secondary, and/or environmental trauma. YES or NO

If you scored four or more "yes" answers above, then you are a prime candidate to begin implementing the Forward-Facing® approach for professional resilience in your life today. If your score was less than that, you will still be able to find wonderful insight, healing, and optimization for your future in education by adopting this five-step process in your daily activities.

FORWARD-FACING® WORKSHEET 2: THE METHODS
OF INVOKING THE RELAXATION RESPONSE

The five methods listed below are arranged to begin with the "easiest" (least intensive) to apply, continuing toward those which require a bit more concentration and practice. They are all equally effective at the acute relaxation portion of self-regulation, and are designed to be performed multiple times a day (or more) as needed.

Method 1: Body scan, a.k.a. the "wet noodle"

This process is executed by simply becoming aware of all the muscles in your body and relaxing them. It can be completed while standing, sitting, or lying down, but we recommend sitting in a chair when you're just starting out.

1. Sit or recline somewhere.
2. Take five seconds and release all of your muscles from head to toe simultaneously, paying special attention to areas of increased tension (i.e., abdominal muscles, throat, chest, et cetera).

One, two, three, four, five.
That's it!

Method 2: Pelvic floor relaxation

As was explained earlier, our pelvic muscles are linked to our fight-or-flight response, and when we're SNS dominant, they are constricted. By releasing them, we initiate a potent and instinctual relaxation response. In this exercise, your goal is to locate and then relax the muscles in your core.

1. Sit down comfortably and place a hand under each side of your bottom.
2. Now feel for the pointed bones that you're sitting upon. These mark the lower boundary of your core.
3. Next, find and touch the two bony points just above your waist on the right and left sides of your body. These mark the upper boundary of your core.
4. Now that you've made a "touch memory" of these four points, imagine connecting them with lines to form a square that encircles your

body. This is your core—the location where your vagal nerve connects to your pelvic floor muscles.

5. Next, take ten seconds and imagine allowing that square to expand
    in all four directions, so that there is no clenching anywhere in the
    middle of it. Completely soften that entire area of your body.

One, two, three, four, five, six, seven, eight, nine, ten.

6. For ten more seconds, focus on the muscles in the center of the
    square, opening and completely releasing them.

One, two, three, four, five, six, seven, eight, nine, ten.

Once you become adept at interoception (sensing your body becoming
activated), you'll be able to practice this acute relaxation method while sitting or standing as part of your daily regimen of self-regulation.

Method 3: Peripheral vision

This method was originally developed by the U.S. military to train snipers. Fortunately, it works just as well for civilians.

1. Find a spot at eye level that's located five to ten feet in front of you.
2. Focus your eyes for five seconds on that spot.

One, two, three, four, five.

3. Now soften your focus until the spot becomes blurry. Hold that for
    five seconds.

One, two, three, four, five.

4. Still facing forward and without moving your eyes, shift your focus to
    your peripheral vision. Do this simultaneously with both eyes.
5. Maintain your peripheral focus for ten seconds.

One, two, three, four, five, six, seven, eight, nine, ten.

6. Repeat steps 1 through 5 five times.

Note: If you're having difficulty shifting your focus from the center to the
periphery, try extending your arms straight out in front of you so that your
hands touch, palms down. Slowly start to move them away from each other,
keeping your eyes fixated forward, until each arm is held straight out on
either side of your body, and you can still see them both in your peripheral
vision. Now hold that peripheral focus for ten seconds.

This is one of the few methods of self-regulation that requires less, rather
than more, interoception. While interoception/bodyfulness is still helpful

at augmenting the effectiveness of this skill, it's not necessary to master a felt-sense awareness of your body to begin the practice of peripheral vision. We've found that this technique works especially well for individuals in service roles that require a lot of interaction with others. You can continue to look at someone, and without their knowledge briefly stop paying direct attention in order to focus on your periphery for a few seconds. Then you can immediately return to the interaction, but with a relaxed and regulated system.

Method 4: Diaphragmatic or regulated "belly" breathing

Also known as belly or abdominal breathing, this is the most common breathing exercise. With diaphragmatic breathing, you're training the body to let your diaphragm do all the work. Your goal here is to breathe through your nose and focus on how your belly fills up with air, and you can do this either sitting up or lying down.

1. Sit comfortably, with your knees bent and your shoulders, head, and neck relaxed.
2. Locate your diaphragm by placing one hand below your rib cage and the other on your upper chest. As you breathe, you will feel your diaphragm rising and falling.
3. Breathe in slowly through your nose so that your stomach moves outward against your hand. Count in your head and make sure the inward breath lasts at least five seconds, paying particular attention to the feeling of the air filling your lungs. The hand on your chest should remain as still as possible.
   One, two, three, four, five.
4. Tighten your stomach muscles, letting them fall inward as you exhale through pursed lips. The hand on your upper chest must remain as still as possible.
5. Repeat steps 1 through 4 five times.

Another simple way to practice diaphragmatic breathing is to lace your fingers together and put them behind your head. Then lean back in your chair and pull your elbows back as far as is comfortable. You should notice that your abdominal muscles are now doing all the work to draw your breath.

Method 5: Soft palate relaxation

Here your goal is to locate and then relax your soft palate, a.k.a. the muscular part at the back of the roof of your mouth.

1. Sit down comfortably and shift your focus to the muscles along the roof of your mouth.
2. Release all the tension in this area.
3. Now expand your focus to include the muscles in your face and jaw.
4. Release the tension in these muscles too.
5. Next, with all of these muscles relaxed, silently say the letter "R" to yourself and try to gently maintain the subtle arch this creates in the roof of your mouth for five seconds.

   One, two, three, four, five.
6. Repeat this exercise five times.

FORWARD-FACING® WORKSHEET 3: SELF-REGULATION PRACTICE AT WORK

It's time to start practicing the skill of self-regulation in the work setting (and at home too). At this point, you should already have chosen the acute relaxation method or methods that are easiest for you to engage in. For the next three days (at least), perform self-regulation five to ten times a day as you go about your normal routine at school. On each occasion, use the log below to write down the level of tension you're feeling before and after self-regulating, which muscles were involved, and the method(s) you used to invoke the relaxation response. (You can also do this in your separate journal or notepad.)

Once the three days are up, you should be familiar with the three components of neuroception, interoception/bodyfulness, and acute relaxation that make up self-regulation, with the Forward-Facing® approach's step one growing to become a habitual part of your daily work and home activities for lasting professional resilience and optimization.

Self-Regulation Log Day 1 (five to ten occasions altogether)
Occasion 1
-Date and time: _____

-Muscle tension on a scale of 0 to 10 (0 = no tension, 10 = highest tension possible): _____

-Tension location (which muscles were tense):

_____

_____

-Acute relaxation method(s) used:

_____

_____

-Results of how you felt afterwards:

_____

_____

Occasion 2

-Date and time: _____

-Muscle tension on a scale of 0 to 10 (0 = no tension, 10 = highest tension possible): _____

-Tension location (which muscles were tense):

_____

_____

-Acute relaxation method(s) used:

_____

_____

-Results of how you felt afterwards:

_____

_____

Occasion 3

-Date and time: _____

-Muscle tension on a scale of 0 to 10 (0 = no tension, 10 = highest tension possible): _____

-Tension location (which muscles were tense):

_____

_____

-Acute relaxation method(s) used:

_____

_____

-Results of how you felt afterwards:

_____

_____

Occasion 4

-Date and time: _____

-Muscle tension on a scale of 0 to 10 (0 = no tension, 10 = highest tension possible): _____

-Tension location (which muscles were tense):

_____

_____

-Acute relaxation method(s) used:

_____

_____

-Results of how you felt afterwards:

_____

_____

Occasion 5

-Date and time: _____

-Muscle tension on a scale of 0 to 10 (0 = no tension, 10 = highest tension possible): _____

-Tension location (which muscles were tense):

_____

_____

-Acute relaxation method(s) used:

_____

_____

-Results of how you felt afterwards:

_____

_____

Self-Regulation Log Day 2 (five to ten occasions altogether)
Occasion 1
-Date and time: _____
-Muscle tension on a scale of 0 to 10 (0 = no tension, 10 = highest tension possible): _____
-Tension location (which muscles were tense):

_____

_____

-Acute relaxation method(s) used:

_____

_____

-Results of how you felt afterwards:

_____

_____

Occasion 2
-Date and time: _____
-Muscle tension on a scale of 0 to 10 (0 = no tension, 10 = highest tension possible): _____
-Tension location (which muscles were tense):

_____

_____

-Acute relaxation method(s) used:

_____

_____

-Results of how you felt afterwards:

_____

_____

Occasion 3

-Date and time: _____

-Muscle tension on a scale of 0 to 10 (0 = no tension, 10 = highest tension possible): _____

-Tension location (which muscles were tense):

_____

_____

-Acute relaxation method(s) used:

_____

_____

-Results of how you felt afterwards:

_____

_____

Occasion 4

-Date and time: _____

-Muscle tension on a scale of 0 to 10 (0 = no tension, 10 = highest tension possible): _____

-Tension location (which muscles were tense):

_____

_____

-Acute relaxation method(s) used:

_____

_____

-Results of how you felt afterwards:

_____

_____

Occasion 5
-Date and time: _____

-Muscle tension on a scale of 0 to 10 (0 = no tension, 10 = highest tension possible): _____

-Tension location (which muscles were tense):

_____

_____

-Acute relaxation method(s) used:

_____

_____

-Results of how you felt afterwards:

_____

_____

Self-Regulation Log Day 3 (five to ten occasions altogether)
Occasion 1
-Date and time: _____

-Muscle tension on a scale of 0 to 10 (0 = no tension, 10 = highest tension possible): _____

-Tension location (which muscles were tense):

_____

_____

-Acute relaxation method(s) used:

_____

_____

-Results of how you felt afterwards:

_____

_____

Occasion 2

-Date and time: _____

-Muscle tension on a scale of 0 to 10 (0 = no tension, 10 = highest tension possible): _____

-Tension location (which muscles were tense):

_____

_____

-Acute relaxation method(s) used:

_____

_____

-Results of how you felt afterwards:

_____

_____

Occasion 3

-Date and time: _____

-Muscle tension on a scale of 0 to 10 (0 = no tension, 10 = highest tension possible): _____

-Tension location (which muscles were tense):

_____

_____

-Acute relaxation method(s) used:

_____

_____

-Results of how you felt afterwards:

_____

_____

Occasion 4
--Date and time: _____

_____

-Muscle tension on a scale of 0 to 10 (0 = no tension, 10 = highest tension possible): _____

-Tension location (which muscles were tense):

_____

_____

-Acute relaxation method(s) used:

_____

_____

-Results of how you felt afterwards:

_____

_____

Occasion 5
-Date and time: _____

-Muscle tension on a scale of 0 to 10 (0 = no tension, 10 = highest tension possible): _____

-Tension location (which muscles were tense):

_____

_____

-Acute relaxation method(s) used:

_____

_____

-Results of how you felt afterwards:

_____

_____

FORWARD-FACING® WORKSHEET 4: CRAFTING YOUR MISSION STATEMENT

In this exercise, your goal is nothing short of defining your mission professionally and personally. Why are you here? Who is your "best self"—the person you could become if the shackles of fear, anger, frustration, and stress were forever banished from your life? How would you fully express your talents and creativity at work and home? What role would you play in helping others become *their* best selves—how would this manifest in school and elsewhere? Now's the time to get out your writing utensil if you haven't already, and your journal or notepad if you're using one.

Preparation for Crafting Your Mission Statement

There are two parts to this preparation portion, with the first one consisting of five questions. Try to come up with at least two good answers for each of the questions below. Keep them short and concise, spending no more than a total of fifteen minutes here.

Part 1

1. Why are you alive? What is your purpose for living on this planet?

_____

_____

_____

2. What do you want to be when you "grow up"? (This can be a professional distinction or a more abstract, generalized description, i.e., "a happy human" or "a positive influence in my students' lives.")

_____

_____

_____

3. What dreams do you have for yourself that are, as yet, unfulfilled?

_____

_____

_____

4. What is *really* important to you?

_____

_____

_____

5. What are your greatest strengths?

_____

_____

_____

Now circle three to five of the answers that feel the most meaningful and accurate to you, reflecting for a minute on what they tell you about yourself, and how your current life and career match up with them.

Part 2

Next, spend a minute or two answering each of the below prompts so that you can begin articulating the key elements of your mission statement. *It is my mission…*

1. To live…

_____

_____

_____

2. To work…

_____

_____

_____

3. To continue…

_____

_____

_____

4. To love…

_____

_____

_____

5. To be…

_____

_____

_____

6. To become…

_____

_____

_____

7. To believe…

_____

_____

_____

8. To promote…

_____

_____

_____

9. To strive…

_____

_____

_____

10. To seek…

_____

_____

_____

Your Mission Statement

Referring to the insights listed above in parts 1 and 2, write a paragraph that most closely defines your current mission on this planet.

My Mission Statement

My mission is to…

_____

_____

_____

_____

_____

_____

_____

_____

_____

_____

_____

_____

_____

_____

_____

_____

_____

Forward-Facing® Worksheet 5: Crafting Your Vision Statement

Close your eyes and picture yourself attending your own retirement party. As you sit on the dais, each attendee stands up in turn to give a short speech honoring you for having achieved your vision. What is each guest saying about you? What qualities or accomplishments are they praising you for? Below are seven guidelines to keep in mind before you begin crafting your vision statement.

1. Your vision statement should consist of at least several sentences written in the present tense. For example, write, "I am financially secure with a stable plan for retirement" rather than, "I will achieve financial security and a stable plan for retirement."

2. State an overarching objective rather than a specific one. For example, write, "I am a well-respected and appreciated educator in my school district who's received multiple honors and distinctions in my career" rather than "I will be chosen as Teacher of the Year at least once."

3. Write in the first person (i.e., "I build long-lasting and supportive relationships with my students, and they feel safe coming to me for assistance.").

4. Make sure your vision statement is compelling enough to keep you motivated and inspired when you encounter setbacks and challenges at school.

5. Remember that you're writing a vision for yourself, not for your spouse, students, colleagues, or anyone else. This is the time to think deeply about what *you* want out of your career and life.

6. Be bold. Don't limit your vision to what you can accomplish now. Consider who you *could* become, and what that person *could* accomplish if they no longer experienced compassion fatigue or burnout in their professional life. Reach for the stars.

7. Most importantly, have fun and recognize there is no "wrong" way to write a vision statement.

Okay, let's start writing!

Your Vision Statement

Referring to the guidelines above, write a paragraph below that most closely defines who you want to be once you've fulfilled (or are fulfilling) your mission. If you feel you need more space, consider writing it in your journal or notepad.

My Vision Statement

My vision is to...

_____

_____

_____

_____

_____

_____

_____

_____

_____

_____

_____

_____

_____

_____

_____

FORWARD-FACING® WORKSHEET 6: CRAFTING YOUR CODE OF HONOR

This exercise will help you establish the moral foundation of an intentional, principle-based life. Your goal is to identify the ethical guidelines you'll be applying in the course of pursuing your mission and achieving your vision.

Preparation for Crafting Your Code of Honor

Start by choosing seven or more words from the list of traits below that most accurately reflect your moral and ethical convictions (or add your own!), and write them down in the spaces below. If you're using a journal or notepad, provide yourself with some empty space underneath each one.

Traits to Choose From

A leader; active; approach vs. avoidance; assertive; altruistic; committed; compassionate; courageous; creative; detailed; effective; efficient; ethical; facilitative; faithful; farsighted; fearless; frugal; generous; honest; hopeful; humorous; joyful; just; lively; loving; optimistic; outspoken; passionate; peaceable; powerful; productive; resilient; responsible; scientific; secure; self-confident; service-oriented; strong; tolerant; tenacious; valiant; warm; witty.

Your Code of Honor

Now write a declarative sentence next to each of the words you've chosen above that states your aspiration to abide by that rule without fail. If "honest" is the word you've chosen, for example, you might write, "I am always honest with myself and others." Of course, as fallible human beings, none of us can adhere to our morals and ethics as fully and faithfully as we might wish. But our goal for now is to set as high a bar as possible for our future behavior. As we continue to practice self-regulation over time, our code of honor and daily behavior will increasingly converge until we are consistently living in accordance with our deepest beliefs and convictions.

My Code of Honor

. I am...

_____

_____

. I am...

_____

_____

. I am...

_____

_____

4. I am...

_____

_____

5. I am...

_____

_____

6. I am...

_____

_____

7. I am...

_____

_____

FORWARD-FACING® WORKSHEET 7: WORKPLACE DETOXIFICATION

Below is a list of all four perceptual shifts that lead to maturation and detoxification of the workplace spoken of earlier. Read each and follow the recommended exercise for a better understanding of what your perceptions look like currently, and to better enable yourself for professional resilience.

1. Real Danger versus Perceived Threat

While at work, ask yourself several times a day: "Am I really in danger right now?" (This is neuroception in the self-regulation process.) If the answer is "no," then dial down the arousal in your body by relaxing the tension in your muscles through one or more of the acute relaxation techniques detailed in chapter six.

If the answer is "yes," then it is even more important that you relax your way back to peak cognitive and motor functioning. (Remember, you are stronger, faster and smarter in a regulated nervous system.)

What percentage of the time do you currently feel you are in *real* danger while at work? _____%

Are there methods that could be deployed to reduce any instances of real danger at work?

Example: "Carrying a radio on me at all times to stay connected with other staff," or "Strengthening my relationships with students to create a supportive and safe environment for myself and everyone else." Write them down below or in a notepad.

_____

_____

_____

_____

2. Demand versus Choice

Notice how frequently you say to yourself or out loud "I have to…" at work. When you begin to shift your perception from which tasks are demanded of you to what you can choose to do or not do, this diminishes much of the stress you experience while at work. What are some work tasks that you currently see as demands?

_____

_____
_____
_____
_____

Do a cost/benefit analysis. How might you change the way in which you view these tasks so that they are no longer demands, and rather necessary facets of the job you've chosen to pursue?

Example: "I choose to grade these tests during my lunch hour while I eat so I can leave right at the end of school today, because in the end, I have to grade them anyway."

I choose to _____

because _____

I choose to _____

because _____

Example: "I choose to be at my duty station every afternoon because I don't want my students to experience an unsafe situation and not have an adult immediately available to help them."
I choose to _____

because _____

I choose to _____

because _____

3. Outcome-Driven versus Principle-Based

Write down several ways you currently make yourself responsible for outcomes that are *beyond* your control:

Example: "I will ensure every student gets a passing grade in my class," or "I will be sure I have one hundred percent of my parents participate in parent-teacher conferences this fall."

_____

_____

_____

_____

_____

Now, see if you can rewrite these to articulate an intention that is *within* your control:

Example: "I will provide support for passing grades for all of my students to the best of my abilities."

_____

_____

_____

_____

_____

4. Relinquishing Entitlement and Other Secondary Gains

Can you identify any entitlements you secretly hold on to because of the "sacrifice" that you make in educating others?

Example: "Because I am so busy and stressed, I expect my friends and family to understand that I can't attend social engagements or communicate with them as much as they'd like me to."

_____

_____

_____

_____

_____

What unconscious "secondary gains" have you received from being a victim of your work?

Example: "My spouse should understand all that I go through and take care of the problems of the household. Those issues are more than I should have to handle."

_____

_____

_____

_____

_____

How are these entitlements and secondary gains improving your quality of life?

_____

_____

_____

_____

_____

Are you prepared to relinquish them?
Yes _____ No _____

5. Acceptance of a Chaotic System

Identify one way in which you find yourself struggling with your work system. How do you allow your unmet expectations of your work system to cause you distress?

Example: "The school should hire more staff members so I don't have to keep adding kids to my classroom when there aren't enough supplies, desks, or chairs for them. I am bothered by this every day I go in to work. What is the district thinking?"

_____

_____

_____

_____

Now try accepting that this is the way that systems behave—they demand more from you than you can give, and they are rarely appreciative of what you *do* give. Relax knowing that you are in no danger when more is demanded of you than you can give. How might you shift your perception in this context toward identifying what *is* within your control to complete effectively?

Example: "I am doing the best with what I have—if I need to find an extra chair or desk unexpectedly, I will try my best. If I can't find exactly what I need, I have the skillset to get creative about a short-term solution until something else can be arranged."

_____

_____

_____

_____

_____

FORWARD-FACING® WORKSHEET 8: SELF-OPTIMIZATION

This next set of exercises are built off mindfulness techniques to help you identify specific areas of stress in your own professional and personal life, so that you can work toward resolving your negative perceptions and strive for happiness and resilience in all situations.

1. Awareness

Identify three situations that cause you stress and practice relaxing and disengaging from the intensity of the situation. Practice "noticing" everything you can about the situation (your thoughts, your body's reaction, how others are acting, etc.) without engaging in the drama.

Example: "I get so frustrated when a parent challenges my decisions about their child. I get so caught up in it, wanting to prove that I'm right and they're wrong. When I think about what is best for the student, I find that I am most effective."

1. _____
   _____
   _____

2. _____
   _____
   _____

3. _____
   _____
   _____

2. Nonjudgmental/Nonevaluative Observation

Notice your thoughts when you are anxious. What are some of the involuntary and patterned thoughts you think during these times? Write them down.

Example: "This stress has caused me to overeat and gain weight, which hasn't made me feel good about myself. I don't like looking or feeling this way, but I don't know how to stop."

_____

_____

_____

_____

How are these negative thoughts predicated on the instinctual desire to help you "survive" the threat (hint: fight, flight, or freeze)? Can you make "good sense" of how your negative/critical thoughts are actually attempting to protect you from perceived threats?

Example: "I know I should eat better and exercise, but I've had a good reason not to—I don't have enough time in the day!"

_____

_____

_____

_____

_____

Practice letting these thoughts go on, by, or through you without engaging with them. Recognize that they are old neural patterns meant to help you through an experience that is being perceived as a threat, but that you now know isn't one. Write down any noticeable changes or shifts in your thinking when you adopt this "observant," nonjudgmental perspective to the negative thoughts.

_____

_____

_____

_____

_____

3. Being in the Present Moment

Notice times when you are anxious. What is the correlation between those times and when your focus has gone to past or future situations? Practice reorienting yourself to the here and now. Now identify a situation at work when you can devote time to being present without any demands being put upon you—a moment to just *be*.

_____

_____

_____

_____

_____

4. Beginner's Mind

Use fewer "I know" statements and allow yourself to approach life with curiosity and a fresh perspective. Identify a situation at work where you can change your "knowing" into curiosity and open-mindedness.

Example: "How can I improve myself in this situation? What can I do better? How can I make things better for others around me? What is there to learn here?"

_____

_____

_____

_____

_____

FORWARD-FACING® *WORKSHEET 9: ESTABLISHING YOUR SUPPORT NETWORK*

We stated earlier how important it is to have a stable support network in place to connect and share your thoughts and experiences with. Feel free to list a few people who you might consider contacting to ask if they'd be interested in filling this role for you—they can be colleagues, mental health professionals, or close friends or family, but they should all be trusted individuals you feel safe with.

_____
_____
_____
_____
_____

Below is a chance to organize your thoughts and craft a "script" for inquiring with someone about whether they are able to be a part of your trusted network of support and accountability partners. Be sure to include a description of self-regulation to share with them so that they can understand what this role would look like. Not only does this protect them from any secondary traumatic stress in listening to your narrative, but it also provides them with the first Forward-Facing® tool for professional resilience in their own life—a win-win!

_____
_____
_____
_____
_____

Forward-Facing® Worksheet 10: Sharing Your Story

This is a place for you to write down your experiences before sharing them with your network. (You might wish to make this a regular activity in your journal or notepad.) These memories can focus on current or past work-related issues, but if they involve any significantly traumatic material such as physical or emotional abuse, grief and loss, and/or anything that remains significantly disturbing from childhood, it's recommended that you connect with a mental health professional to work through these memories together. Save this space for journaling about those workplace experiences that remain in your consciousness and are mildly to moderately dysregulating, practicing self-regulation as you write.

_____

_____

_____

_____

_____

_____

_____

_____

_____

_____

_____

_____

_____

_____

_____

_____

_____

FORWARD-FACING® WORKSHEET 11: SELF-CARE AND REVITALIZATION ASSESSMENT

Under each of the five sections below or in your separate notebook, we ask that you rate your current frequency with that particular activity using the scale provided (0 = never; 4 = frequently). After you've scored the items listed for each category, go back through all of them and pick one that you will intentionally focus on over the coming month, with the goal of raising your score by one more point on the scale.

Scale
0 = Never; 1 = Rarely; 2 = Occasionally; 3 = Moderately; 4 = Frequently

1. Physical Self-Care and Revitalization
This area focuses upon developing and maintaining a healthy body. It's all about moving toward (instead of away from) health and fitness. You don't need to eat a solely plant-based diet or participate in high-intensity boot camps multiple times each week to reap the benefits of intentional and gradual engagement in physical activity—but a good bit of attention applied to this area produces significant benefits.

_____ 1. Mild aerobic activity (<110 heartbeats per minute). Strolling, golfing, bicycling (<10 miles per hour), et cetera, for less than twenty minutes less than three times per week.

_____ 2. Moderate aerobic activity (110 – 140 heartbeats per minute). Walking (3.5+ miles per hours), jogging, bicycling (15 – 20 miles per hour), tennis, team sport games, etc., for more than twenty minutes three times per week.

_____ 3. Eating regularly (three times per day; no more than 2,400 calories).

_____ 4. Eating healthily (balanced diet, lowered carbs, fiber, fruits and vegetables, et cetera).

_____ 5. Anaerobic exercise (toning muscles, gym workout, carrying weights while walking, etc., one or more times per week).

_____ 6. Wellness checkups and preventative medicine.

_____ 7. Massage.

_____ 8. Outdoor recreation.

_____ 9. Sexual engagement.

_____ 10. Getting enough sleep.

11. Other: _____

12. Other: _____

2. Psychological Self-Care and Revitalization

This area of self-care is focused upon enhancing and optimizing psychological health and cognitive functioning. Clarity, better memory, quick wit, goodwill, being slow to anger, and having peace of mind are all results of a well-maintained psychological system. Focusing a little effort in this area can make life much easier and more satisfying for educators.

_____ 1. Intentionally facing (instead of avoiding) perceived threats with relaxed muscles.

_____ 2. Reading literature unrelated to work.

_____ 3. Puzzles (crosswords, Sudoku, word puzzles, et cetera), neural feedback practice (brain games and training on websites like Lumosity), videogames, et cetera.

_____ 4. Adult education activities.

_____ 5. Journaling (formal classes or informal).

_____ 6. Psychotherapy/life-coaching.

_____ 7. Meditation/mindfulness (formal or informal).

_____ 8. Self-regulating/relaxing muscles and refocusing when you find yourself perseverating or obsessing about something.

_____ 9. Reading self-help books/manuals.

10. Other: _____

11. Other: _____

3. Emotional Self-Care and Revitalization

Educators of all kinds spend a lot of time in chaotic—and thus traumatizing—environments, oftentimes around others who are anxious or traumatized as well. It's important to counter-balance the intensity of this environment with activities and surroundings that soothe and revive us emotionally.

_____ 1. Spending time in nature and/or gardening.

_____ 2. Connecting with positive people who support you.

_____ 3. Doing something new and exciting.

_____ 4. Engaging in financial planning, budgeting, and other activities for a stable financial future.

_____ 5. Building something.

_____ 6. Scheduling trips (day or extended) and activities that you enjoy regularly.

_____ 7. Anonymously being of service to someone.

_____ 8. Intentionally cultivating deeper and more fulfilling relationships with your partner and/or your support network.

_____ 9. Attending a support group.

_____ 10. Playing—with an animal or pet, kids, games with friends, or online with others.

11. Other: _____

12. Other: _____

Spiritual Self-Care and Revitalization

Spiritual self-care and revitalization is the process of discovering and deepening meaning, security, hope, faith, belief, and joy in your life. This can be done through formalized processes (such as attending church, synagogue, or yoga practice) or informal processes (such as walking meditation, prayer/meditation, or writing). Anything that enhances your connection to something greater than yourself and provides purpose and meaning to your life could be considered spiritual self-care.

_____ 1. Attending religious or spiritual services.

_____ 2. Yoga classes (also a powerful tool for developing interoception/bodyfulness and self-regulation).

_____ 3. Qigong, tai chi, or other martial arts training.

_____ 4. Prayer/meditation.

_____ 5. Listening to and/or playing music.

_____ 6. Taking a class in spiritual methods (i.e., mindfulness, Transcendental Meditation, Gnosticism, philosophy, et cetera).

_____ 7. Practicing gratitude (i.e., daily list of five things for which you are grateful as a discipline of cultivating happiness).

_____ 8. Practicing humility.

_____ 9. Reading books that feed your soul.

_____ 10. Watching films that feed your soul.

11. Other: _____

12. Other: _____

Professional Self-Care and Revitalization

There are a variety of simple steps to take and healthy boundaries to set in a professional space to make it work _for_ us rather than against us. With continued education and self-development efforts and genuine feedback shared with those who make decisions in our institutional systems, you can feel confident and supported in your chosen career.

_____ 1. Identifying professional development training that will make your work easier and provide you with greater competence and confidence.

_____ 2. Scheduling training in one or more of these skill areas over the next year.

_____ 3. Seeking out professional and/or peer supervision, consultation, and/or support.

_____ 4. Discussing with administration (collaboratively and non-reactively) ways to improve ergonomics and climate of your school district.

_____ 5. Becoming a resource in your district for positive, solution-focused, and resilient action.

_____ 6. Scheduling and utilizing breaks throughout the day (i.e., regularly making time for lunch, planning periods, bathroom breaks, et cetera).

_____ 7. Interviewing coworkers who are competent and resilient. Discovering what they have done to become and remain successful.

_____ 8. Organizing a consortium of coworkers to explore ways to make your professional environment more resilient and able to provide better education to students.

_____ 9. Organizing and arranging your workspace so that it is comfortable and conducive for you.

_____ 10. Identifying books and research articles that will enhance your skills and knowledge and making time to read a little each month.

11. Other: _____

12. Other: _____

Your Forward-Facing® Professional Resilience Plan

1. Self-Regulation.

Self-regulation is the ability to monitor and regulate your ANS, activating only the amount of energy necessary for the task. This process requires three activities—neuroception, interoception, and acute relaxation—done within a few-second window while remaining fully engaged in professional, personal, and all other activities of daily living. Releasing tension in your core muscles is an excellent method to quickly achieve this, but becoming aware of and releasing the tension in *all* muscles of your body is successfully practicing self-regulation. You cannot experience stress with relaxed muscles, as proven by reciprocal inhibition.

Identify five situations in your personal and/or professional life in which you are habitually dysregulated, and make a commitment to confront these situations with intentionally relaxed muscles over the next month. (Example: "When I get an email from a parent or coworker and my pulse rises.") Feel free to refer to your answers from Forward-Facing® Worksheet 3 for ideas.

1. _____
   _____
2. _____
   _____
3. _____
   _____
4. _____
   _____
5. _____
   _____

2. Intentionality.

Intentionality is the ability to follow your personal covenant while maintaining integrity across the landscape of your life, both professionally and personally. It is shifting away from reactivity and impulsive behaviors toward chosen and intentional behaviors.

Identify two situations where you habitually respond reactively and find yourself derailed from your mission, vision, and code of honor while breaching your integrity (one professional and one personal). Make the commitment to self-regulate during the confrontation with the perceived threat(s) embedded in these situations to replace reactivity with intentionality. You can refer to your personal covenant documents in Forward-Facing® Worksheets 4, 5, and 6 for direction.

1. Describe a specific **professional** behavior (usually aggression or avoidance) that constitutes the breach of your integrity. (Example: "I become impatient and angry with a student.")

_____

_____

_____

_____

_____

What is the trigger/perceived threat(s)? (Example: "The student disregarded my request to put their phone away during class.")

_____

_____

_____

_____

_____

What is your intentional behavior in this situation? (Example: "I strive to have patience with my students and understand that they are children first and foremost, per my code of honor. If they are disregarding my politely voiced request to put their phone away after I've asked already, I will follow the class rules I've set out ahead of time of taking their phone for the rest of the period without getting dysregulated or allowing it to derail me from that day's lesson.")

_____

_____

_____

_____

_____

2. Describe a specific **personal** behavior (usually aggression or avoidance) that constitutes the breach of your integrity.

_____

_____

_____

What is the trigger/perceived threat(s):

_____

_____

_____

What is your intentional behavior in this situation:

_____

_____

_____

3. Perceptual Maturation.

Your workplace is not the cause of your stress. Instead, it is your perception of your workplace and the happenings therein that cause your stress. It is difficult to get workplaces to change to meet your specifications; it is much simpler to change your perceptions to more satisfying and ergonomic ways of seeing. You can significantly lessen the toxicity of your work by changing some of your perceptions and meanings by answering the questions below. Look back at the exercises in chapter eight as well as your responses to Forward-Facing® Worksheets 7 and 8 for reference if needed.

Workplace Detoxification

1. Real Danger versus Perceived Threat. How often during each day do you encounter a real and present danger? How often during the day do you perceive threat? What is the ratio of real dangers to perceived threats? When you stop to consider these questions, it becomes clear that you perceive threat *much* more frequently than you encounter real danger. Reminding yourself that this is true is a good beginning for evolving and detoxifying your perception of the environment.

Ask yourself several times each day during the next month: *Am I really in danger right now?*

How does asking and answering this question impact your stress levels in those situations? Describe:

_____

_____

_____

2. Demand versus Choice. What is demanded of you in your work? Answer: *nothing!* You retain choice in every single situation for the rest of your life. Your ability to move away from perceiving tasks at work, requests from your boss, or added trainings as a demand upon you and instead perceiving them as opportunities to evaluate the costs/benefits of doing or not doing the them before going forward will significantly lessen the effects of a toxic workplace upon you.

You can begin to develop this skill by replacing language like "I have to…" with "I choose to…" This simple shift frees you from conscription and bondage where you are forced, against your will, to complete tasks to a voluntary action that enriches your quality of life. This works especially for the tasks you do *not* want to complete.

Name five tasks at work that you very much dislike doing but that you do anyway.

1. _____

   _____

2. _____

   _____

3. _____

   _____

4. _____

   _____

5. _____

   _____

For the next week try **choosing** to do these tasks while keeping a relaxed body and positive attitude. What is different when you choose to do them?

_____

_____

_____

Next, identify five tasks that you catch yourself saying "I have to..."

1. _____

   _____

2. _____

   _____

3. _____

   _____

4. _____

   _____

5. _____

   _____

For the next week try **choosing** to do these tasks while keeping a relaxed body and positive attitude. What is different when you choose to do them?

_____

_____

_____

3. Outcome-Driven versus Principle-Based. There are very few outcomes that you are able, by an act of will, to make happen in the complex world of educating. Outcomes—good or bad—are influenced by a myriad of factors all beyond your ability to predict or control. When you make yourself responsible for outcomes in others' lives or even in your own life, you will find yourself having threat responses each time you encounter something that jeopardizes the wished-for outcome. The ability to relinquish outcomes in favor of embracing a commitment to bring your personal best—skills, attention, compassion, willingness—to a situation can significantly lessen the level of stress created by the need to have a situation turn out any particular way.

Identify five situations in your work where you find yourself preoccupied or obsessed with achieving a particular outcome (i.e., students' test scores, parent-teacher conferences, recognition from others, et cetera).

1. _____

2. _____

3. _____

4. _____

5. _____

For the next week practice re-attenuating your focus away from outcomes like these, identifying five principle-based behaviors you can practice instead.

1. _____

2. _____

3. _____

4. _____

5. _____

What impact does this change have upon your quality of life?

_____

_____

_____

4. Relinquishing Entitlement and Secondary Gains. Professionals impaired by work-related stress can develop diminished functioning of the neocortical areas of their brains. This impairment can gradually and increasingly result in educators perceiving themselves to be victims of their work, and from this perspective to develop a sense of entitlement, believing they should be given more than they are getting from their work. They believe that their workplace owes them certain self-perceived things, like a less stressful environment, more pay, more time off, fewer students, and/or more resources to get their jobs done.

While it is true that we should expect our leadership to work toward enhancing operations and resources at our places of work, the holding of embittered entitlement and the perception of being a victim saps stamina, positive outlook, and resilience. Letting go of the entitlements and the underlying victim stance that supports them can immediately enhance resilience and quality of life.

Entitlement

Write down a list of all the things your work as an educator entitles you to that you are not getting from your workplace. (Example: "With my degree, I shouldn't have to do many of the menial tasks that I am expected to do.")

1. _____
_____
2. _____
_____
3. _____
_____
4. _____
_____
5. _____
_____
6. _____
_____
7. _____
_____
8. _____
_____

Which of these are you willing to let go of for the next week?

1. _____
_____

2. _____

3. _____

4. _____

5. _____

For the next week, practice going to your workplace as a place where nothing is owed to you. Where you are there because you have chosen to be there. Where your workplace is not responsible for your quality of life. What impact does this make?

_____

_____

_____

Indulgences

What self-harmful indulgences do you allow yourself because of your "stressful" work?

1. _____

2. _____

3. _____

4. _____

5. _____

Which of these are you willing to relinquish and substitute with a healthy alternative? (See chapter ten for self-care and revitalization techniques and ideas.)

1. _____

_____

2. _____
_____
3. _____
_____
4. _____
_____
5. _____
_____

5. Acceptance of a Chaotic System. Human systems, especially in education, are chaotic, anxious, and demanding. It has always been and will likely remain this way. Educators who have not yet matured into a resilient professional lifestyle often perceive the demands, anxiety, lack of appreciation, and system politics as a personal affront. As educators evolve into resilience, they find that they can stop fighting what is and begin to accept—just for today—that this is the way things are, while at the same time continuing to advocate and work toward positive change in their environments.

Make a quick list of all the happenings in your workplace that anger, frustrate, irritate, distress, or bother you in any way. (Example: "I become annoyed when I spend so much time planning out really good lessons and then unexpected situations like fire drills or assemblies disrupt my entire plan.")

1. _____
_____
2. _____
_____
3. _____
_____
4. _____
_____
5. _____
_____
6. _____
_____
7. _____
_____

8. _____

_____

Which of these are you willing to practice acceptance with—just for that day—instead of struggling and continuing to hold distress in your body while those things are not changing?

1. _____

2. _____

3. _____

Identify three concrete actions—no matter how small—you can make over the next week to improve the quality of life in your workplace for both you and others.

1. _____

2. _____

3. _____

Personal Optimization
Mindfulness
List three recent situations when you intentionally engaged in mindfulness practice—whether that was returning to your breath and the current moment, approaching things with a "beginner's mind" of curiosity and positivity, practicing nonjudgmental observation of yourself or others, or something else.

1. _____

2. _____

3. _____

The Science of Happiness

Spend two minutes a day describing a positive experience from the last twenty-four hours. This tactic transforms your thinking from task-based to meaning-based, and promotes a viewpoint that is engaged and focused instead of searching for the next thing to do. Write one down here to practice if you would like.

_____

_____

_____

Exercise at least three times a week for twenty minutes; not only is it physically beneficial, but it trains your brain to believe your behavior and choices are important and impactful for the rest of your day. List below the days and types of exercise you chose.

1. _____

2. _____

3. _____

Write down three things you are grateful for every day in a journal, on your phone, or anywhere you can refer to later. Research says this will greatly increase your optimism and success rates. Practice below if you would like.

1. _____

2. _____

3. _____

Take two minutes to meditate and focus on your breathing, fully disengaging from any multitasking you may have been doing. This decreases your stress and resets your brain so that you can address each task one at a time, with optimized neocortical functioning.

Write one short email when you wake up in the morning to a colleague, friend, or family member praising them and what they have been doing.

From Other-Validated to Self-Validated Caregiving

A subtle but powerful protective factor for burnout and compassion fatigue is addressing this issue of other- versus self-validation in the life of the educator. When our worth is determined by someone other than ourselves, we are in danger of losing it if that person does not approve of or appreciate us.

Identify four situations where you perceive threat from another person's judgment or potential criticism.

1. _____
   _____
2. _____
   _____
3. _____
   _____
4. _____
   _____

Identify in which of the above situations you find yourself changing your behavior to avoid or lessen the potential risk of judgment or criticism.

1. _____
   _____
2. _____
   _____
3. _____
   _____

If you were to become intentional and self-validated in these situations, what would you have to say to yourself?

_____
_____
_____

Write a letter to yourself from the voice of "the Great Administrator" telling you all that you have wished to hear from some external source. Provide yourself with all the validation for which you have ever longed. No criticisms—just identifying all of the positive things you have done and do regularly. Provide yourself with the support that you wish you had. Once done, put it in an envelope and mail it to yourself. When it is delivered back to you, read it with a relaxed body and an attitude of compassion and curiosity.

4. Support and Connection.

Throughout this book we have discussed the importance of developing, maintaining, and utilizing a support network. Now it is time to put it into action, using your answers to the Forward-Facing® Worksheets 9 and 10 for reference.

1. Safety Net. Identify one person who knows you well, cares about you, sees you regularly, and—maybe most importantly—is resilient themselves. Seek this person out over the next couple of weeks and invite them to be your "safety net." You may wish to use the following as a guide:

"Hey, I recently learned that I am at high risk for compassion fatigue and work-related stress. I learned that it is important to have at least one person who knows me well watching my back. Of all the people I know who could do this, your name was at the top of my list. Because the effects are hard to detect in ourselves, I am asking you to just passively notice if you see me starting to become symptomatic. That might be things like irritability, anger, complaining a lot, jittery, obsessed with something—anything that looks like stress. The symptoms can go the other way also, like withdrawal, isolation, depression, chronic fatigue, or disengagement. If you see me consistently— over a few weeks or months—displaying these negative effects, I ask that you would confront me. Chances are if I am in one of those places, I will not be very open to hearing your confrontation. I ask that you remind me of this conversation and do not give up confronting me until I commit to do something about it. Even though it may strain the ties of our friendship/relationship, you may save my life. I will gladly do the same for you, if you like."

Identify the one person to seek out to be your safety net:

1. _____

2. Sharing Narratives. In chapter three we discussed secondary traumatic stress—the post-traumatic stress that comes from witnessing the trauma and/or suffering of others. If you have frequent exposure to students (or their families) who are experiencing one or both of these, then you are high-risk for secondary traumatic stress. The bad news is that this type of traumatization can produce a wide array of symptoms, many of which can be debilitating. The good news is that it is easily resolved by sharing the narratives of these painful encounters with peers (or a hired professional) while retaining a relaxed-muscle body. By doing this, the memories of the painful experiences are desensitized and generate fewer symptoms. You may wish to use the following script as a template to guide your conversation:

"Hey, I just learned that I might be high-risk for compassion fatigue, and that preventing compassion fatigue requires that I regularly share my narratives with another person. I'd like for you to be that person. If you are willing, I'd like to show you this thing I learned about how to keep your body relaxed while you are listening to me so that you don't get sick from my stories [teach self-regulation: neuroception + interoception/bodyfulness + acute relaxation technique]. I promise you I will always ask permission from you and allow you time to prepare yourself before I start talking with you about these issues— I won't hijack you. I would ask that you make yourself available sometime within seventy-two hours after I initially reach out, either in person or by telephone. When we meet, I will have everything I need to share organized into a twenty-minute narrative. I ask that you just listen and do not interrupt. If you have insights, comments, or suggestions I would love to hear them after I have completed my narrative. If you are willing to do this for me, I am more than happy to reciprocate. I will offer the same thing—I only ask that you ask me first, and I will make myself available to you within seventy-two hours as well."

Identify three peers or professionals (i.e., mental health) who you will seek out to fill this role:

1. _____
   _____

2. _____
   _____

3. _____
   _____

3. Accountability. This important asset is developed and utilized to support you through your implementation and maintenance of intentionality. It is nearly impossible to live an intentional, principle-based life in isolation. We need support. Utilizing this support to celebrate our successful confrontations with situations where we have previously been out of alignment with our integrity is important, as it facilitates our continued progress. It is also equally (if not more so) important to have a cadre of safe and supportive individuals to whom we can turn when we are in breach of our integrity. We have discovered that this practice of "telling on ourselves" is an integral part of living an intentional life.

Identify three people you will recruit to fill this role (note—these may be some of the same people you are utilizing in other roles).

1. _____
   _____
2. _____
   _____
3. _____
   _____

4. Social Support. These are the people that you wish to include as part of your wider-reaching social support network. These should be people you feel safe and comfortable around, and share a camaraderie with. After spending time with the people you identify in this group, you should feel revitalized, hopeful, cared about, and joyful.

Identify three to five people who fit these requirements with whom you will seek to deepen connection.

1. _____
   _____
2. _____
   _____
3. _____
   _____
4. _____
   _____

5. _____

_____

5. Self-Care and Revitalization.

We must intentionally refuel our bodies, minds, and spirits so that we can confront the rigors of our work. By regularly engaging these activities, you should find that you are able to burn a bright light that shines into the lives of others who are suffering and never burns out. Looking back to chapter ten's self-care and revitalization self-assessment, we ask that you identify one activity from each of the five categories that you will intentionally increase your engagement in over the next month.

Physical self-care and revitalization.
1. _____

Psychological self-care and revitalization.
1. _____

Emotional self-care and revitalization.
1. _____

Spiritual self-care and revitalization.
1. _____

Professional self-care and revitalization.
1. _____

APPENDIX II:

"FIND YOUR ACE SCORE" SELF-ASSESSMENT

Prior to your eighteenth birthday:

1. Did a parent or other adult in the household often or very often...
Swear at you, insult you, put you down, or humiliate you?
Or
Act in a way that made you afraid that you might be physically hurt?
No _____
If Yes, enter 1 _____

2. Did a parent or other adult in the household often or very often...
Push, grab, slap, or throw something at you?
Or
Ever hit you so hard that you had marks or were injured?
No _____
If Yes, enter 1 _____

3. Did an adult or person at least five years older than you ever...
Touch or fondle you or have you touch their body in a sexual way?
Or
Attempt or actually have oral, anal, or vaginal intercourse with you?
No _____
If Yes, enter 1 _____

4. Did you often or very often feel that...
No one in your family loved you or thought you were important or special?
Or
Your family didn't look out for each other, feel close to each other, or support each other?

No _____
If Yes, enter 1 _____

5. Did you often or very often feel that...
You didn't have enough to eat, had to wear dirty clothes, and had no one to protect you?
Or
Your parents were too drunk or high to take care of you or take you to the doctor if you needed it?
No _____
If Yes, enter 1 _____

6. Were your parents ever separated or divorced?
No _____
If Yes, enter 1 _____

7. Was your mother or stepmother:
Often or very often pushed, grabbed, slapped, or had something thrown at her?
Or
Sometimes, often, or very often kicked, bitten, hit with a fist, or hit with something hard?
Or
Ever repeatedly hit over at least a few minutes or threatened with a gun or knife?
No _____
If Yes, enter 1 _____

8. Did you live with anyone who was a problem drinker or alcoholic, or who used street drugs?
No _____
If Yes, enter 1 _____

9. Was a household member depressed or mentally ill, or did a household member attempt suicide?
No _____

If Yes, enter 1 _____

10. Did a household member go to prison?
No _____
If Yes, enter 1 _____

Now add up your "Yes" answers: _____
_____

Put the total here: _____ This is your Adverse Childhood Experiences
or "ACE" score

APPENDIX III:

COACHING, TRAINING, AND CERTIFICATIONS IN FORWARD-FACING

The Forward-Facing® Institute in Phoenix, Arizona, provides training to professionals and nonprofessionals in a wide array of Forward-Facing® topics.

We offer a group experience for anyone interested in deepening their practice and engagement with self-regulation and intentionality. This group, called Forward-Facing® Me, provides a six-week immersion into Forward-Facing® living. The group is limited to twelve participants per cycle and is offered multiple times each year.

For individuals wanting personalized assistance implementing Forward-Facing® into their personal and/or professional lives, we offer individual coaching/consultation by certified professional Forward-Facing® coaches. These coaches are skilled in helping anyone who is struggling with any aspect of the Forward-Facing® process accelerate their process into rapid success. Our coaches have helped hundreds of people, just like you, implement this process into their lives and quickly enjoy the benefits of Forward-Facing® living.

Individual sessions are also available with the authors of this book.

For those interested in going further, we offer a training and certification program that teaches anyone to become a coach and/or consultant in Forward-Facing®. The Forward-Facing® Institute offers virtual and in-person education and training that can lead to the following designations:

- Certified Forward-Facing® Coach for Health and Wellness
- Certified Forward-Facing® Coach for Professional Leadership and Resilience
- Certified Forward-Facing® Consultant for Health and Wellness
- Certified Forward-Facing® Consultant for Professional Leadership and Resilience

If you would like further information about any of the services, trainings, or certifications at the Forward-Facing® Institute, please reach out to us at www.forward-facing.com.

Acknowledgments

Cheryl

I would like to thank my son, Ian, for the tremendous love and joy he brings to my life, as well as the support of family, friends, colleagues, and other educators who have given my life meaning every step of the way.

Rebecca

I would like to acknowledge my teacher leaders, specifically Bonnie Rhodes and Eva Stevens. Through your sustained support and belief in me, I was able to grow and learn beyond my wildest dreams. Thank you.

Eric

First and foremost, I wish to acknowledge, thank, and extend eternal gratitude to my friend and editor, Ashley R. Carlson (www.utopiaediting.com). Without Ashley, it is doubtful that any of my work would have made it beyond my own head. She has consistently helped me formulate, organize, clarify, and articulate these transformative ideas and practices into clear and cogent language so that these Forward-Facing® books could get published. I will forever be in her debt.

Additionally, I wish to thank the first two authors of this book: Cheryl Fuller and Rebecca Leimkuehler. They share almost eighty years of experience in all phases of K-12 education, and have both embraced Forward-Facing® as a path forward in evolving our educational processes and delivery in the United States. I am honored and humbled that they have agreed to participate in this process of adapting my work for the educational community.

Finally, I wish to thank all the educators that have contributed to my social, emotional, and educational success and wellbeing.

About the Authors

Cheryl Fuller, M.Ed., has experienced many years of joy in the world of education as a teacher, counselor, principal, and professional development consultant. Additionally, she has had the honor of working as a professor at Duke University with those just joining the teaching field. Recently with the release of her own trauma narrative, *Peace by Piece*, she bridged her personal experience with trauma with her professional certifications and interest in trauma and grief work. She now works with schools and districts across the country on introducing trauma-informed practices into schools, and providing skills for educators to support them in building professional resilience and healing their compassion fatigue symptoms. While she works remotely from her home in North Carolina, she also enjoys travel and visiting schools across the U.S. and in other countries. When she's not traveling, Cheryl lives in a small, peaceful lake home in the company of her three "chugs" (Chihuahua-pug mixes), and a Tuxedo cat. To connect with Cheryl for support in reaching personal and professional life goals, educational trainings, and much more, she can be reached at www.cherylfuller.org.

Rebecca Leimkuehler, M.Ed., started her educational path earning a Bachelor of Education, with multiple endorsements focusing on reading and language acquisition. She furthered her studies with a Master of Education in Administration and Supervision, and went on to earn a second master's degree in Organizational Psychology through Grand Canyon University. With the focused goal of building better people, Rebecca's introduction to the Adverse Childhood Experiences (ACE) study put her on a course that was undeniable. It answered many questions she'd been asking about human behavior, and provided a framework for understanding the behavioral challenges Rebecca kept encountering in both adults and children as the principal of a K-5 elementary school. With this new knowledge in place, Rebecca made it a top priority to transform her school and others into trauma-informed ones, and the journey began in November of 2015. Along the way, a lot of learning has occurred. The work has been equally rewarding and beautiful, while being terribly difficult and

messy at the same time. As a leader, Rebecca has learned, cried, laughed, taken "brain breaks," and done yoga with students, parents, and staff. She recognizes that no educator has all the answers, but that they'll never stop striving for success. Creating a safe, welcoming, and trauma-informed school environment is and always will be a top priority for Rebecca, as she's personally experienced the importance of connecting with others, being mindful of every moment, using nonviolent communication, and ensuring restorative practices for all.

J. Eric Gentry, Ph.D., DAAETS, FAAETS, is an internationally recognized leader in the study and treatment of traumatic stress and compassion fatigue. His Ph.D. is from Florida State University, where he studied with Professor Charles Figley—a pioneer of these two fields. Dr. Gentry was original faculty, curriculum designer, and Associate Director of the Traumatology Institute at Florida State University. He became the co-director in 2001 and moved this institute to the University of South Florida, where it became the International Traumatology Institute. In 2010, he began the International Association of Trauma

Professionals—a training and certification body—for which he was the Vice President. Formerly serving as the Vice President of the Arizona Trauma Institute, Dr. Gentry is currently the President and CEO of the Forward-Facing® Institute and owner of Compassion Unlimited—a private psychotherapy, training, and consulting practice in Phoenix, Arizona.

BIBLIOGRAPHY

Achor, Shawn. "5 Ways to Turn Happiness Into an Advantage." Psychology Today. Published August 23, 2011. https://www.psychologytoday.com/us/blog/the-happiness-advantage/201108/5-ways-turn-happiness-advantage.

American Federation of Teachers. *A Decade of Neglect: Public Education Funding in the Aftermath of the Great Recession*. Washington D.C.: American Federation of Teachers, 2018. Accessed May 30, 2021. https://www.aft.org/sites/default/files/decade-of-neglect-2018.pdf.

Bauer, Jack, and George Bonanno. "Continuity amid Discontinuity: Bridging One's Past and Present in Stories of Conjugal Bereavement." *Narrative Inquiry* 11, no. 1 (2001): 123. doi:10.1075/ni.11.1.06bau.

Benson, Herbert. *The Relaxation Response*. New York: HarperCollins, 1975.

Blazer, Christie. *Teacher Burnout*. Miami: Miami-Dade County Public Schools Research Services Office of Assessment, Research, and Data Analysis, 2010. Accessed August 25, 2021. https://files.eric.ed.gov/fulltext/ED536515.pdf.

Cherry, Kendra. "What is Happiness?" Very Well Mind. published October 26, 2020. https://www.verywellmind.com/what-is-happiness-4869755.

Cohn, Michael A., Barbara L. Fredrickson, Stephanie L. Brown, Joseph A. Mikels, and Anne M. Conway. "Happiness Unpacked: Positive Emotions Increase Life Satisfaction by Building Resilience," *Emotion* 9, no. 3 (2009): 361, doi:10.1037/a0015952.

DeSilver, Drew. "U.S. Students' Academic Achievement Still Lags That of Their Peers in Many Other Countries." Pew Research Center. Published February 15, 2017. https://www.pewresearch.org/fact-tank/2017/02/15/u-s-students-internationally-math-science/.

De Souza, Jane Carla, Ivanise Cortez de Sousa, Aline Belísio, and Carolina V. M. Azevedo. "Sleep Habits, Daytime Sleepiness, and Sleep Quality of High School Teachers." *Psychology and Neuroscience* 5, no. 2 (2012): 257. doi:10.3922/j.psns.2012.2.17.

Dewitt, Ellen. "Lowest-Paying Jobs That Require a Bachelor's Degree." Stacker. Published May 20, 2021. https://stacker.com/stories/4095/lowest-paying-jobs-require-bachelors-degree.

Dizon-Ross, Elise, Susanna Loeb, Emily Penner, and Jane Rochmes. "Stress in Boom Times: Understanding Teachers' Economic Anxiety in a High-Cost Urban District." *AERA Open* 5, no. 4 (2019): 1. doi:10.1177/2332858419879439.

Ecker, Bruce, Robin Ticic, and Laurel Hulley. *Unlocking the Emotional Brain: Eliminating Symptoms at Their Roots Using Memory Reconsolidation*. New York: Routledge, 2012.

Ellerson, Noelle M. *Education Cuts Have Yet to Heal: How the Economic Recession Continues To Impact Our Nation's Schools*. Alexandria: AASA, The School Superintendents Association, 2015. Accessed May 30, 2021. https://files.eric.ed.gov/fulltext/ED569200.pdf.

Figley, Charles R., ed. *Compassion Fatigue: Coping with Secondary Traumatic Stress Disorder in Those Who Treat the Traumatized*. New York: Routledge, 2013.

Flannery, Mary Ellen. "Teachers Paying for Their Own Substitutes? Believe It or Not, It Happens." National Education Association. Published May 31, 2019. https://www.nea.org/advocating-for-change/new-from-nea/teachers-paying-their-own-substitutes-believe-it-or-not-it.

Foa, Edna B., Terence M. Keane, Matthew J. Friedman, and Judith A. Cohen, eds. *Effective Treatments for PTSD: Practice Guidelines from the International Society for Traumatic Stress Studies*. New York: Guilford Press, 2008.

Fogoros, Richard N. "Anatomy of the Vagus Nerve." Verywell Health. Published October 31, 2019, https://www.verywellhealth.com/vagus-nerve-anatomy-1746123.

Fredrickson, Barbara L. "The Role of Positive Emotions in Positive Psychology: The Broaden-and-Build Theory of Positive Emotions." *American Psychologist* 56, no. 3 (2001): 218. doi:10.1037/0003-066X.56.3.218.

Future Ed Interviews. "How Do School Spending Cuts Affect Student Achievement?" McCourt School of Public Policy: Georgetown University. Published January 18, 2018. https://www.future-ed.org/work/how-do-school-spending-cuts-affect-student-achievement/.

Gentry, J. Eric, Anna B. Baranowsky, and Robert Rhoton. "Trauma Competency: An Active Ingredients Approach to Treating Post-Traumatic Stress Disorder." *Journal of Counseling and Development* 95, no: 3 (2017): 279. doi:10.1002/jcad.12142.

Göksoy, Süleyman, and Türkan Argon. "Conflicts at Schools and Their Impact on Teachers." *Journal of Education and Training Studies* 4, no. 4 (2016): 197. doi:10.11114/jets.v4i4.1388.

Greenberg, Mark T., Joshua L. Brown, and Rachel M. Abenavoli. *Teacher Stress and Health*. University Park: The Pennsylvania State University, 2016. Accessed May 30, 2021. https://www.rwjf.org/en/library/research/2016/07/teacher-stress-and-health.html.

Hanson, Rick. *Hardwiring Happiness: The New Brain Science of Contentment, Calm, and Confidence*. New York: Harmony, 2013.

Harding, Sarah. "Is Teachers' Mental Health and Wellbeing Associated with Students' Mental Health and Wellbeing?" *Journal of Affective Disorders* 242 (2019): 180. doi:10.1016/j.jad.2018.08.080.

Hinojosa, David. "Essential Building Blocks for State School Finance Systems and Promising State Practices." Learning Policy Institute. Published December 5, 2018. https://learningpolicyinstitute.org/product/state-school-finance-systems-report.

Hruza, Melissa. "How Much Do Teachers Spend on Supplies?" AdoptAClassroom.org. Published July 29, 2021. https://www.adoptaclassroom.org/2021/07/29/how-much-do-teachers-spend-on-supplies/.

Jackson, C. Kirabo, Cora Wigger, and Heyu Xiong. *The Costs of Cutting School Spending: Lessons from the Great Recession*. Cambridge: Education Next Institute, Inc., 2020. Accessed May 30, 2021. https://www.educationnext.org/costs-cutting-school-spending-lessons-from-great-recession/.

Jones, Christina, Richard D. Griffiths, Gerry Humphris, and Paul M. Skirrow. "Memory, Delusions, and the Development of Acute Post-Traumatic Stress Disorder-Related Symptoms After Intensive Care." *Critical Care Medicine* 29, no. 3 (2001): 573-580. doi:10.1097/00003246-200103000-00019.

Klaxton, Gary, Larry Levitt, Rabah Kamal, Tricia Neuman, Jennifer Kates, Josh Michaud, Wyatt Koma, et al. "How Many Teachers Are at Risk of

Serious Illness If Infected with Coronavirus?" Kaiser Family Foundation. Published July 10, 2020. https://www.kff.org/coronavirus-covid-19/issue-brief/how-many-teachers-are-at-risk-of-serious-illness-if-infected-with-coronavirus/.

Kwon, Kyong-Ah. "Are Early Childhood Teachers Happy and Healthy? This Research Study Will Find Out." EdSurge. Published October 9, 2019. https://www.edsurge.com/news/2019-10-09-are-early-childhood-teachers-happy-and-healthy-this-research-study-will-find-out.

Larimer, Sarah. "'Kids are Freezing': Amid Bitter Cold, Baltimore Schools, Students Struggle." The Washington Post. Published January 5, 2018. https://www.washingtonpost.com/local/education/kids-are-freezing-amid-bitter-cold-baltimore-schools-students-struggle/2018/01/05/8c213eec-f183-11e7-b390-a36dc3fa2842_story.html.

Leachman, Michael, Kathleen Masterson, and Eric Figueroa. A Punishing Decade for School Funding. Washington D.C.: Center on Budget and Policy Priorities, 2017. Accessed May 30, 2021. https://www.cbpp.org/research/state-budget-and-tax/a-punishing-decade-for-school-funding.

Llopis-Jepsen, Celia. "5 Reasons the Kansas Supreme Court Found the State's School Funding Unconstitutional." KCUR. Published October 9, 2017. https://www.kcur.org/education/2017-10-09/5-reasons-the-kansas-supreme-court-found-the-states-school-funding-unconstitutional.

Mishel, Lawrence, and Sylvia A. Allegretto. The Teacher Pay Gap is Wider Than Ever. Washington D.C.: Economic Policy Institute, 2016. Accessed May 30, 2021, https://www.epi.org/publication/the-teacher-pay-gap-is-wider-than-ever-teachers-pay-continues-to-fall-further-behind-pay-of-comparable-workers/.

National Center for Education Statistics. Enrollment Trends. Washington D.C.: U.S. Department of Education, 2019. Accessed May 30, 2021. https://nces.ed.gov/fastfacts/display.asp?id=65.

National Center for Education Statistics. Public School Teacher Spending on Classroom Supplies. Washington D.C.: U.S. Department of Education, 2018. Accessed June 30, 2021. https://files.eric.ed.gov/fulltext/ED583062.pdf.

Nittler, Kency. "Does Low Pay Shut Teachers out of the Housing Market?" National Council on Teacher Quality. Published October 17, 2017.

https://www.nctq.org/blog/October-2017:-Does-low-pay-shut-teachers-out-of-the-housing-market.

Pearson, Geraldine S. "'Please Don't Hurt Yourself': Managing Youth Suicide Risk During the COVID-19 Pandemic." *Journal of the American Psychiatric Nurses Association* 27, no. 4 (2021): 269-270. doi:10.1177/10783903211023731.

Piquero, Alex R. Wesley G. Jennings, Erin Jemison, Catherine Kaukinen, and Felicia Marie Knaul. "Domestic Violence During the COVID-19 Pandemic - Evidence From a Systematic Review and Meta-Analysis." *Journal of Criminal Justice* 74 (2021): 1-10. doi:10.1016/j.jcrimjus.2021.101806.

Porges, Stephen W. *The Polyvagal Theory: Neurophysiological Foundations of Emotions, Attachment, Communication, and Self-Regulation*. New York: W.W. Norton & Company, 2011.

Porges, Stephen W. "Neuroception: A Subconscious System for Detecting Threats and Safety." *Zero to Three* 24, no. 5 (2004): 19-24. https://pdfs.semanticscholar.org/44e4/004fb363b42a17b92035971fe0 97ae29cccb.pdf?_ga=2.170612576.1537256157.1567868036-437478209.1567868036.

Przystac, Carley. "Diversity in STEM Fields Is Key to Stopping Climate Change." Roosevelt Institute. Published October 2, 2015. https://rooseveltinstitute.org/2015/10/02/diversity-in-stem-fields-is-key-to-stopping-climate-change/.

Rodriguez, Tori. "Impact of the COVID-19 Pandemic on Adolescent Mental Health." Psychiatry Advisor. Published April 30, 2021. https://www.psychiatryadvisor.com/home/topics/child-adolescent-psychiatry/adolescent-mental-health-issues-are-further-exacerbated-by-the-covid-19-pandemic/.

Schneider, Kirk. "Toward a Humanistic Positive Psychology: Why Can't We Just Get Along?" Psychology Today. Published November 29, 2010. https://www.psychologytoday.com/us/blog/awakening-awe/201011/toward-humanistic-positive-psychology-why-cant-we-just-get-along.

Selye, Hans. "Stress without Distress." In *Psychopathology of Human Adaptation*, edited by George Serban, 137-146. Boston: Springer, 1976.

Smiley Amanda. "Why School Wellness Isn't Just for Kids: Many Teachers are Stressed and Depressed." Occupational Health and Safety

Magazine. Published February 7, 2020. https://ohsonline.com/
Articles/2020/02/07/Why-School-Wellness-Isnt-Just-for-Kids-Many-
Teachers-are-Stressed-and-Depressed.aspx?Page=1.

Sorensen, Lucy, and Helen F. Ladd. "Teacher Turnover and the Disruption of
Teacher Staffing." The Brookings Institution. Published April 29, 2019.
https://www.brookings.edu/blog/brown-center-chalkboard/2019/04/29/
teacher-turnover-and-the-disruption-of-teacher-staffing/.

Stevens, Francis L., Robin A. Hurley, and Katherine H. Taber. "Anterior
Cingulate Cortex: Unique Role in Cognition and Emotion." *The Journal
of Neuropsychiatry and Clinical Neurosciences* 23, no. 2 (2011): 121-
125. doi:10.1176/jnp.23.2.jnp121.

Sulea, Coralia, Răzvan Filipescu, Alexandra Horga, Ciprian Ortan,
and Gabriel Fischmann. "Interpersonal Mistreatment at Work
and Burnout among Teachers." *Cognition, Brain, Behavior: An
Interdisciplinary Journal* 16, no. 4 (2012): 553. https://www.
researchgate.net/profile/Coralia-Sulea/publication/234012886_
Interpersonal_mistreatment_at_work_and_burnout_among_teachers/
links/0deec52b182e1a052f000000/Interpersonal-mistreatment-at-work-
and-burnout-among-teachers.pdf.

Sutcher, Leib, Linda Darling-Hammond, and Desiree Carver-Thomas.
"Understanding Teacher Shortages: An Analysis of Teacher Supply and
Demand in the United States." *Education Policy Analysis Archives* 27,
no. 35 (2019): 4. doi:10.14507/epaa.27.3696.

Sutcher, Leib, Linda Darling-Hammond, and Desiree Carver-Thomas. *A
Coming Crisis in Teaching? Teacher Supply, Demand, and Shortages in
the U.S.* Palo Alto: Learning Policy Institute, 2016. Accessed May 30,
2021. https://learningpolicyinstitute.org/product/coming-crisis-teaching.

Takashima, Atsuko, Karl Magnus Petersson, Femke Rutters, Indira
Tendolkar, Ole Jensen, M. J. Zwarts, Bruce L. McNaughton, and Grisel
Mariom Fernández. "Declarative Memory Consolidation in Humans:
A Prospective Functional Magnetic Resonance Imaging Study."
Proceedings of the National Academy of Sciences 103, no. 3 (2006):
756-761. doi:10.1073/pnas.0507774103.

Tan, Siang Yong, and Angela Yip. "Hans Selye (1907–1982): Founder of the
Stress Theory." *Singapore Medical Journal* 59, no. 4 (2018): 170-171.
doi:10.11622/smedj.2018043.

The National Commission on Teaching and America's Future. *Policy Brief: The High Cost of Teacher Turnover*. Washington D.C.: The National Commission on Teaching and America's Future, 2007. Accessed May 30, 2021. https://files.eric.ed.gov/fulltext/ED498001.pdf.

Torpey, Elka. "Projections for Teachers: How Many Are Leaving the Occupation?" U.S. Bureau of Labor Statistics. Published October 2018. https://www.bls.gov/careeroutlook/2018/data-on-display/how-many-teachers-are-leaving.htm?view_full.

Troncale, Joseph. "Your Lizard Brain." Psychology Today. Published April 22, 2014. https://www.psychologytoday.com/us/blog/where-addiction-meets-your-brain/201404/your-lizard-brain.

Tschiesner, Reinhard, Sarah Tauber, Pastore Martina, and Alessandra Farneti. "Pupils' Interpersonal Problems and Occupational Stress in Teacher. Preliminary Results." *Procedia - Social and Behavioral Sciences* 140 (2014): 197. doi:10.1016/j.sbspro.2014.04.409.

U.S. Bureau of Labor Statistics. "Employment in STEM Occupations." Accessed May 30, 2021. https://www.bls.gov/emp/tables/stem-employment.htm.

Warren, Debby. "Lead in the Drinking Water in Public Schools: Our American Way of Life." Nonprofit Quarterly. Published September 25, 2019. https://nonprofitquarterly.org/lead-in-the-drinking-water-in-public-schools-our-american-way-of-life/.

Weiss, Elaine, and Emma García. *Challenging Working Environments ('School Climates'), Especially in High-Poverty Schools, Play a Role in the Teacher Shortage*. Washington D.C.: Economic Policy Institute, 2019. Accessed August 20, 2021. https://www.epi.org/publication/school-climate-challenges-affect-teachers-morale-more-so-in-high-poverty-schools-the-fourth-report-in-the-perfect-storm-in-the-teacher-labor-market-series/.

Will, Madeline. "Teachers Are More Likely to Experience Depression Symptoms Than Other Adults." Education Week. Published June 15, 2021. https://www.edweek.org/teaching-learning/teachers-are-more-likely-to-experience-depression-symptoms-than-other-adults/2021/06.

Wolpe, Joseph. "Psychotherapy by Reciprocal Inhibition." *Integrative Psychological and Behavioral Science* 3, no. 4 (1968): 234-240. doi:10.1007/BF03000093.

Wolpe, Joseph. "Reciprocal Inhibition as the Main Basis
    of Psychotherapeutic Effects." *Archives of Neurology
    and Psychiatry* 72, no. 2 (1954): 205-226. doi:10.1001/
    archneurpsyc.1954.02330020073007.
World Health Organization. "Burn-Out an 'Occupational Phenomenon':
    International Classification of Diseases." World Health Organization.
    Published May 28, 2019. https://www.who.int/news/item/28-05-2019-
    burn-out-an-occupational-phenomenon-international-classification-of-
    diseases.
Woudstra, Marit Helen, Estie Janse van Rensburg, and Maretha Visser.
    "Learner-to-Teacher Bullying as a Potential Factor Influencing Teachers'
    Mental Health." *South African Journal of Education* 38, no. 1 (2018): 1.
    doi:10.15700/saje.v38n1a1358.
Yerkes, Robert M., and John D. Dodson. "The Relation of Strength of
    Stimulus to Rapidity of Habit-Formation." *Journal of Comparative
    Neurology and Psychology* 18, no. 5 (1908): 459-82. doi:10.1002/
    cne.920180503.

ENDNOTES

1   Geraldine S. Pearson, "'Please Don't Hurt Yourself': Managing Youth Suicide Risk During the COVID-19 Pandemic," *Journal of the American Psychiatric Nurses Association* 27, no. 4 (2021): 269, doi:10.1177/10783903211023731.

2   Tori Rodriguez, "Impact of the COVID-19 Pandemic on Adolescent Mental Health," Psychiatry Advisor, published April 30, 2021, https://www.psychiatryadvisor.com/home/topics/child-adolescent-psychiatry/adolescent-mental-health-issues-are-further-exacerbated-by-the-covid-19-pandemic/.

3   Alex R. Piquero, Wesley G. Jennings, Erin Jemison, Catherine Kaukinen, and Felicia Marie Knaul. "Domestic Violence During the COVID-19 Pandemic - Evidence From a Systematic Review and Meta-Analysis," *Journal of Criminal Justice* 74 (2021): 1, doi:10.1016/j.jcrimjus.2021.101806.

4   Leib Sutcher, Linda Darling-Hammond, and Desiree Carver-Thomas, *A Coming Crisis in Teaching? Teacher Supply, Demand, and Shortages in the U.S.* (Palo Alto: Learning Policy Institute, 2016), accessed May 30, 2021, https://learningpolicyinstitute.org/product/coming-crisis-teaching.

5   Debby Warren, "Lead in the Drinking Water in Public Schools: Our American Way of Life," Nonprofit Quarterly, published September 25, 2019, https://nonprofitquarterly.org/lead-in-the-drinking-water-in-public-schools-our-american-way-of-life/.

6   Sarah Larimer, "'Kids are Freezing': Amid Bitter Cold, Baltimore Schools, Students Struggle," The Washington Post, published January 5, 2018, https://www.washingtonpost.com/local/education/kids-are-freezing-amid-bitter-cold-baltimore-schools-students-struggle/2018/01/05/8c213eec-f183-11e7-b390-a36dc3fa2842_story.html.

7   Ellen Dewitt, "Lowest-Paying Jobs That Require a Bachelor's Degree," Stacker, published May 20, 2021, https://stacker.com/stories/4095/lowest-paying-jobs-require-bachelors-degree.

8   U.S. Bureau of Labor Statistics, "Employment in STEM Occupations," accessed May 30, 2021, https://www.bls.gov/emp/tables/stem-employment.htm.

9   Carley Przystac, "Diversity in STEM Fields Is Key to Stopping Climate Change," Roosevelt Institute, published October 2, 2015, https://rooseveltinstitute.org/2015/10/02/diversity-in-stem-fields-is-key-to-stopping-climate-change/.

10 Amanda Smiley, "Why School Wellness Isn't Just for Kids: Many Teachers are Stressed and Depressed," Occupational Health and Safety Magazine, published February 7, 2020, https://ohsonline.com/Articles/2020/02/07/Why-School-Wellness-Isnt-Just-for-Kids-Many-Teachers-are-Stressed-and-Depressed.aspx?Page=1.

11 Michael Leachman, Kathleen Masterson, and Eric Figueroa, *A Punishing Decade for School Funding* (Washington D.C.: Center on Budget and Policy Priorities, 2017), accessed May 30, 2021, https://www.cbpp.org/research/state-budget-and-tax/a-punishing-decade-for-school-funding.

12 Celia Llopis-Jepsen, "5 Reasons the Kansas Supreme Court Found the State's School Funding Unconstitutional," KCUR, published October 9, 2017, https://www.kcur.org/education/2017-10-09/5-reasons-the-kansas-supreme-court-found-the-states-school-funding-unconstitutional.

13 Noelle M. Ellerson, *Education Cuts Have Yet to Heal: How the Economic Recession Continues To Impact Our Nation's Schools* (Alexandria: AASA, The School Superintendents Association, 2015), accessed May 30, 2021, https://files.eric.ed.gov/fulltext/ED569200.pdf.

14 American Federation of Teachers, *A Decade of Neglect: Public Education Funding in the Aftermath of the Great Recession* (Washington D.C.: American Federation of Teachers, 2018), accessed May 30, 2021, https://www.aft.org/sites/default/files/decade-of-neglect-2018.pdf.

15 Lawrence Mishel and Sylvia A. Allegretto, *The Teacher Pay Gap is Wider Than Ever* (Washington D.C.: Economic Policy Institute, 2016), accessed May 30, 2021, https://www.epi.org/publication/the-teacher-pay-gap-is-wider-than-ever-teachers-pay-continues-to-fall-further-behind-pay-of-comparable-workers/.

16 Elka Torpey, "Projections for Teachers: How Many Are Leaving the Occupation?" U.S. Bureau of Labor Statistics, published October 2018, https://www.bls.gov/careeroutlook/2018/data-on-display/how-many-

teachers-are-leaving.htm?view_full.

17 Leib Sutcher, Linda Darling-Hammond, and Desiree Carver-Thomas, "Understanding Teacher Shortages: An Analysis of Teacher Supply and Demand in the United States," *Education Policy Analysis Archives* 27, no. 35 (2019): 4, doi:10.14507/epaa.27.3696.

18 Lucy Sorensen and Helen F. Ladd, "Teacher Turnover and the Disruption of Teacher Staffing," The Brookings Institution, published April 29, 2019, https://www.brookings.edu/blog/brown-center-chalkboard/2019/04/29/teacher-turnover-and-the-disruption-of-teacher-staffing/.

19 The National Commission on Teaching and America's Future, *Policy Brief: The High Cost of Teacher Turnover* (Washington D.C.: The National Commission on Teaching and America's Future, 2007), accessed May 30, 2021, https://files.eric.ed.gov/fulltext/ED498001.pdf.

20 National Center for Education Statistics, *Enrollment Trends* (Washington D.C.: U.S. Department of Education, 2019), accessed May 30, 2021, https://nces.ed.gov/fastfacts/display.asp?id=65.

21 C. Kirabo Jackson, Cora Wigger, and Heyu Xiong, *The Costs of Cutting School Spending: Lessons from the Great Recession* (Cambridge: Education Next Institute, Inc., 2020), accessed May 30, 2021, https://www.educationnext.org/costs-cutting-school-spending-lessons-from-great-recession/.

22 Jackson, Wigger, and Xiong, *Costs of Cutting School Spending*.

23 Future Ed Interviews, "How Do School Spending Cuts Affect Student Achievement?" McCourt School of Public Policy: Georgetown University, published January 18, 2018, https://www.future-ed.org/work/how-do-school-spending-cuts-affect-student-achievement/.

24 David Hinojosa, "Essential Building Blocks for State School Finance Systems and Promising State Practices," Learning Policy Institute, published December 5, 2018, https://learningpolicyinstitute.org/product/state-school-finance-systems-report.

25 Drew DeSilver, "U.S. Students' Academic Achievement Still Lags That of Their Peers in Many Other Countries," Pew Research Center, published February 15, 2017, https://www.pewresearch.org/fact-tank/2017/02/15/u-s-students-internationally-math-science/.

26 Jane Carla de Souza et al., "Sleep Habits, Daytime Sleepiness, and Sleep Quality of High School Teachers," *Psychology and Neuroscience* 5, no.

2 (2012): 257, doi:10.3922/j.psns.2012.2.17.

27 Kyong-Ah Kwon, "Are Early Childhood Teachers Happy and Healthy? This Research Study Will Find Out," EdSurge, published October 9, 2019, https://www.edsurge.com/news/2019-10-09-are-early-childhood-teachers-happy-and-healthy-this-research-study-will-find-out.

28 Gary Klaxton et al., "How Many Teachers Are at Risk of Serious Illness If Infected with Coronavirus?" Kaiser Family Foundation, published July 10, 2020, https://www.kff.org/coronavirus-covid-19/issue-brief/how-many-teachers-are-at-risk-of-serious-illness-if-infected-with-coronavirus/.

29 Mark T. Greenberg, Joshua L. Brown, and Rachel M. Abenavoli, *Teacher Stress and Health* (University Park: The Pennsylvania State University, 2016), accessed May 30, 2021, https://www.rwjf.org/en/library/research/2016/07/teacher-stress-and-health.html.

30 Madeline Will, "Teachers Are More Likely to Experience Depression Symptoms Than Other Adults," Education Week, published June 15, 2021, https://www.edweek.org/teaching-learning/teachers-are-more-likely-to-experience-depression-symptoms-than-other-adults/2021/06.

31 Sarah Harding et al., "Is Teachers' Mental Health and Wellbeing Associated with Students' Mental Health and Wellbeing?" *Journal of Affective Disorders* 242 (2019): 180, doi:10.1016/j.jad.2018.08.080.

32 Marit Helen Woudstra et al., "Learner-to-Teacher Bullying as a Potential Factor Influencing Teachers' Mental Health," *South African Journal of Education* 38, no. 1 (2018): 1, doi:10.15700/saje.v38n1a1358. National Center for Education Statistics, *Enrollment Trends* (Washington D.C.: U.S. Department of Education, 2019), accessed June 30, 2021, https://nces.ed.gov/fastfacts/display.asp?id=65.

33 National Center for Education Statistics, *Public School Teacher Spending on Classroom Supplies* (Washington D.C.: U.S. Department of Education, 2018), accessed June 30, 2021, https://files.eric.ed.gov/fulltext/ED583062.pdf.

34 Melissa Hruza, "How Much Do Teachers Spend on Supplies?" AdoptAClassroom.org, published July 29, 2021, https://www.adoptaclassroom.org/2021/07/29/how-much-do-teachers-spend-on-supplies/.

35 Hruza, "Teachers Spend on Supplies?"

36 Mary Ellen Flannery, "Teachers Paying for Their Own Substitutes? Believe It or Not, It Happens," National Education Association, published

May 31, 2019, https://www.nea.org/advocating-for-change/new-from-nea/teachers-paying-their-own-substitutes-believe-it-or-not-it.

37 Kency Nittler, "Does Low Pay Shut Teachers out of the Housing Market?" National Council on Teacher Quality, published October 17, 2017, https://www.nctq.org/blog/October-2017:-Does-low-pay-shut-teachers-out-of-the-housing-market.

38 Elise Dizon-Ross et al., "Stress in Boom Times: Understanding Teachers' Economic Anxiety in a High-Cost Urban District," *AERA Open* 5, no. 4 (2019): 1, doi:10.1177/2332858419879439.

39 Reinhard Tschiesner et al., "Pupils' Interpersonal Problems and Occupational Stress in Teacher. Preliminary Results," *Procedia - Social and Behavioral Sciences* 140 (2014): 197, doi:10.1016/j.sbspro.2014.04.409.

40 Süleyman Göksoy and Türkan Argon, "Conflicts at Schools and Their Impact on Teachers," *Journal of Education and Training Studies* 4, no. 4 (2016): 197, doi:10.11114/jets.v4i4.1388.

41 Elaine Weiss and Emma García, *Challenging Working Environments ('School Climates'), Especially in High-Poverty Schools, Play a Role in the Teacher Shortage* (Washington D.C.: Economic Policy Institute, 2019), accessed August 20, 2021, https://www.epi.org/publication/school-climate-challenges-affect-teachers-morale-more-so-in-high-poverty-schools-the-fourth-report-in-the-perfect-storm-in-the-teacher-labor-market-series/.

42 Coralia Sulea et al., "Interpersonal Mistreatment at Work and Burnout among Teachers," *Cognition, Brain, Behavior: An Interdisciplinary Journal* 16, no. 4 (2012): 553, https://www.researchgate.net/profile/Coralia-Sulea/publication/234012886_Interpersonal_mistreatment_at_work_and_burnout_among_teachers/links/0deec52b182e1a052f000000/Interpersonal-mistreatment-at-work-and-burnout-among-teachers.pdf.

43 World Health Organization, "Burn-Out an 'Occupational Phenomenon': International Classification of Diseases," World Health Organization, published May 28, 2019, https://www.who.int/news/item/28-05-2019-burn-out-an-occupational-phenomenon-international-classification-of-diseases.

44 Christie Blazer, *Teacher Burnout* (Miami: Miami-Dade County Public Schools Research Services Office of Assessment, Research, and Data Analysis, 2010), accessed August 25, 2021, https://files.eric.ed.gov/full-

text/ED536515.pdf.

45 Charles R. Figley, ed., *Compassion Fatigue: Coping with Secondary Traumatic Stress Disorder in Those Who Treat the Traumatized* (New York: Routledge, 2013), 2.

46 Atsuko Takashima et al., "Declarative Memory Consolidation in Humans: A Prospective Functional Magnetic Resonance Imaging Study," *Proceedings of the National Academy of Sciences* 103, no. 3 (2006): 756, doi:10.1073/pnas.0507774103; Christina Jones et al., "Memory, Delusions, and the Development of Acute Post-Traumatic Stress Disorder-Related Symptoms After Intensive Care," *Critical Care Medicine* 29, no. 3 (2001): 573, doi:10.1097/00003246-200103000-00019.

47 Bruce Ecker, Robin Ticic, and Laurel Hulley, *Unlocking the Emotional Brain: Eliminating Symptoms at Their Roots Using Memory Reconsolidation* (New York: Routledge, 2012).

48 Should you encounter these roadblocks, please reach out to the Forward-Facing® Institute at: www.forward-facing.com, and we will assist you in finding a qualified clinician in your area who can help.

49 Joseph Wolpe, "Psychotherapy by Reciprocal Inhibition," *Integrative Psychological and Behavioral Science* 3, no. 4 (1968): 234, doi:10.1007/BF03000093.

50 Joseph Wolpe, "Reciprocal Inhibition as the Main Basis of Psychotherapeutic Effects," *Archives of Neurology and Psychiatry* 72, no. 2 (1954): 205, doi:10.1001/archneurpsyc.1954.02330020073007.

51 Edna B. Foa, Terence M. Keane, Matthew J. Friedman, and Judith A. Cohen, eds., *Effective Treatments for PTSD: Practice Guidelines from the International Society for Traumatic Stress Studies* (New York: Guilford Press, 2008).

52 Herbert Benson, *The Relaxation Response* (New York: HarperCollins, 1975).

53 Stephen W. Porges, "Neuroception: A Subconscious System for Detecting Threats and Safety," *Zero to Three* 24, no. 5 (2004): 19, https://pdfs.semanticscholar.org/44e4/004fb363b42a17b92035971fe097ae29cccb.pdf?_ga=2.170612576.1537256157.1567868036-437478209.1567868036.

54 Kendra Cherry, "What is Happiness?" Very Well Mind, published October 26, 2020, https://www.verywellmind.com/what-is-happi-

ness-4869755.

55 Kirk Schneider, "Toward a Humanistic Positive Psychology: Why Can't We Just Get Along?" Psychology Today, published November 29, 2010, https://www.psychologytoday.com/us/blog/awakening-awe/201011/ toward-humanistic-positive-psychology-why-cant-we-just-get-along.

56 Rick Hanson, Hardwiring Happiness: The New Brain Science of Contentment, Calm, and Confidence (New York: Harmony, 2013).

57 Shawn Achor, "5 Ways to Turn Happiness Into an Advantage," Psychology Today, published August 23, 2011, https://www.psychologytoday.com/us/blog/the-happiness-advantage/201108/5-ways-turn-happiness-advantage.

58 Jack Bauer and George Bonanno, "Continuity amid Discontinuity: Bridging One's Past and Present in Stories of Conjugal Bereavement," Narrative Inquiry 11, no. 1 (2001): 123, doi:10.1075/ni.11.1.06bau.

59 Barbara L. Fredrickson, "The Role of Positive Emotions in Positive Psychology: The Broaden-and-Build Theory of Positive Emotions," American Psychologist 56, no. 3 (2001): 218, doi:10.1037/0003-066X.56.3.218.

60 Michael A. Cohn et al., "Happiness Unpacked: Positive Emotions Increase Life Satisfaction by Building Resilience," Emotion 9, no. 3 (2009): 361, doi:10.1037/a0015952.

61 J. Eric Gentry et al., "Trauma Competency: An Active Ingredients Approach to Treating Post-Traumatic Stress Disorder," Journal of Counseling and Development 95, no: 3 (2017): 279, doi:10.1002/jcad.12142.